Living in Christ

saint mary's press

The Bible

The Living Word of God

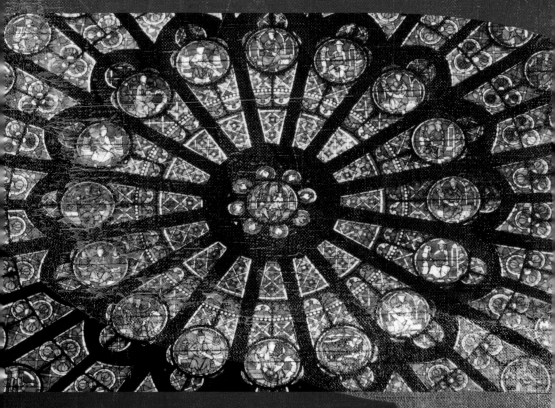

Robert Rabe

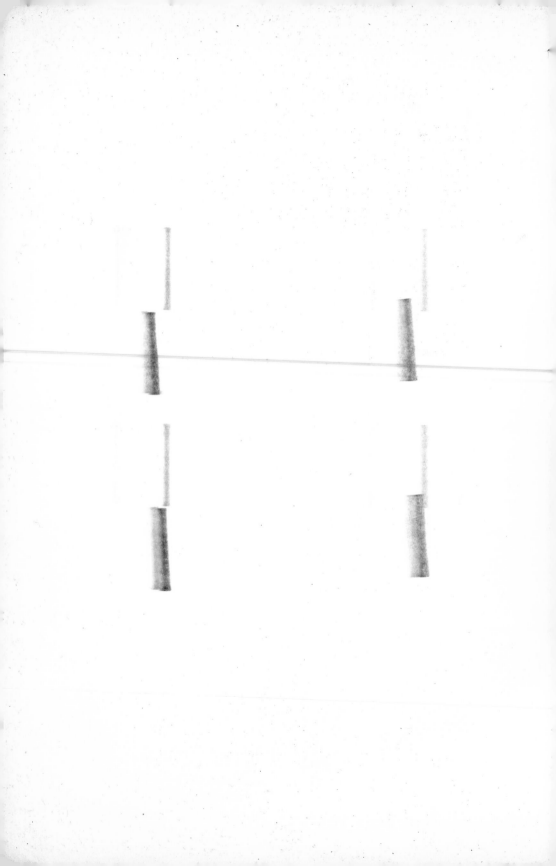

Living in Christ

The
Bible

The Living Word of God

Robert Rabe

saint mary's press

The Subcommittee on the Catechism, United States Conference of Catholic Bishops, has found this catechetical text, copyright 2011, to be in conformity with the *Catechism of the Catholic Church.*

Nihil Obstat: Rev. William M. Becker, STD
Censor Librorum
December 13, 2010

Imprimatur: † Most Rev. John M. Quinn, DD
Bishop of Winona
December 13, 2010

The nihil obstat and imprimatur are official declarations that a book or pamphlet is free of doctrinal or moral error. No implication is contained therein that those who have granted the nihil obstat or imprimatur agree with the contents, opinions, or statements expressed, nor do they assume any legal responsibility associated with publication.

The publishing team included Gloria Shahin, editoral director; Steven McGlaun, development editor; Brian Singer-Towns, consultant; Javier Bravo, contributing editor; Maura Thompson Hagarty, theological reviewer; Roxane Kadrlik Chlachula, contributing author; Chris Wardwell, contributing author; prepress and manufacturing coordinated by the production departments of Saint Mary's Press.

Printed in the United States of America

1144 (PO2861)

ISBN 978-0-88489-906-8

Contents

Section 3: Revelation in the Old Testament

Section 4: Revelation in the New Testament

Section 5:
The Scriptures and the Life of Faith

Introduction

"In the beginning . . ." (Genesis 1:1)

These are the first words in the Bible, and it is fitting that they should be the first words in this book. The beginning point for any exploration of our faith is discovering that God has revealed himself to us. This course starts by exploring God's Revelation, which is communicated to us through Tradition and Scripture. The course will focus on Sacred Scripture, the Bible. As the editor for this book I am excited to welcome you to what can be an amazing encounter with the living Word of God.

I imagine that in your home there is at least one Bible. In my home there are three. Two of them belonged to my grandparents. Those Bibles sit in a prominent space on a shelf in my home office. When my grandparents passed away, I asked for their Bibles because, for me, they are a special connection to a part of my past. They remind me of my family and my history. They remind me of the love my grandparents had for each other and passed on to my parents and to me. When I first acquired these Bibles I sat down and leafed through their pages. I found passages that had been marked as important by my grandparents. I discovered old family pictures of my parents and relatives I did not know. I came across documents that were tucked into the Bibles for safe keeping. I do not open these Bibles much anymore because I want them stay intact. However, I am very aware of these treasured possessions, and deeply grateful for them.

The third Bible in my office is the one I use personally and for my work. I consult this Bible often. I have important passages marked. I have notes tucked into it. The pages are getting tattered from use. This Bible plays a part in my spiritual and professional life almost every day, always bringing me closer to God.

These three Bibles—the ones reverently placed on a shelf and rarely touched anymore and the one pulled off the shelf and consulted daily—are a good example of what Scripture is in my life. It is a connection to my personal history and the history of the faith I hold so dear. It helps me know where I come from, what I was created for, and of God's enduring goodness in reaching out to me and to all his people to lead us to salvation. My hope is that Scripture can do the same for you—that it will connect your life today to the history of our salvation and to the promise of eternal life, and that it will help you grow in your relationship with God, and guide you in how to live your life and bring the Good News of Jesus Christ to others.

You are going to learn a great deal about God and Scripture during this course, with this book as the starting point. But this book, and a single semester, cannot teach you everything there is to know about God's Revelation. Seeking this understanding is a life-long journey. I constantly discover new insights in my well-worn Bible. My hope is that through this course and lifelong study of Scripture, you too will continually encounter the living Word of God.

Peace and Blessings,
Steven McGlaun, editor

Revelation

Part 1

The Desire to Know God

We are created with a longing, a yearning, for God. Each of us yearns for a life of meaning and truth, which can find fulfillment only in our supreme, good, and loving God. God desires that we know him. It is easy to become distracted by worldly promises and definitions of happiness, goodness, and beauty, but God continually invites and challenges us to renounce the distortions of this world and fix our eyes on the infinite truth found in him alone. There is only one answer, one choice, if we want to be truly happy in this life and the next. That answer is God—our God who knew us before we were born, knows our thoughts before we speak them, and leads us on the path to salvation.

The articles in this part address the following topics:

1 Longing for God

Hunger . . . thirst . . . yearn . . . crave . . . long . . . need! When we use these words, we speak of the **desire** to fill an emptiness, a void, in our lives. We all have the need to satisfy this inner longing. Because this inner longing is "written in the human heart" (*Catechism of the Catholic Church [CCC]*, 27) by God, people experience a restlessness that only God can satisfy. To be human is to embark on a journey of wandering, as the Israelites did during the Exodus, knowing that the one true direction and destination is God alone.

Humanity as Religious Beings

Each one of us is a religious being. Whether we realize it or not, our **vocation** (from the Latin, meaning "to call") as religious beings is to live fully human lives—lives in which we know, love, and freely choose God. When we call humans religious beings, we are saying they are made by and for God, "to live in communion with God" (*CCC,* 45). Within the human heart is a place—a God-shaped hole—desiring to be filled with God's infinite love. From the moment of conception, we were knitted in our "mother's womb" (Psalm 139:13) with a desire for truth and happiness that only God

desire
From the Latin *desidero,* "to long for what is absent or lost."

vocation
A call from God to all members of the Church to embrace a life of holiness. Specifically, it refers to a call to live the holy life as an ordained minister, as a vowed religious (sister or brother), in a Christian Marriage, or in single life.

Pray It!

Holy Desire for God

Have you ever felt a desire for silence and prayer? God's love draws us to him and calls us to respond to him with love. Sometimes we experience his love as a yearning in our heart. Saint Teresa of Ávila, the first woman Doctor of the Church, wrote about how God reaches out to us every day. The next time you are in prayer, reflect on the following words of Saint Teresa:

> This Lord of ours is so anxious that we should desire him and strive after his companionship that he calls us ceaselessly, time after time, to approach him; and this voice of his is so sweet. . . . His appeals come through the conversations of good people, or from sermons, or through the reading of good books . . . through sicknesses and trials, or by the means of truths which God teaches us at times when we are engaged in prayer; however feeble such prayers may be, God values them highly.

can satisfy. We find expressions of this desire in both the Sacred Scriptures and in the lives of the saints.

The Book of Psalms, in the Old Testament, illuminates that we are religious beings with longings that can find meaning and rest only in the knowledge and wisdom of God. Psalm 42 speaks of the quest for God in this way: "As the deer longs for streams of water, / so my soul longs for you, O God. / My being thirsts for God, the living God" (verses 2–3). The psalmist, writer, and composer compares thirst for God to a deer that is parched, longing for refresh-

Saint John of the Cross and Saint Teresa of Ávila

Both Saint John of the Cross and Saint Teresa of Ávila were sixteenth-century mystics who sought to reform the Carmelite religious order. Their goal was to establish a deeper life of prayer and austerity for the order"s members. The reform eventually led to the establishment of the Discalced ("without shoes") Carmelites. The two saints are considered Doctors of the Church,

along with thirty-one other saints and holy people, because of their abundant writings on doctrine and the spiritual life. John is known for his writings *Ascent of Mount Carmel*, *The Dark Night*, and *The Living Flame of Love*. Teresa is most notable for authoring *The Way of Perfection* and *The Interior Castle*.

ing and plentiful water. In Psalm 23 we find a people desiring a shepherd who gives strength, provides protection, and sets a banquet of love.

The lives of the saints illustrate humanity's "quest for God" (*CCC*, 28), a people moving toward God at all times to find completion. Saint John of the Cross (1542–1591) wrote: "One dark night, fired with love's urgent longings. . . . O night that has united the Lover with his beloved" (*The Collected Works of Saint John of the Cross*, pages 358–359). In this poetic line, John speaks of his soul's burning desire to be united with God, the Lover. Saint Teresa of Ávila (1515–1582) states, "In the measure you desire Him, you will find Him." According to both saints, persistent longing and authentic desire are the direct paths to God.

Going Toward God

In the words of Saint Augustine of Hippo (354–430), "The whole life of a good Christian is a holy desire to see God as He is." Because we came from God and are going toward him, our ultimate desire is union with him. As religious beings, our whole spiritual journey is characterized by an unceasing craving to know the saving hand of God. When we respond to the invitation to live in communion with God, we become more fully the people he created us to be. ✝

2 God's Invitation

We spend much of our time on earth building relationships. Science, psychology, and our experiences tell us healthy relationships are necessary for us to survive and thrive. The heart of any healthy relationship is a strong, intimate bond, closeness, or union, challenging us to become people of compassion and faith. The most important relationship we have is with God. Sacred Scripture reminds us of the critical importance of knowing God and his mighty power to save us (see Philippians 3:8–11).

Incarnation

From the Latin, meaning "to become flesh," referring to the mystery of Jesus Christ, the divine Son of God, becoming man. In the Incarnation, Jesus Christ became truly man while remaining truly God.

salvation

From the Latin *salvare,* meaning "to save," referring to the forgiveness of sins and assurance of permanent union with God, attained for us through the Paschal Mystery—Christ's work of redemption accomplished through his Passion, death, Resurrection, and Ascension. Only at the time of judgment can a person be certain of salvation, which is a gift of God.

God constantly calls us to relationship with him. *Pastoral Constitution on the Church in the Modern World* (*Gaudium et Spes,* 1965) states that "from the very circumstance of his origin man is already invited to converse with God" (19). In other words we are invited into communion with God and to experience the grace of his saving love. God wants to know, love, and hold us. Therefore, he "never ceases to draw man to himself" (*CCC,* 27).

Jesus Christ: God's Greatest Invitation

Because God so longs for a relationship with us, he reached out in a radical way. In the **Incarnation** the Word of God became flesh in the person of Jesus Christ. Through Jesus Christ, "God has revealed himself and given himself" (*CCC,* 68) to human beings in a new way so we may heed and understand the message of **salvation.** In fact, the meaning of the name Jesus is "God saves." In and through Jesus Christ, God has "provided the definitive, superabundant answer to the questions that man asks himself about the meaning and purpose of his life" (68). The Incarnation of the Son of God is about God's love for humanity. Because of his love for us, God sent his only Son, who is God himself, to invite us into a life-giving relationship with him. God's dwelling among us is a further extension of his invitation to communion and eternal salvation. Although we build many relationships throughout life, no relationship is greater than the one we have with our God. ✝

Catholic Wisdom

Facts about Pope John XXIII

Did you know that Pope John XXIII's name was Angelo Giuseppe Roncalli? Roncalli came from a family of sharecroppers and knew the value of hard work. In 1915 he was drafted to serve his country as a sergeant in the medical corps as a priest. The guidance of the Holy Spirit, his deep spirituality, and his ministry in the Church gave him an understanding of the importance of renewal in the Church.

Gaudium et Spes

In 1962 Pope John XXIII opened the Second Ecumenical Council of the Vatican. This Council became known as Vatican Council II. This Council, like all Ecumenical Councils, was a gathering of the Church's bishops from all around the world, convened by the Pope. Pope John XXIII wanted the Church to respond in a relevant manner to the cares and concerns of people in a rapidly changing world. Vatican II ended in 1965. Among the many documents written at Vatican II was *Gaudium et Spes*. This document is also known as *Pastoral Constitution on the Church in the Modern World*. It had the goal of "scrutinizing the signs of the times" and "interpreting them in the light of the Gospel" (4). Among the many issues addressed were the dignity of the human person, the necessity of community in an individualistic world, and human beings' relationship to the universe. It also dealt with the Church's role in the formation of people, the sanctity of marriage and family life, and economic and social justice.

© Franklin McMahon/CORBIS

3 Happiness in God Alone

"What do I need to be truly happy in this lifetime?" All people encounter this question at some point. Most of us struggle with it throughout our entire lives. In our culture the media offer various answers to this question. They range from expensive homes, cars, and clothing to lives of promiscuous sex and experimentation with drugs and alcohol. Even though people buy into these cultural approaches to happiness, they are still unhappy. Why?

The promises of this world are empty, lacking depth and meaning. Therefore they often provide momentary satisfaction or relief but eventually leave us looking for a fix to our unhappy and aching spirits. We may try to fill the void of unhappiness with the greatest and latest cell phone, computer, fashion trend, and so on. Through advertising, the media have been able to convince people that material goods answer our dissatisfactions with life. All these things, though good in moderation, will still leave us looking for true happiness.

According to Saint Augustine, we need not look anywhere for happiness but to God, "for our hearts are restless until they rest" in him. Happiness and truth can be found only when we live "in communion with God" (*CCC*, 45).

The Beatitudes

Blessed are the poor in spirit,
    for theirs is the kingdom of heaven.
Blessed are they who mourn,
    for they will be comforted.
Blessed are the meek,
    for they will inherit the land.
Blessed are they who hunger and thirst for righteousness,
    for they will be satisfied.
Blessed are the merciful,
    for they will be shown mercy.
Blessed are the clean of heart,
    for they will see God.
Blessed are the peacemakers,
    for they will be called children of God.
Blessed are they who are persecuted for the sake of righteousness,
    for theirs is the kingdom of heaven.

Blessed are you when they insult you and persecute you and utter every kind of evil against you [falsely] because of me. Rejoice and be glad, for your reward will be great in heaven.

(Matthew 5:3–12)

God always takes the first step in calling us to live in communion with him. Responding to God's call means we remove the promises and distractions of this world and focus on him in order to have a clearer sense of his vision and path.

God is "our first origin and our ultimate goal" (*CCC*, 229). He is our beginning and our destiny. Thus happiness is found only in a life fully committed to him. Being fully commited to God means putting our faith in him. The Holy Spirit works in us and helps us to believe by preparing us to receive the gift of faith. This is God's supernatural gift of faith, which leads us to choose God with our whole hearts and minds, so we neither prefer "anything to him" nor "substitute anything for him" (229). When we make this choice, we will want to live a life based on the Beatitudes—recognizing that true happiness is found in God alone. Jesus Christ, God's infinite Word and Wisdom, gave us the Beatitudes as a key for living in true happiness. ✞

4 Saint Augustine and the Four Objects of Love

Have you ever noticed that some people get along with everyone? It seems that the more friends they have, the more friends they make. This is possible because within our heart and soul is a tremendous capacity to love. The more we love, the more love we have to give—within limits, of course.

Love, sometimes referred to as *caritas*, from a Latin term meaning "charity," is equated with the emotions of affection, reverence, and blessing. Love describes the manifestation of God's presence in creation. As Christians our primary call is to give and accept love. Underlying much of the Christian understanding of love are the words and wisdom of Saint Augustine of Hippo, an early Father and Doctor of the Church, who proclaimed that there are four objects we should love: God, our neighbors, ourselves, and our bodies.

God

"You shall love the Lord, your God, with all your heart, with all your soul, and with all your mind" (Matthew 22:37). Jesus Christ himself says this is the Greatest Commandment.

Before we can love anything or anyone, we must first love God, who breathed life into our bodies. But love does not start with us. We are only able to love because God loved us first. Once we respond to him and give ourselves fully to him, the love that flowed from the wounds of Jesus Christ on the cross will inflame our hearts with a fire that cannot be extinguished.

> **"The way of salvation is easy; it is enough to love."**
>
> (Margaret of Cortona, 1247–1297)

Neighbors

According to Augustine, if we do not love our neighbors, we do not love God. Loving our neighbors does not mean we always agree with their attitudes and actions. It means we revere and respect them because God has created every person "in his image" (Genesis 1:27). After all, Jesus did exclaim that the second Greatest Commandment is: "You shall love your neighbor as yourself"(Matthew 22:39).

Saint Augustine taught that our love should focus on God, our neighbors, ourselves, and our bodies. Which of these four is easiest for you to love? Which is hardest?

© Summerfield Press/CORBIS

Selves

To love ourselves is to love God. Self-love is the realization that God is imprinted on our heart, waiting, wanting to be displayed to the world in a beautiful and magnificent way. Knowing that Jesus Christ gave himself for our salvation points to our infinite worth and value—God himself died for us. Love of self must not become selfish or contrary to God's will but should empower us to move beyond ourselves and build the Reign of God, where everyone can see their own value.

> **"At the end of life, we will be judged by love."**
>
> (Saint John of the Cross, 1542–1591)

Bodies

Augustine said, "When God created the body, He showed a greater regard for beauty than for necessity." In other words, our bodies are one of God's great artistic masterpieces. These bodies, which will be resurrected someday, manifest God's greatness, goodness, and glory. Because of this reality, we must hold our bodies in high esteem. The body bears God's creative hand. Therefore "it is animated by a spiritual soul, and it is the whole human person that is intended to become, in the body of Christ, a temple of the Holy Spirit"[1] (*CCC*, 364). ✝

Live It!

Loving by Listening

One way you can love is by listening well. Listening is more than just physical hearing. Good listening is a gift that takes time and energy. It demands your full presence and attentiveness. It is sometimes difficult to listen, especially when the person speaking is in pain.

Listening also fits in with Saint Augustine's four objects of love. Listening to God in prayer and in his Word is essential in the life of a Christian. Listening to your neighbor is love too. If anyone has ever attentively listened to your problems, you know what a wonderful gift it is to be able to get things off your chest. Listening to yourself—your own fears, needs, hopes, and dreams—is important in discerning your vocation in life. Athletes will attest to the importance of listening to our bodies, which speak to us in many ways. Take time to listen well. It's an act of love!

Review

1. What is the vocation of every human being?

2. How did Saint Augustine summarize the goal of a good Christian?

3. What is the Incarnation? Why is it important?

4. What were the goals of the Vatican Council II document *Gaudium et Spes*?

5. What do we find when we respond to God's call to live in communion with him?

6. What did Jesus give us as a framework or as the keys for living in true happiness?

7. According to Saint Augustine, what are the four objects of love?

Part 2

Natural Revelation

God painted all creation with the truth of his existence. He also created us with the ability to know him by using our thinking ability, our reason. Through creation and reason, we can come to know God. This is called natural revelation, meaning that we can logically and reasonably deduce the existence of God through the natural order. God shaped all living things as a sign and symbol of his desire to be known through his magnificent universe.

Natural revelation is pointed to in the Scriptures and in the wisdom of the Church Fathers. It is also pointed to in the "proofs" developed by scholastic theologians and in the teachings of recent Church Councils. However, historical conditions and the consequences of Original Sin often hinder the ability of the human mind to fully come to know the truth about God through natural revelation. Something more is needed. God, in his wisdom and goodness, provided Divine Revelation for us. This is God's communication about himself and his plan for humanity, which he has made known to us most fully by sending his own Divine Son, Jesus Christ.

The articles in this part address the following topics:

5 The Sacred Scriptures and Natural Revelation

natural revelation
The process by which God makes himself known to human reason through the created world. Historical conditions and the consequences of Original Sin, however, often hinder our ability to fully know God's truth through natural revelation alone.

"The heavens declare the glory of God; / the sky proclaims its builder's craft"(Psalm 19:2). God reveals himself in many and varied ways. We can come to know God by contemplating his wondrous and majestic universe. The process by which God makes himself known through the natural and created order is called **natural revelation.** Within each person lies the capacity to understand God "as the origin and the end of the universe" (*CCC,* 32). From the sun and moon to the trees and changing seasons, from the uniqueness of every person to the endless energy that flows through all living things, God's existence is proclaimed in all creation. The Old and New Testaments of the Bible emphasize natural revelation by calling attention to God's glory in the universe he created.

Natural Revelation in the Old Testament

The Sacred Scriptures are filled with countless passages pointing to the Christian understanding of natural revelation. In the account of Creation, found in the Book of Genesis, we hear about God's creative action during seven days. At the end of each day, after God has tirelessly worked to splash the earth with color and life, he sees how good and beautiful his creations are. The goodness of every created

Live It!

Seeing God in All Things

When creating a yearbook spread for the senior class, the editor decided to ask a few seniors to take pictures of their rooms at home so they could be added to the spread. The spread asked the reader to guess which seniors the rooms belonged to. Not surprisingly, those who knew the seniors the best could easily identify the rooms with their owners. Isn't it funny how the manner in which you decorate your room can say a lot about you? After all, you are the interior designer.

The same is true with God and his creation. All of creation is able to tell us something about the one who made it. Take time to listen to what creation is telling you about God. Make a plan to take in the next available sunset. Go to a hill or open area and just take it in with all its colors. Then take a moment to see God's imprint in it.

thing points to the Absolute and Supreme Good, God. Light, darkness, water, sky, earth, plants, trees, sun, moon, stars, animal life, and human beings —God's most important creation—all point to God as "the first cause and final end of all things" (*CCC*, 34).

The Book of Wisdom has a passage that mentions people who were unable to recognize God from the things they could see. The passage describes as foolish those "who from the good things seen did not succeed in knowing him who is" (13:1). They didn't recognize that all created things point to the Creator. When we take time to wonder and marvel at "the world's order and beauty" (*CCC*, 32), we are able to see the work of God, who is Creator of Heaven and earth.

Natural Revelation in the New Testament

Just as the Old Testament sheds light on our understanding of natural revelation, so too does the New Testament. The Book of Acts of the Apostles details the growth of the early Church under the direction of the Holy Spirit. In Acts of the Apostles, Saint Paul speaks of a God who "fixed the ordered seasons and the boundaries of their regions" (17:26). Paul said this to point the Athenians to a magnificent truth: God is alive, real, and continually revealing himself throughout all creation.

Saint Paul affirms that God made himself evident in all creation. In his Letter to the Romans, Paul writes this about God: "Ever since the creation of the world, his invisible attributes of eternal power and divinity have

Creation itself gives witness to the glory of God, the Creator. What in creation causes you to think about God and give thanks to God?

© Andrey.tiyk / shutterstock.com

been able to be understood and perceived in what he has made"(1:20). Acts of the Apostles and Romans, along with many other New Testament writings, point to our capacity to know God through the natural order. The Sacred Scriptures direct our eyes and heart toward the world and all its inhabitants, which enable us to recognize God's existence and presence. ☩

Pierre Teilhard de Chardin

Pierre Teilhard de Chardin was a French theologian who lived between 1881 and 1955. He was a member of the Society of Jesus, or the Jesuits. The Jesuits are a group of priests and religious brothers following the ideas and spirituality of Saint Ignatius of Loyola. Teilhard was schooled in theology and science. As both a mystic and a scientist, Teilhard sought to reconcile the world of religious thought with the rapidly increasing scientific data characteristic of the time in which he lived. One of his most significant contributions to the Church's understanding of natural revelation is the belief that creation reveals the sacred face and blazing heart of God.

6 Natural Revelation and the Wisdom of the Church Fathers

"Creation is a great book. . . . [God] set before your eyes the things he had made. . . . Heaven and earth cry out to you, 'God made me!'" These words of Saint Augustine, an influential Father of the Church, assert that the universe and created order point to the existence of God. Augustine invites us to open the "book of creation" and discover the presence of God. Along with Augustine, the other **Fathers of the Church** affirm the notion of natural revelation—knowledge of God in and through the natural world, informed by human reason. As the *Catechism* states, "by the natural light of human reason" (47), we can know God, the Creator and Lord, through the magnificence and glory of his creation. Historical conditions and the consequences of Original Sin, however, often diminish our ability to fully know God's truth through natural revelation alone. This is why Divine Revelation is needed.

The Universe as a Sign of God

Essential to the theology and spirituality of the Church Fathers is the idea that the universe provides visible evidence of God's existence. Therefore when we notice a beautiful sunset, enjoy the changing colors of a tree, or recognize the cycle of life, we can arrive at a deeper "knowledge of God as the origin and the end" (*CCC*, 32) of all creation. Saint Gregory of Nyssa (335–394) was a Church Father and bishop. He recognized that as people come to know God through the created universe, their desire for God grows stronger and deeper. According to the Church Fathers, because the universe shows God's existence, it draws us into a closer relationship with him.

Fathers of the Church (Church Fathers)

During the early centuries of the Church, those teachers whose writings extended the Tradition of the Apostles and who continue to be important for the Church's teachings.

Human Being as the Image of God

Many Church Fathers, especially Saint Athanasius (293–373), Saint Gregory of Nazianzen (325–389), Saint Gregory of Nyssa, and Saint Augustine of Hippo (354–430), coupled the idea that God can be known through natural revelation with the belief that humanity is the summit of creation. In others words, the Church Fathers saw human beings as the high point of God's creative action in the world. After all, the

Pray It!

Your Presence in Creation

God,
Help me to see that all creation flows from you.
You reveal yourself in the wind, in the stars and planets of the night sky.
All living plants and animals remind me of your glory.

Although my life is sometimes chaotic, I marvel at the order in the universe.

The majestic mountains, the tree-lined forests, and the vast beaches that line our oceans give witness to the peace and harmony you place within creation.

Remind me often that I am your child, for you created me in your image and likeness.

Help me to develop my capacity to love, to seek the truth, and to use my freedom wisely.

And as I continue to see the beauty and wonder of all your creation, may it lead me to a deeper longing for you.

Amen.

Middle Ages

Also known as the medieval period, the time between the collapse of the Western Roman Empire in the fifth century AD and the beginning of the Renaissance in the fourteenth century.

scholastic theology

The use of philosophical methods to better understand revealed truth. The goal of scholastic theology is to present the understanding of revealed truth in a logical and systematic form.

Book of Genesis tells us God created us in his image. To look at humans in all their complexities is to see God. He is the fashioner of our souls. Saint Irenaeus (130–202), made this point in his famous quotation: "Man fully alive is the glory of God."

Seeing God Revealed in All Creation

Saint Augustine stressed that, "even the tiniest insect cannot be considered attentively without astonishment and without praising the Creator." The Church Fathers truly recognized the imprint of God on everything created, especially on human beings. Nothing created by God, "even the tiniest insect," is insignificant. From the smallest to the largest of his creations, God's existence and glory are manifested. We can know him through the work of his hands. This is the fruit of the scriptural understanding of natural revelation. The Church Fathers proclaim the undeniable truth of God revealed in nature. When we recognize God's Revelation in all creation and listen to God's call to the deepest parts of our beings, we can be certain that God exists and that he is "the cause and the end of everything" (*CCC*, 46). ✝

Timeline of the Church Fathers

- Saint Athanasius (293–373), Bishop of Alexandria
- Saint Gregory of Nazianzen (325–389), Archbishop of Constantinople
- Saint Basil the Great (329–379), Archbishop of Caesarea in Cappadocia, Asia Minor, located in modern-day Turkey
- Saint Gregory of Nyssa (335–394), Bishop of Nyssa in Cappadocia, located in modern-day Turkey
- Saint Ambrose (340–397), Bishop of Milan
- Saint John Chrysostom (347–407), Archbishop of Constantinople
- Saint Jerome (347–419), of Bethlehem
- Saint Augustine (354–430), Bishop of Hippo Regius, now Annaba, located in Algeria
- Saint Gregory the Great (540–604), Bishop of Rome

7 Natural Revelation and Scholastic Theology

During the **Middle Ages,** new ways of providing logical arguments to demonstrate the existence of God emerged. The centuries with particular influence were the twelfth, thirteenth, and fourteenth centuries. These centuries gave rise to **scholastic theology,** a theological approach that used philosophical methods to better understand revealed truth. Grounded in the Scriptures and the Church Fathers' understanding of natural revelation, scholastic theologians also relied heavily on the use of reason and logic. These great thinkers of the Middle Ages maintained that through the use of our minds, we could logically develop "converging and convincing arguments" (*CCC*, 31) to attain truth and certainty about God and the human experience.

The goal of scholastic theology is to present the understanding of revealed truth in a logical and organized form. It is recognized as an energizing force behind current arguments regarding the genuineness of God's existence.

What do you think is significant about the two objects Saint Thomas Aquinas is holding in this painting?

Saint Thomas Aquinas: The Five Proofs

One of the most prominent individuals in the development of scholastic theology was Saint Thomas Aquinas. He was a Dominican friar, prolific writer, and Doctor of the Church. His most notable written work is called the *Summa Theologica*. The *Summa Theologica* is a twenty-one volume work on theology and faith. One of Aquinas's many accomplishments in the area of philosophy and theology is *The Five Proofs of God's Existence.* According to Aquinas the reality of God can be proved, or logically demonstrated, in five ways.

© National Gallery, London / Art Resource, NY

First Proof: The First Mover

The first proof or argument is known as the First Mover. It draws on the idea that the universe constantly moves. Because everything continuously moves and changes, human beings can logically deduce or see a need for a "First Mover," who set everything in motion and guides the actions of humanity. We call that First Mover "God."

Second Proof: Causality

The second proof of God's existence is referred to as Causality, or First Efficient Cause. By reflecting on the cycle of life, we realize that all things are caused by something else. We equally realize that nothing can create itself. Therefore common sense tells us there is an Ultimate Cause or First Efficient Cause, which is uncaused, or not created by something else. This uncaused First Cause is God.

Third Proof: Contingency

The third proof is based on a theory of contingency. This argument states that the universe contains many contingent things—that is, things that came into existence because of something else. But if everything were contingent, there would have to be a time where nothing would exist. This point in time would have been in the past. But things do exist. If they exist they cannot do so without a Necessary Being. A Necessary Being is one who creates but is not created. That Necessary Being, which gives life to all beings, is God.

Fourth Proof: Perfection

The fourth proof finds its strength in our understanding of perfection. Most of us can point out the imperfections of the world and humanity. In naming imperfections we acknowledge there are varying degrees of beauty, goodness, and knowledge. The question then becomes, How do we know perfect beauty, goodness, and knowledge? According to Aquinas, we know perfection because there is one all-perfect being, God, who sets the infinite standard for wisdom and truth.

Fifth Proof: Intelligent Being

The fifth and final proof asserts that the world is characterized by remarkable order. This proof asserts that it is apparent that there are things in the universe that on their own have no intelligence. Yet regardless of their lack of intelligence, they still act toward and achieve their end. One can then deduce that if things that lack intelligence still achieve their end, something that does have an intelligence and knowledge of their end and directs all things to their appropriate end must exist. This something can be seen as the intelligent designer behind our complex universe. We name this intelligent designer and magnificent architect God.

The Proofs Point to God's Existence

All five proofs logically point to the existence of God as the First Mover, First Cause, Necessary Being, Model of Perfection, and Intelligent Being. In the words of the *Catechism*, each argument emphasizes that we "can come to know that there exists a reality which is the first cause and final end of all things, a reality 'that everyone calls "God"'"[2] (34). ✝

A Different Lens

Saint Anselm of Canterbury (1033–1109) was a monk and theologian. He proposed a rational and logical argument for the existence of God. His argument provided a proof that uses reason alone to assert the existence of God. Anselm's proof predates Aquinas's five proofs, and scholars today study it widely. Anselm's argument, which is presented in his work titled *Proslogion*, is as follows:

1. God is "that than which nothing greater can be thought."
2. It is greater to exist in reality than to exist merely in the mind.
3. Then God must exist in reality, not only in mind and understanding.

8 Natural Revelation: Vatican Council I to the Present

Echoed throughout Church history is the assertion that God "can be known with certainty from the created world by the natural light of human reason"[3] (*CCC*, 36). However, at

Ecumenical Council

A gathering of the Church's bishops from around the world to address pressing issues in the Church. Ecumenical councils are usually convened by the Pope or are at least confirmed or recognized by him.

conscience

The "interior voice," guided by human reason and divine law, that leads us to understand ourselves as responsible for our actions, and prompts us to do good and avoid evil. To make good judgments, one needs to have a well-formed conscience.

Vatican Council II

The Ecumenical or general Council of the Roman Catholic Church that Pope John XXIII (1958–1963) convened in 1962 and that continued under Pope Paul VI (1963–1978) until 1965.

various points in the Church's history the reality of natural revelation encountered opposition.

Between December 1869 and October 1870, Vatican Council I, the twentieth **Ecumenical Council** of the Church, was held. One of the main issues the Council attended to before being cut short due to outside circumstances was the relationship between faith and reason. Regarding this issue, there were those who claimed that human reason lacked the capacity to grasp religious knowledge. In other words, large parts of the population challenged the Church's teaching that God can be known in and through creation informed by human reason. In the constitution *Dei Filius* (1870), the Council affirmed that "God, the first principle and last end of all things, can be known with certainty from the created world by the natural light of human reason" (2).

A Deeper Understanding

The philosopher Immanuel Kant (1724–1804) was noted for saying, "Have the courage to use your own reason!" This motto and the assertions of Vatican Council I gained the attention of the philosopher and theologian John Henry Cardinal Newman. Cardinal Newman lived between 1801 and 1890. He developed a theory known as the convergence of probabilities. This theory asserts that a number of probable hints, or indicators, point to the existence of God. These indicators range from people's experiences of beauty and goodness to the mystery of our world, from the voice of **conscience** to the enjoyment of freedom. The theory also asserts that no indicator alone necessarily proves the existence of God. Instead it claims that when the indicators are combined, they produce a powerful argument. The strength of these probable indicators together arrives at the same conclusion: God exists.

Karl Rahner (1904–1984) was a Jesuit theologian. He largely influenced the Catholic understanding of natural revelation. His work during **Vatican Council II** and his writings presented the idea that any time human beings experience limitation in knowledge, freedom, or perfection, there is an underlying awareness of God as Absolute Mystery. In speaking of God as mystery, Rahner used the image of a horizon. When we gaze at the horizon, we are not directly looking at the horizon. It is not actually something we can see. It

Modern theologian Karl Rahner speaks of God as the "horizon of being." How would you explain what this means to someone who has never heard the phrase?

© Iakov Kalinin / shutterstock.com

is where the sky and sea only appear to meet. It is beyond us, but it is the background of everything we see. Just as we do not see the horizon directly, we are unable to see God directly. Nonetheless, he is always there. He is Absolute Mystery and forms the backdrop and setting to the stage of our lives. Rahner believed we come to know God through the universe, which is marked by deep mystery and complexity. Natural revelation coupled with human reason helps to give us an awareness of a God of awesome depth who wants to be known. ☥

Catholic Wisdom

Vatican Council II Attendees

Did you know that Pope Benedict XVI and Pope John Paul II both were present at Vatican Council II (1962–1965)? At the time of the Council, Pope John Paul II, who was born in 1920, was a bishop, and Pope Benedict XVI, who was born in 1927, was a priest. Pope John Paul II was one of more than twenty-six hundred bishops who participated. Pope Benedict XVI contributed to the Council as a theological expert.

The Wisdom of Vatican Council II

The People of God believes that it is led by the Lord's Spirit, Who fills the earth. Motivated by this faith, it labors to decipher authentic signs of God's presence and purpose in the happenings, needs and desires in which this People has a share along with other men of our age. For faith throws a new light on everything, manifests God's design for man's total vocation, and thus directs the mind to solutions which are fully human.

(*Pastoral Constitution on the Church in the Modern World* [*Gaudium et Spes,* 1965], 11)

Review

1. What is natural revelation?

2. How does the Book of Wisdom support the concept of natural revelation?

3. Why is natural revelation alone insufficient for us to know God fully?

4. How do the Church Fathers explain human beings' place as the summit of creation?

5. What was the goal of scholastic theology?

6. List and give a brief explanation of the five proofs for the existence of God given by Saint Thomas Aquinas.

7. What was reasserted by the Pope and bishops at Vatican Council I about the relationship between faith and reason?

Part 3

Divine Revelation

As we have seen, God makes himself known to people in many ways through natural reason. In the fullness of his love, God has also freely chosen to directly reveal himself and his plan for humanity. The Scriptures are the written accounts of God's Revelation to the Jewish people and the first Christians.

The Bible itself is not the fullness of Divine Revelation. The definitive and most exquisite moment in the Revelation of God took place when the Word of God, the Second Person of the Trinity, became flesh. Jesus Christ is the fullness of Divine Revelation and salvation. He forged a new path for all of us to follow. This is the same path the Apostles and their successors, the bishops, would carry on. Guided by the Holy Spirit, the Church is called to continually teach and live the mysteries revealed by Christ. Together, Sacred Scripture and Sacred Tradition are the means by which Divine Revelation is transmitted to every generation.

The articles in this part address the following topics:

salvation history

The pattern of specific events in human history in which God clearly reveals his presence and saving actions. Salvation was accomplished once and for all through Jesus Christ, a truth foreshadowed and revealed throughout the Old Testament.

Divine Revelation

God's self-communication through which he makes known the mystery of his divine plan. Divine Revelation is a gift accomplished by the Father, Son, and Holy Spirit through the words and deeds of salvation history. It is most fully realized in the Passion, death, Resurrection, and Ascension of Jesus Christ.

theophany

God's manifestation of himself in a visible form to enrich human understanding of him. An example is God's appearance to Moses in the form of a burning bush.

9 Salvation History: God's Revelation

Many of us are lucky enough to have storytellers in our families. From these people we learn our family history. We may hear the stories of how our parents fell in love and how our grandparents survived tough times. We may also hear stories of pain and conflicts within the family, caused by selfishness and greed. If we listen carefully, these stories help us to understand who we are, whom to model our lives after, and what family pitfalls to avoid.

But we are also part of a much larger and more important history. The Church calls this salvation history, which tells how God's saving hand has been at work in and through human history. In one sense we can say that all human history is salvation history. By this we mean that the one true God—Father, Son, and Holy Spirit—has been present and active in the lives of his people since the beginning of time. But more specifically, **salvation history** is the pattern of specific events in human history in which God clearly reveals his presence and saving actions. Salvation was accomplished once and for all through Jesus Christ, a truth foreshadowed and revealed through the Old Testament.

At the heart of salvation history is **Divine Revelation**. Over time God revealed the fullness of his loving plan to save the human race from our bondage to sin and death. "God has revealed himself to man by gradually communicating his own mystery in deeds and in words" (*CCC,* 69). Divine Revelation, also called supernatural Revelation, is a window into the wisdom and knowledge of God. Although Divine Revelation is gradual, it culminated and took form "in the person and mission of the incarnate Word, Jesus Christ" (53). Out of a desire to fully disclose himself and his plan, God provides us "access to the Father, through Christ, the Word made flesh, in the Holy Spirit"[4] (51). He did this so we can share in his divine nature, the eternal life of God. God alone has revealed to us the central mystery of the Christian faith, the mystery of the Most Holy Trinity, by revealing himself as Father, Son, and Holy Spirit.

In the unfolding of salvation history, God invites us into communion with the blessed Trinity. Therefore he communicates "his own mystery in deeds and in words" (*CCC,* 69). Salvation history tells about God, who heals, refreshes, trans-

forms, reveals, and saves us. God revealed his name to our
ancestors in ways beyond human imagination—from
the time the divine name was disclosed to Moses in the
theophany of the burning bush to the time the angels' heralded the name of Jesus Christ, God Incarnate.

Out of love for his children, God has "provided the
definitive, superabundant answer to the questions that man
asks himself about the meaning and purpose of his life"
(*CCC*, 68). God reveals himself, especially in Jesus Christ,
who is himself God, so we may know and love him beyond
our "own natural capacity" (52). Yet in spite of his Revelation
of himself, God "remains a mystery beyond words"(230).
He stretches our hearts and minds so there is immeasurable
space for divine knowledge and love. We can never fully
grasp God. Human words and language can never capture
the magnificence of our transcendent God.

In the words of John Henry Cardinal Newman (1801–
1890), "As prayer is the voice of [human beings] to God, so
revelation is the voice of God to man." Divine Revelation
is the voice of God, who has revealed himself as Truth and
Love. He is trying to get our attention and attract our souls.
God wants us to know truth, beauty, goodness, and peace.
He knows these can be found only in his revealed Word of
Life, Jesus Christ. Divine Revelation is about God's love for
his most perfect creations, each of us. ☦

Live It!

God's Hand in My History

If we believe God's saving hand has been active throughout all of history, then that
means it has been active in our own individual lives as well. God is often present to
us through the people and events in our lives. Prayerfully reflecting on this can be a
good spiritual exercise.

One way to do this is by charting your own personal history as a journaling activity. Begin by reflecting back on your life. Then tell your story in terms of the people
or events that have brought you closer to God. Remember that our relationship
with God is not always sweet and rosy. Even the events we might have perceived
as negative at one point can strengthen our relationship with God. How do you see
God's hand working in your life?

Story of a Soul

Saint Thérèse of Lisieux (1873–1897), known as the Little Flower of Jesus, was a Carmelite nun and a woman of profound wisdom. Her life on this earth was brief, but she became known to the world through her autobiography, *Story of a Soul*. Her superiors had recognized her unique holiness and directed her to write it. In the book she shares with us the many ways God revealed himself to her simple soul. She describes a path called "the little way," in which she explains how every charitable action performed for God is a manifestation of God's existence.

The manner in which God made himself known to Saint Thérèse is known as private revelation. This is distinct from Divine Revelation. Private revelations help people live more fully at certain times in history, but they do not add to or change Christ's definitive Revelation.

© MalibuBooks / shutterstock.com

10 Salvation History in the Old Testament

The Sacred Scriptures—the Old and New Testaments—root us in God's Divine Revelation to, and saving action on behalf of, those who have gone before us. The words of our ancestors in faith continually reveal the truth of God. Salvation history, as written about in the Scriptures, reveals God's love for his people. Every time we read or hear the Word of God, we are led ever deeper into the mystery and wonder of God.

Old Testament Highlights

Salvation history begins with our first parents, who have the symbolic names Adam and Eve. Realizing there is "constant evidence of himself in created realities"[5] (*CCC*, 54), God wanted to further manifest himself to our first parents. He invited them "to intimate communion with himself and clothed them with resplendent grace and justice" (54). Even when Adam and Eve turned away from God in sin, God remained faithful to his People, and "promised them salvation (cf. *Genesis* 3:15) and offered them his covenant" (70). The sin of Adam and Eve is called **Original Sin**. It led to the loss of original holiness, made humans subject to death, and made sin universally present in the world. This universally present sin led to further sin among God's People. The sins of his People resulted in broken communities and families and in separation from God. Yet, despite their sinful actions, God still heard the cries of his People and offered them the hope of salvation.

Salvation history continues with the story of Noah. We hear how sin has spread throughout the whole world, making all people wicked and corrupt. God intends to destroy his creation through a great Flood. However, God gives Noah, the one remaining good and righteous man, instructions on how to build an ark that will save him and his family from disaster. The instructions and the rainbow that appears at the end of the Flood symbolize God's **covenant** with all living beings—a covenant fertilized and nourished by God's self-disclosure that "will remain in force as long as the world lasts" (*CCC*, 71).

Salvation history continues by telling how generations after the Flood, humanity had been scattered and divided

Original Sin
From the Latin *origo*, meaning "beginning" or "birth." The term has two meanings: (1) the sin of the first human beings, who disobeyed God's command by choosing to follow their own will and thus lost their original holiness and became subject to death, (2) the fallen state of human nature that affects every person born into the world.

covenant
A solemn agreement between human beings or between God and a human being in which mutual commitments are made.

Pray It!

Proclaiming the Word of God

Each time we gather to celebrate the Mass, we hear the Word of God. Lectoring, or proclaiming the sacred Word during the Mass, is one of the ways some members of the assembly are called to participate. Lectors proclaim the first and second readings. In preparation lectors immerse themselves in the Scripture passages by reading them and praying with them. Perhaps God is calling you to serve as a lector. Pray about it and, if you are interested, let your pastor or campus minister know.

by God. He did this because of human pride symbolized by the building of the Tower of Babel. Now God begins his plan to reconcile all humanity with himself by calling a special people to be his light to the nations. Thus he enters into a Covenant with the **patriarch** Abraham. God appears to Abraham in a vision, promising him descendants more numerous than the stars. God makes this promise even though Abraham's wife, Sarah, is barren, or unable to have children. Because Abraham is a man of great faith and righteousness, he obeys God. His obedience results in a bloodline of charismatic patriarchs, including Isaac and Jacob. It also results in Abraham's gaining land that yields in abundance.

Salvation history continues with the account of Moses and the Exodus. God, as liberator of the Israelites from Egyptian slavery, enters into a Covenant with Abraham's descendants, who are now known as the Israelites. As the people's part of the Covenant, God gives Moses the Law at Mount Sinai. The Law is summarized in the Ten Commandments. Christians call this Law the Old Law. This Covenant gives the people an identity as the Chosen, Holy Children of God. Through Divine Revelation God promises to remain faithful to the Covenant and never to cease calling the Israelites to be faithful.

Although God revealed his will and plan to Adam, Eve, Abraham, and Moses, humanity's inclination to sin stood in the way of God's plan. The Israelites continued to turn

The account of Noah and the Flood is an important part of salvation history. Why did sin become so widespread? How does the story give us hope?

© Philadelphia Museum of Art/CORBIS

away from the Covenant and the Law. In response God
revealed himself to the **prophets,** men like Isaiah, Jeremiah,
and Ezekiel. He called the prophets to speak God's Word and
to announce the "radical redemption of the People of God,
purification from all their infidelities, a salvation which will
include all nations"[6] (*CCC,* 64).

Further Hints of Salvation

Wisdom literature is the ancient Israelite writings that extol
the virtue of wisdom. This literature also gives practical advice on what it means to be wise. Wisdom literature
speaks of a God who intervenes and discloses himself in the
events of people's lives. We find God's divine wisdom crying
"aloud in the streets" (Proverbs 1:20), trying to catch the
attention of his beloved children.

Wisdom is sometimes personified in the wisdom literature (see Proverbs 1:20–21 and Wisdom 6:12–14). This personification of wisdom finds its realization in Jesus Christ,
the Son of God, who is the Wisdom of God (see 1 Corinthians 1:30). ☨

11 Jesus Christ: The Fullness of All Revelation

The Sacred Scriptures reveal to us that Jesus Christ is the
Son of God (see Matthew 3:17). This title describes the
unique and eternal relationship between God the Father and
his Son, Jesus Christ. Christ is the only Son of the Father,
and he is God himself. He is the perfect image of the Father
and the fullness of Divine Revelation (see John 14:8–11).
"God has revealed himself fully by sending his own Son,
in whom he has established his covenant for ever. The Son
is his Father's definitive Word; so there will be no further
Revelation after him" (*CCC,* 73). God's Word "became flesh
/ and made his dwelling among us" (John 1:14). Jesus Christ
is "the Father's one, perfect, and unsurpassable Word. In him
he has said everything; there will be no other word than this
one"(*CCC,* 65). Because Christ, the Son of God, humbled
himself in taking on our humanity, we have been invited into
communion with the Blessed Trinity in a whole new way.

patriarch
The father or leader
of a tribe, clan, or
tradition. Abraham,
Isaac, and Jacob were
the patriachs of the
Israelite people.

prophet
A person God chooses
to speak his message
of salvation. In the
Bible, primarily a
communicator of a
divine message of
repentance to the
Chosen People, not
necessarily a person
who predicted the
future.

wisdom literature
The Old Testament
Books of Proverbs,
Job, Ecclesiastes, Sir-
ach, and the Wisdom
of Solomon.

Trinity

From the Latin *trinus,* meaning "threefold," referring to the central mystery of the Christian faith that God exists as a communion of three distinct and interrelated divine Persons: Father, Son, and Holy Spirit. The doctrine of the Trinity is a mystery that is inaccessible to human reason alone and is known through Divine Revelation only.

The Light Shines

All salvation history, as contained in the Sacred Scriptures, speaks of one single Word, a transforming Word. This Word is God himself, the Second Divine Person of the **Trinity**, who came to dwell among us by assuming a human nature. The same Word that created the universe and revealed himself to the sacred writers of the Scriptures is Jesus Christ. All of the Scriptures bear witness to Jesus Christ—the First and Last, the definitive Word of Revelation. There is no greater Word, and no greater Word can ever be conceived.

And We Saw His Glory

In the life of Jesus Christ, we see the glory of God. The Word being born in a lowly stable, the Word welcoming the sinner, the Word healing pain and naming demons, the Word washing the feet of friends, the Word hanging on a cross, and the Word rising—these reveal a God who chose to disclose himself by taking on our humanity. God's Word, by revealing himself in the flesh, nursed our pain, bandaged our limitations, and counseled our souls.

Full of Grace and Truth

Jesus Christ is our "instruction manual" for interpreting all creation and its final end. In studying the life of Jesus Christ, who reveals the New Covenant, we come to know the fullness of salvation. We cannot fully understand this plan in this lifetime, but by pursuing a relationship with Jesus Christ, we come to know his free offer of grace, which enlightens the human mind and heart.

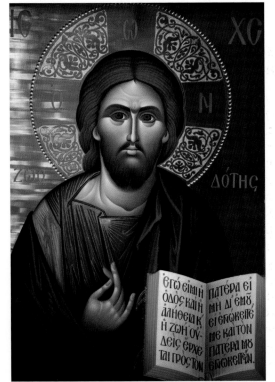

© Julian Kumar / GODONG/Godong/Corbis

In this Greek icon, the top letters—IC XC—are abbreviations for the Greek spelling of Jesus Christ. The three letters in the halo—O W N—are abbreviations for "He Who Is." Jesus is holding the Gospel of John. What do these titles and symbols tell us about Jesus Christ?

The Gospels use many images to convey the truth of Jesus' identity, the culmination of Divine Revelation. Shepherd, Friend, Savior, Doctor, Bread, Vine, Gate, and Light—all these images point to Jesus, the Son of God, who perfectly reflects and reveals his Father. He is the Word that can free us from all that enslaves us and takes away our freedom. What greater word has ever been spoken? None! Taken from the writings of Saint Patrick of Ireland (387–493), let us "bind" ourselves to Christ—the Eternal Word of God. ✝

A Prayer of Commitment: "Saint Patrick's Breastplate"

I bind to myself today
The virtue of the Incarnation of Christ with that of his Baptism,
The virtue of His Crucifixion with that of His Burial,
The virtue of His Resurrection with that of His Ascension,
The virtue of His Coming on the Judgment Day.

12 The Transmission of Divine Revelation

"What I say to you in the darkness, speak in the light; what you hear whispered, proclaim on the housetops" (Matthew 10:27). Jesus Christ, the fullness of Divine Revelation, commanded the Apostles to tell all people and all nations what they had heard and seen regarding the salvation of God. He entrusted them with the gift of the Holy Spirit to empower them to authentically teach and interpret the sacred truths revealed through his teachings and actions during his earthly life and through the events of the Paschal Mystery—his Passion, death, Resurrection, and Ascension. As they moved from village to village, city to city, the Apostles, under the inspiration of the Holy Spirit, helped more and more people to believe in Jesus Christ through their preaching and writing. This handing on, or transmission, of the truths that Jesus Christ taught is known as **Sacred Tradition** and will continue "under the inspiration of the Holy Spirit, to all generations, until Christ returns in glory" (*CCC*, 96).

Sacred Tradition
From the Latin *tradere*, meaning "to hand on." Refers to the process of passing on the Gospel message. It began with the oral communication of the Gospel by the Apostles, was written down in the Scriptures, and is interpreted by the Magisterium under the guidance of the Holy Spirit.

© iStockphoto.com / Duncan Walker

At the Last Supper, Jesus commanded the Apostles to "do this in memory of me" (Luke 22:19). The Apostles fulfilled this command even at the cost of their lives.

Through the process of **Apostolic Succession,** the authority of the original Apostles is passed on to their successors, the bishops of the Church. Every bishop of the Church can trace his special authority back to the original Apostles in an unbroken chain of succession through the laying on of hands in the Sacrament of Holy Orders as instituted by Christ. The office of bishop is permanent, because at ordination a bishop is marked with an indelible, sacred character. In the Sacrament the Holy Spirit empowers a bishop with the gifts needed to fulfill his role in the Church, including the gift of authentically teaching and interpreting Sacred Scripture and Sacred Tradition.

Through Tradition and the leadership of the bishops as teachers and interpreters, the Church, in "her doctrine, life, and worship"[7] (*CCC*, 78), proclaims the redemption found in Jesus Christ. It is through the doctrine, life, and worship of the Church that she "perpetuates and transmits to every generation all that she herself is, all that she believes"[8] (*CCC*, 78).

In fulfilling this mission, the Church is guided by the Holy Spirit. The God who spoke to people of the past, "continues to converse"[9] (*CCC*, 79) with men and women through the Holy Spirit. The Holy Spirit ignites the hearts of believers with a fire. The Holy Spirit enlivens and manifests all that was revealed in the Word made flesh—Jesus Christ. Jesus promised to send the Holy Spirit as our Advocate when the hour of his glorification had arrived (see John 14:15–17). The Holy Spirit proceeds from the Father and the Son, and

Catholic Wisdom

Apostolic Succession: The Symbol of the Keys

Perhaps you have noticed a papal flag in your school or parish. One of the symbols you will notice on the flag is two keys. The keys symbolize the responsibility that Christ gave to Saint Peter, the first Pope (see Matthew 16:19). One key is silver, representing power in the world, and the other is gold, representing spiritual power. All popes have the keys in their coat of arms as a symbol of Apostolic Succession.

guides the Church into the fullness of God's revealed truth, and opens the hearts and minds of God's people to know the truth that he has revealed and to faithfully live as his own people.

Two Pillars

Sacred Scripture and Sacred Tradition are intimately bound together. They are two pillars of strength. They hold up the Church as a light for all to know the mystery of Christ. These two pillars, the written, inspired Word of God and the living transmission of the Word of God, communicate effectively the whole of God's Revelation. Neither pillar can be understood without the other. They make up a single sacred deposit of the Word of God. Therefore both "are to be accepted and venerated with the same sense of loyalty and reverence" (*Dogmatic Constitution on Divine Revelation* [*Dei Verbum*, 1965], 9).

The **Deposit of Faith** is the heritage of faith contained in Sacred Scripture and Sacred Tradition. The task of interpreting the Deposit of Faith is entrusted to the **Magisterium,** the living teaching office of the Church, made up of the Pope and all the bishops in communion with him, under the guidance of the Holy Spirit. The bishops of the Church, both individually and collectively, have the obligation and the right to authentically teach and interpret Scripture and Tradition. Thus the Magisterium, rooted in its teaching authority and moved by the Holy Spirit, defines the **dogma,** or doctrine, of the faith.

Faith is necessary for salvation. Our faith is in Jesus Christ and the One who sent him. "For God so loved the world that he gave his only begotten Son, so that everyone who believes in him might not perish but have eternal life" (John 3:16). The Deposit of Faith contained in the Scriptures and Tradition nurtures our faith with the sacred truth revealed by God.

The Vocation of All

Saint Vincent of Lerins (fifth century) stated: "Keep the talent of the Catholic faith inviolate and unimpaired. What has been faithfully entrusted, let it remain in your possession, let it be handed on." By virtue of our Baptism, we are all called

Apostolic Succession
The uninterrupted passing on of apostolic preaching and authority from the Apostles directly to all bishops. It is accomplished through the laying on of hands when a bishop is ordained in the Sacrament of Holy Orders as instituted by Christ. The office of bishop is permanent, because at ordination a bishop is marked with an indelible, sacred character.

Deposit of Faith
The heritage of faith contained in Sacred Scripture and Sacred Tradition. It has been passed on from the time of the Apostles. The Magisterium takes from it all that it teaches as revealed truth.

Magisterium
The Church's living teaching office, which consists of all bishops, in communion with the Pope.

dogma
Teachings recognized as central to Church teaching, defined by the Magisterium and accorded the fullest weight and authority.

© Christopher Futcher / shutterstock.com

to treasure our faith as a price-less gem. We are to hold it in the treasure chest of our lives. We are also to share the gem with others. In this way we can bring forth the light and radi-

We all share in the responsibility to learn about God's revealed truth and to share it with others. Besides in classes at school, how do you continue to learn about your faith?

Mary, the Mother of God

© Victorian Traditions / shutterstock.com

Within the Tradition of the Church lies a special devotion to the Blessed Virgin Mary. Devotion to the Blessed Mother is celebrated in liturgical feasts and others prayers, such as the Rosary. Because of the teachings of the Apostles, we have come to realize the significant role Mary played in salvation. By saying yes to an angel, Mary opened the doors to Heaven. She miraculously conceived by power of the Holy Spirit and gave birth to Jesus Christ, the Eternal Son of God made man. Thus Mary remained a virgin through the conception and birth of Jesus and throughout her entire life. Mary is honored as the *Theotokos*, Greek for "God-bearer," a title affirming that as the mother of Jesus Christ, who is God himself, she is the Mother of God. The Scriptures and Tradition lift up Mary as a model of humble faith and amazing courage.

ance of Jesus revealed through Sacred Scripture and Sacred Tradition. The Church "cannot err in matters of belief" (*Dogmatic Constitution on the Church* [*Lumen Gentium,* 1964], 12), because the Holy Spirit guides her in the ways of truth and righteousness. Gifted by Apostolic Succession and led by the universal call to holiness, the entire Church—which includes each one of us—must speak what she has heard, in the light and from the housetops. ✝

13 Sacred Scripture and Sacred Tradition

redemption
From the Latin *redemptio,* meaning "a buying back," referring, in the Old Testament, to Yahweh's deliverance of Israel and, in the New Testament, to Christ's deliverance of all Christians from the forces of sin.

It is common to hear the teachings of the Catholic Church challenged with a question such as, Why do Catholics have beliefs and practices that are not in the Bible? In reality Sacred Tradition teaches the fullness of Divine Revelation. It began with the preaching of the Gospel by the Apostles, was written in the Scriptures, continues to be handed down and lived out in the life of the Church, and is interpreted by the Magisterium under the guidance of the Holy Spirit. Thus the Scriptures developed from Sacred Tradition. However, the Bible by itself does not communicate everything God reveals through Sacred Tradition.

As Catholics we are blessed in recognizing that God chooses to disclose the truths of Revelation through both Sacred Tradition and the Sacred Scriptures. "There exists a close connection and communication between Sacred Tradition and Sacred Scripture," both of them "flowing from the same divine wellspring" (*Divine Revelation,* 9). They communicate the whole of God's **redemptive** and reconciling love. Together "Sacred Tradition and Sacred Scripture make up a single sacred deposit of the Word of God" (10). This deposit of the Word of God enables the Church to contemplate God who is the "source of all of her riches" (*CCC,* 97).

Tradition helps us to understand the Revelation of Jesus Christ found in the Scriptures. As true successors to the Apostles and guided by the Holy Spirit, the bishops, in communion with the Pope, witness and give further understanding to God's self-revelation in the Church's "teaching, life and worship" (*Divine Revelation,* 8). In conversation with the Scriptures, Tradition passes on the message of the Gospel to be lived out in the life of the Church. The Church's Magisterium has a unique responsibility to interpret both Scripture and Tradition under the guidance of the Holy Spirit.

Again, all that is part of Sacred Tradition is a manifestation of what was disclosed through Jesus' teachings and

The Words of Saint John Chrysostom, Doctor of the Church

"'Therefore, brethren, stand fast and hold the traditions that you have been taught, whether by word or by our letter" (2 Thessalonians 2:15). From this it is clear that they did not hand down everything by letter, but there was much also that was not written. Like that which was written, the unwritten too is worthy of belief. So let us regard the tradition of the Church also as worthy of belief. Is it a tradition? Inquire no further.

actions during his earthly ministry and the events of the Paschal Mystery—his Passion, death, Resurrection, and Ascension. Nothing taught or proclaimed by the Church ever contradicts the truth of Jesus Christ. In the words of the *Catechism*, Sacred Tradition and Sacred Scripture "makes present and fruitful in the Church the mystery of Christ, who promised to remain with his own 'always, to the close of the age'"[10] (80). What an amazing Church to be a part of! ☦

Review

1. What is Divine Revelation?

2. What is salvation history?

3. What is Original Sin, and what are some of the consequences of Original Sin?

4. What is Sacred Tradition?

5. What is the relationship between the Sacred Scriptures, Sacred Tradition, and Revelation?

6. What is the Deposit of Faith?

7. What is the Magisterium? What is the Magisterium's responsibility in regard to the Scriptures and Tradition?

Interpretation and Overview of the Bible

Part 1

Understanding the Scriptures

The Sacred Scriptures are the account of God's saving hand at work in human history and experience. God is the Bible's sole and supreme author, and all that is taught and proclaimed in Sacred Scripture is free from error regarding the truths he wishes to reveal for the sake of our salvation. The Holy Spirit inspired the human authors of the sacred books, who made full use of their human knowledge and intelligence to communicate the particular truths entrusted to them. Even though written in the language and styles of particular times and cultures, all of Sacred Scripture reveals the truth of who God is and of his work of salvation.

The canon of the Bible consists of forty-six Old Testament books and twenty-seven New Testaments books. The contents of the canon were discerned based on their authentic Revelation and truth. Inspired by God, inerrant in truth, defined in number, and appearing in different translations, the words of both the Old and New Testaments lead to right understanding of God's Incarnate Word.

The articles in this part address the following topics:

Divine Inspiration
The divine assistance the Holy Spirit gave the authors of the books of the Bible so the authors could write in human words the salvation message God wanted to communicate.

biblical inerrancy
The doctrine that the books of the Scriptures are free from error regarding the truth God wishes to reveal through the Scriptures for the sake of our salvation.

14 Divine Inspiration and Biblical Inerrancy

Writers sometimes talk about a time when they were inspired. This usually means that some person or event helped them to write something unique or to write especially well. Maybe you have felt that way at some time.

But the Bible's inspiration is unique. The Holy Spirit, the Third Person of the Trinity, inspired the human authors who wrote the Bible's books. This is called **Divine Inspiration.** God himself is the ultimate author of the Sacred Scriptures. Thus, the books of the Sacred Scriptures "without error teach that truth which God, for the sake of our salvation, wished to see confided to the Sacred Scriptures" (*Divine Revelation,* 11).

The Author of the Sacred Scriptures

God chose ordinary and often unsuspecting people to write the books of the Bible. The Holy Spirit "breathed into" (this is the literal meaning of *inspired*) human beings the ways and truths of God. Does this mean the human authors were only human word processors, writing down the words the Holy Spirit dictated to them? The answer is no. They kept full use of their human knowledge and creativity. The Bible's human authors were true authors. But in a truly marvelous way, God acted in them and through them as they wrote about the origins of creation and sin, the relevance of wisdom and prophecy, and the saving work of Jesus Christ, the eternal Son of God made man.

Faithfully and Without Error

Within the words of the Scriptures lies the delicacy of God's wisdom. His wisdom is absolute and without error. Even though human authors wrote the books of the Bible, God is the ultimate author, and the saving truths God willed us to know are inerrant (without error). In other words, the books of the Bible manifest and teach the truths of faith accurately and without mistake. This is called **biblical inerrancy.**

Through the Medium of Their Words

In the Sacred Scriptures, we come to know the amazing works of God, the Father, Son, and Holy Spirit. God's Revelation is understandable to us because in the Sacred Scriptures he speaks to us using human words. It is a sign of God's tremendous respect for us that he uses human language, words, and symbols as vehicles of his saving grace.

We must, however, take into account that culture and time affect the Bible's words. The human authors used the languages and thinking of their times. We need to study "the conditions of their time and culture, the literary genres in use at that time, and the modes of feeling, speaking, and narrating then current" (*CCC*, 110) to understand what the authors intended to communicate. As we study the cultures in which the books of the Bible were written, we note that the human authors may not have been aware of the deeper truths God was intending to communicate. Just understanding what they intended to communicate is not enough. For a correct interpretation of the Sacred Scriptures, we must also look for the truth that God wanted to reveal to us through the human authors' words. "Sacred Scripture must be read and interpreted in the light of the same Spirit by whom it was written"[1] (*CCC*, 111). ✟

The Bishop of Milan

Saint Ambrose was the Bishop of Milan, a diocese in Italy. He is a Father and Doctor of the Church who devoted much of his life to the study of the Sacred Scriptures. He delved into the Sacred Scriptures in an attempt to make them relevant and accessible to everyday people of faith. He was recognized as a powerful preacher, compassionate minister, prominent leader, and inspirational writer. He was so influential that Saint Augustine of Hippo attributes to the sermons of Saint Ambrose his own decision to be baptized.

15 From the Spoken to the Written Word

Communication is essential to the survival of the human race. People have spent the past several thousand years developing new ways to exchange stories, thoughts, and feelings. Today we make those exchanges through cell phones, e-mail messages, text messages, television, radio, and iPods. We have developed these devices to help us effectively com-

oral tradition
The handing on of the message of God's saving plan through words and deeds.

written tradition
Under the inspiration of the Holy Spirit, the synthesis in written form of the message of salvation that has been passed down in the oral tradition.

municate with one another. However, even with these new methods, there are still three basic forms of communication: nonverbal deeds and actions, the spoken word, and the written word. These types of communication were instrumental in the development of the Sacred Scriptures as we know them today.

Before anything can ever be spoken about or written down, human beings must have an experience. Central to the experiences of people during Old Testament times was their relationship with God. They experienced God as Creator, Liberator, and Covenant Maker. They also experienced God as Patriarchal Warrior, Father, Beloved Spouse, Dancing Wisdom, and Herald of Hope. Grounded in the heritage and wisdom of the past, the people of the Gospels personally saw and interacted with the Word made flesh, Jesus Christ. They gathered around Jesus with attentive ears and hearts, listening to and loving his healing words. Their journey was different from that of the people of the Old Testament. Yet both were instructed to tell the world about God's saving action.

The Spoken Word

The Israelites' experience of God was originally handed down orally. Some of the methods used were prophesying, preaching, storytelling, and poetry. Their experience of God was also handed down through the manner in which they worshipped and kept the covenants made by God and his People. This handing on of truth-carrying and wisdom-filled words and deeds from generation to generation is called

Pray It!

Lament, Thanksgiving, and Praise!

The Psalms tell us about the Israelites' relationship with God. The Book of Psalms contains many kinds of prayer, including prayers of lament, thanksgiving, and praise. The Book of Psalms can be a great source for us when we pray.

Take some time to go through the Book of Psalms. Have a notebook handy and jot down the numbers of Psalms that catch your attention. Then, next time you pray, have your Bible and notebook ready and pray with the Psalms. Here are some suggestions to help you get started: Psalm 23, 109:105–112, 118, 121, 144, and 150.

oral tradition. Narratives of God's wonderful work on behalf of humanity were told in groups, families, and other gatherings. During Old Testament times, few people could read and write. Consequently the people relied heavily on the spoken words of their ancestors.

In New Testament times, language was developing dramatically. Writing was becoming more accessible. At first it was the proclaimed Word of Jesus that was so powerful and transforming. In fact, he sent his followers with the charge to proclaim the Word of God. In the Gospel of Mark, Jesus said, "Go into the whole world and proclaim the gospel to every creature"(16:15). The Acts of the Apostles speaks of the Holy Spirit's coming to the Apostles in "tongues as of fire"(2:3) so they could speak of God's great love. Notice that both passages emphasize speaking rather than writing.

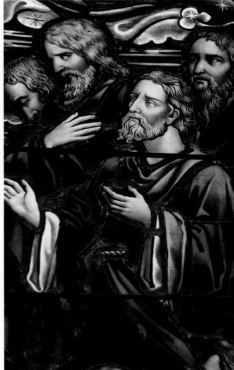

© iStockphoto.com / Leah-Anne Thompson

The Written Word

The people, in both Old and New Testament times, wanted to preserve God's message of salvation. Therefore they began the **written tradition.** This involved the writing down, with the inspiration of the Holy Spirit, God's Revelation to his children. The early Christians were especially concerned about protecting and safeguarding the message of Jesus Christ. They were concerned because many of the people who knew Jesus personally were being persecuted and put to death for their faith. The people did not want to lose the perspective and testimonies of these witnesses to the life and mission of our Lord and Savior, Jesus Christ.

From experience to speech to writing, the record of salvation history has been told. The spoken and written traditions have communicated the deep seed of God's wisdom for more than two thousand years. These traditions continue to pave the way into a new millennium, a new day. ☩

The Apostles preached the Good News to others after Jesus' Ascension. How do you see the Good News being shared today?

Three Stages in the Formation of the Gospels

1. **The life and teachings of Jesus:** Jesus, the Son of God, walked the earth, teaching and preaching the truth of salvation.

2. **The oral tradition:** The Apostles, enlightened by the Holy Spirit, handed on to their hearers all that Jesus had revealed.

3. **The written Gospels:** Under the guidance of the Holy Spirit and without error, the Evangelists synthesized in writing what had been handed on orally or had already been written regarding the Incarnate Word of God, Jesus Christ.

© Brooklyn Museum/Corbis

16 When Was It Written?

Have you ever had an experience that seemed insignificant at the time, but later you realized its importance? We may not recognize the saving action of God until we have time to reflect on all that has happened to us. This is equally true for the authors of the Bible.

The ancient Israelites and first Christians often did not write down their personal experiences or their ancestors' dealings with God. They did not understand these experiences' larger implications. Through the intervention and inspiration of the Holy Spirit, the authors of biblical texts began to realize the need to write down their people's experiences of God manifested in creation, freedom, Covenant, and Incarnation. Therefore many of the biblical books were written down years, even centuries, after the events they describe had happened (see chart "When Was It Written?").

Most books do not appear in the Bible in the order in which they were written. A number of Paul's letters (Romans, First and Second Corinthians, Galatians, Philippians, Colossians, and First and Second Thessalonians), were most likely written around AD 50–60. This was before the Gospels of Matthew, Mark, Luke, and John were written (AD 62–100). However, it makes sense to place the Gospels first, because they are eyewitness accounts of Jesus' life. Paul's letters cover the life of early Christians after the death and Resurrection of Jesus Christ. We must not become lost and overburdened by historical dates or the arrangement of books. We should instead pay attention to the overarching truth and cohesive picture of our compassionate God woven through the words of the Sacred Scriptures. It is good to have a sense of history and accuracy. It is better to know the ultimate, never ending, triumphant love God offers his People. ✝

Live It!

Check Out the Background

Learning when a book was written can shed light on its interpretation. For example, Mark probably wrote the first Gospel sometime around AD 65–70. During this period the faith of some Christians was being tested by Roman persecutions. This may be the reason the Gospel of Mark has a strong emphasis on Jesus' faithfulness to his mission even when he was misunderstood and persecuted.

As another example, consider John's Gospel, most likely the last Gospel written, sometime around AD 90–100. During this time many Jewish Christians were rejected by Jews who did not believe that Jesus was the Messiah. They were no longer allowed to worship in the synagogues. The Gospel of John emphasizes the importance of believing in Jesus and contains several accounts of the conflicts between Jesus and the Jewish leaders who did not believe in him. This was probably intended to remind the early Christians to remain steadfast in their faith despite the rejection they faced, and that this experience was not unique to their time.

When Was It Written?		
Book	**Period Covered**	**Date Written**
Genesis	Creation–1500 BC	900–500 BC
Exodus	1500–1250 BC	900–500 BC
Prophetic Books	922–300 BC	865–300 BC
Gospels	5 BC–AD 30	AD 62–100
Paul's Letters	AD 51–100	AD 51–100

17 Setting the Canon of Scripture

The Bible has been, and continues to be, the most read book in the world. The Bible is a collection of *biblia sacra* (Latin for "sacred books"). The books of the Bible contain the truth of God's Revelation, composed by human authors under the inspiration of the Holy Spirit. The **canon** of the Bible is the official collection of inspired books. It is an integral part of the Church's tradition. The canon of the Catholic Bible is composed of forty-six Old Testament books and twenty-seven New Testament books. The pages of the Sacred Scriptures contain God's self-revelation to human beings. The Sacred Scriptures lay the foundation for the beliefs, practices, and customs of the Catholic faith.

There are times when some of the popular media and literature place before us stories about newly discovered "gospels." The contents of these "gospels" often contradict the truths we read in the Sacred Scriptures and the tenets (system of belief) of Christianity. For this reason it is important for us to understand how the authentic canon was chosen. "It was by the apostolic Tradition that the Church discerned which writings are to be included in the list of the sacred books"[2] (*CCC*, 120). The early bishops, who were the successors to the Apostles, used four standards to discern the validity of a book. A book had to pass all four standards to be considered divinely inspired and canonical (part of the sacred canon). These four standards were especially used in the case of the New Testament writings.

The first standard dealt with the apostolic origin. A book passed this standard if it was based on the preaching and teaching of the Apostles and their closest companions.

The second standard centered on the universal acceptance of the book. Was the book accepted and received by all major Christian communities in the Mediterranean world? If Christians accepted it universally, then it passed this standard.

The third standard revolved around the early Christian community's use of the texts. Were they being used in Christian liturgical celebrations? More important, was it being used when they gathered for **the Eucharist,** also called the Mass? If early Christians were weaving the books into their entire worship, then the early bishops concluded that the texts enhanced the prayer lives of the people.

The final standard involved delving deeply into the book to see if its message was consistent with other Christian and Hebrew, or Jewish, writings.

Knowing the standards the bishops used in determining the canon of the Bible helps us to understand why some books were not selected. For instance, the **Gnostic** gospels were rejected because they placed little importance on the suffering and death of Jesus. The suffering and death of Jesus are essential in understanding God's full plan of salvation. They must be emphasized for us to comprehend the amazing and redemptive work of our God. The canon of the Sacred Scriptures is the true, authoritative record of God's saving plan. ✝

canon
The collection of books the Church recognizes as the inspired Word of God.

the Eucharist
The celebration of the entire Mass. The term sometimes refers specifically to the consecrated bread and wine that have become the Body and Blood of Christ.

Gnostic
Referring to the belief that salvation comes from secret knowledge available to only a select few.

Three Councils, One Decision

Three main Councils were instrumental in forming the canon of the Sacred Scriptures we know today. They were the Council of Hippo (393), the Council of Carthage (397), and the Ecumenical Council of Trent (1543–1563). These Councils contributed something unique to the discussion about the authenticity of particular books. Most interesting is that each in its own way came to the same conclusive list of inspired books to include in the canon of the Bible. It was not until the Ecumenical Council of Trent that an infallible definition regarding the books included in the canon was declared.

18 Different Translations: The Same Revelation

Hebrew, Greek, Aramaic, Latin, Spanish, French, Chinese, English—the world is filled with many languages and dialects. Translating one language to another is one of the most daunting tasks a person can undertake. This is the task of individuals who translate the Bible from its original languages of Hebrew, Aramaic, and Greek. Because we place such high value on the inspired words in the Bible, translations are always completed by many people working with numerous ancient texts. The people working on a particular translation bring their expertise and knowledge of the language to the task. The result is a diversity of biblical translations and versions, but the truths of Divine Revelation are the same.

The Greek translation of the Old and the New Testament was used for many centuries in the early Church. After Saint Jerome translated the Bible into Latin, the Church used that translation for over a thousand years. Jerome's translation of the Bible into Latin is known as the Latin Vulgate.

Yet if you go to a book store today, you will find many different versions of the Bible in many different languages. A particular version may exist to serve a particular purpose. One translation's purpose might be to stay as faithful as possible to the original words for accuracy. Another translation might use more contemporary words and phrases for easier understanding. For this reason we consider a number of translations to be trustworthy and sound.

Although there are others, four Catholic biblical translations are widely used in modern English: the New American Bible with Revised New Testament and Revised Psalms

Catholic Wisdom

The New American Bible

Have you ever wondered which translation of the Bible is used by Catholics most often in the United States? The New American Bible (NAB) translation is probably used most often. The NAB is the translation used in this book. It is the same translation that is on the Web site of the United States Conference of Catholic Bishops. The NAB is also the translation that is used in the *Lectionary* and *Book of the Gospels* that are read from at the Mass.

Different Translations of Matthew 5:13–16

New American Bible **The Similes of Salt and Light** You are the salt of the earth. But if salt loses its taste, with what can it be seasoned? It is no longer good for anything but to be thrown out and trampled underfoot. You are the light of the world. A city set on a mountain cannot be hidden. Nor do they light a lamp and then put it under a bushel basket; it is set on a lampstand, where it gives light to all in the house. Just so, your light must shine before others, that they may see your good deeds and glorify your heavenly Father.	New Revised Standard Version **Salt and Light** You are the salt of the earth; but if salt has lost its taste, *how can its saltiness be restored?* It is no longer good for anything, but is thrown out and trampled under foot. You are the light of the world. A city built on a hill cannot be hid. No one after lighting a lamp puts it under the bushel basket, but on the lampstand, and it gives light to all in the house. In the same way, let your light shine before others, so that they may see your good works and give glory to your Father in heaven.
New Jerusalem Bible **Salt for the Earth and Light for the World** You are salt for the earth. But if salt loses its taste, what can make it salty again? It is good for nothing, and can only be thrown out to be trampled under people's feet. You are light for the world. A city built on a hill-top cannot be hidden. No one lights a lamp to put it under a tub; they put it on the lamp-stand where it shines for everyone in the house. In the same way your light must shine in people's sight, so that, seeing your good works, they may give praise to your Father in heaven.	Good News Translation **Salt and Light** You are like salt for the whole human race. But if salt loses its saltiness, there is no way to make it salty again. It has become worthless, so it is thrown out and people trample on it. You are like a light for the whole world. A city built on a hill cannot be hid. No one lights a lamp and puts it under a bowl; instead it is put on the lampstand, where it gives light for everyone in the house. In the same way your light must shine before people, so that they will see the good things you do and praise your Father in heaven.

(NAB); the New Revised Standard Version (NRSV), Catholic Edition; the *New Jerusalem Bible (NJB)*; and the Good News Translation in Today's English Version, Second Edition (GNT). Four translations, one message of saving love.

Though the NAB is the approved lectionary text for the United States, the NRSV is the approved lectionary text for Canada. The NJB is widely used outside the United States and is a wonderful asset to prayer because of its poetic nature. The GNT uses a more basic vocabulary and is more conversational in style. Note the different biblical translations of Matthew 5:13–16 in the chart on page 57. Which do you find most appealing? ✝

Review

1. What is divine inspiration?

2. Who is the ultimate author of the Sacred Scriptures? Explain the relationship between the ultimate author and the human authors of the Sacred Scriptures.

3. What is the relationship between divine inspiration and biblical inerrancy?

4. What is the total number of books in the official canon of the Bible? How are these books divided?

5. List the three stages that were part of the formation of the Gospels.

6. What standards did the early bishops use to discern which books belong in the canon of the Bible?

Part 2

Interpreting Scripture

The Scriptures, the Old Testament and the New Testament, make known to us the truth of who God is and his plan for our salvation. The truth God reveals in Scripture must be interpreted throughout time. The authentic interpretation of Scripture is entrusted to the Magisterium, the teaching office of the Church. The Magisterium interprets the meaning of a particular text by reading and interpreting it within the Tradition and teachings of the Church. It also interprets a text "in the sacred spirit in which it was written" (*Divine Revelation,* 12). The Church also considers the cultures and conditions in which a biblical passage was written. She articulates an authentic understanding of salvation grounded in Jesus Christ. Christ is the fullness of Revelation because he is God himself. The Church also teaches us how to relate the truths of Divine Revelation to science and history. "There can never be any real discrepancy between faith and reason"[3] (CCC, 159).

The articles in this part address the following topics:

19 A Vocation to Interpret and Teach

Have you ever had a discussion with friends about your religious beliefs? People have strong feelings about religious beliefs, especially about what the Bible teaches about certain things. Understanding the truth that God wants to reveal in the Scriptures is important and can be a tremendous challenge. With the grace of the Holy Spirit, the Magisterium of the Church provides us with the proper guidance and wisdom.

The Magisterium is the "living, teaching office of the Church"[4] (*CCC*, 85). It has been given the sole authority to authentically interpret the words of the Sacred Scriptures. The Holy Spirit guides the Magisterium—the bishops in communion with the Pope—in this task. The Magisterium guards and explains the truths revealed in the Bible.

Under the guidance of the Magisterium, the Church seeks to hear and understand what God reveals through the words of Sacred Scripture. This involves prayerfully listening to the same Spirit who inspired the human authors of the Bible. "Interpretation of the inspired Scripture must be attentive above all to what God wants to reveal through the sacred authors for our salvation. What comes from the Spirit is not fully 'understood except by the Spirit's action' (cf. Origen, *Hom. in Ex.* 4, 5: J. P. Migne, ed., Patrologia Graeca (Paris, 1857–1866) 12, 320)" (*CCC*, 137).

Interpreting and explaining Sacred Scripture is a grave responsibility, and many who are not bishops are engaged

Live It!

Sacred Scripture and Personal Prayer

Reading the Bible as part of personal prayer and reflection is an important way to grow in faith. When we read a Bible passage, we must consider it in the context of the history of our salvation. We must also consider the intention of the original author and what God intends to reveal. One way for us to gain understanding of what God wants to communicate to us through Scripture is to look to the teachings of the Magisterium. Through the Church's guidance, we can grow in our understanding of God's love for us, communicated through his words and deeds in the Scriptures, and of how we can respond to him with love in the way we live our lives each day.

Three Defining Moments

1943 *Divino Afflante Spiritu*

This encyclical, issued by Pope Pius XII, allowed a limited use of modern methods of biblical criticism. The teaching authority of the Church began to recognize the need to examine the influence of literary techniques and forms on the deeper meaning of biblical passages.

1965 *Dogmatic Constitution on Divine Revelation (Dei Verbum)*

Vatican Council II issued this dogmatic constitution. *Dei Verbum* further explored the relationship between literary devices and the intended meaning of the Word of God. It also strongly emphasized the need to study the cultures in which the books of the Bible were written. This would help in understanding what God wants to communicate to us. The Council cautioned those working in biblical interpretation that all study of a particular text must be situated within the whole history of salvation.

1993 *Interpretation of the Bible in the Church*

The Pontifical Biblical Commission built on the teachings of *Divino Afflante Spiritu* and *Dei Verbum* by laying out several approaches and methods of interpretation. Among these methods were the textual, historical, literary, source, and redaction methods. It explained the senses of the Scriptures (literal, spiritual, and allegorical, moral, and anagogical). It developed a list of characteristics of Catholic interpretation. Among the list of characteristics of Catholic interpretation was the role of Tradition, the task of the interpreter, and the relevance of other theological disciplines.

in this work. Those who do biblical interpretation, such as scholars and priests, are called to follow the Magisterium's principles of interpretation, and of course the interpreters' research, teaching, and preaching are subject to the judgment of the Magisterium. The work of biblical interpreters serves the Church by helping us to gain a better understanding of the meaning of Sacred Scripture. The principles of interpretation are helpful to all—especially students—who read and seek to understand the Bible. We'll explore several principles of interpretation in upcoming articles.

The Magisterium is strengthened by its direct link to the Apostles. It "is not superior to the Word of God, but is its servant"[5] (*CCC*, 86). As servant, one role of the Magisterium is to guide all of the faithful in the task of bringing to light all that God reveals and of announcing the great love of our saving God. We trust the Holy Spirit, who directs the Magisterium in its interpretation of the Sacred Scriptures and guides the efforts of all the faithful to understand and share the message of the Scriptures. As Saint Thomas More (1478–1535), an English martyr under King Henry VIII of England, stated so well: "The Church of Christ has always, and never fails in, the right understanding of Scripture, so far as is necessary for our salvation." ✝

20 Biblical Exegesis

People often ask, "Why do I have to read the Bible?" This question might be followed by this statement: "I have nothing in common with the people of the Bible. Times have changed." It is true that times have changed, but in reality we still struggle with the same issues as people did then: jealousy, idolatry, disbelief, hypocrisy, selfishness, and so on. Although we may not recognize the similarities between ourselves and our ancestors in faith, closer study of Scripture helps us understand the events portrayed in Scripture and relate them to our lives today. The process of interpreting and critically explaining a passage from Sacred Scripture is called **biblical exegesis.** Biblical exegesis involves thoughtful and rigorous interpretation of the Scriptures and what God is communicating to us through his Words. Biblical exegesis dispels the myth that the people and lessons of the Bible are outdated and affirms that the inspired Word of God continues to speak to us and guide us.

Pray It!

The Guidance of the Holy Spirit

A good practice to have when reading the Scriptures is to pray to the Holy Spirit for guidance. Pray the following prayer to the Holy Spirit the next time you pray with the Scriptures:

Come, Holy Spirit, fill the hearts of your faithful. Enkindle in them the fire of your love.
Send forth Your Spirit, and they will be created,
And you will renew the face of the earth.
Let us pray:
Lord, by the light of the Holy Spirit, you have taught the hearts of the faithful. In the same Spirit, help us to relish what is right and always rejoice in your consolation. We ask this through Christ our Lord. Amen.

Biblical exegesis is primarily the work of biblical scholars—men and women with advanced degrees in biblical studies. Although any person can strive to develop an understanding of the Word of God in the Bible, these professionals are fluent in Greek or Hebrew, or both, and often specialize in particular areas of exegesis. For example, a scholar might be an expert in the cultural beliefs of biblical people or he or she might have expertise in the interpretation of Paul's letters. Biblical exegetes also teach and create Bible study resources such as dictionaries, commentaries, and professional journals.

biblical exegesis
The critical interpretation and explanation of a biblical text.

Bridging the Gap

Biblical scholars work hard at bridging the gap between the people of yesterday, today, and tomorrow. They "must be attentive to what the human authors truly wanted to affirm and to what God wanted to reveal to us by their words"[6]

The Fruit of Their Labors

The publication of Bible commentaries is a significant contribution of biblical scholarship. Bible commentaries draw on the work of biblical scholars and their tireless exegetical studies. They detail the meaning of the stories and lessons of the Sacred Scriptures. From a study of the cultures in which the stories were written to their significance today, biblical scholars have provided resources that aid in spreading the truth and wisdom of God's Word. Two of the most popular and reputable Bible commentaries are *The Collegeville Bible Commentary* (Liturgical Press, 1992) and *The New Jerome Biblical Commentary* (Prentice Hall, 1989).

analogy of faith
The coherence of individual doctrines with the whole of Revelation. In other words, as each doctrine is connected with Revelation, each doctrine is also connected with all other doctrines.

(*CCC,* 109). They must study the culture and context in which the author of a particular book of the Bible lived to more fully develop their understanding of the meaning of Scripture, the intentions of a biblical author. The scholar must also look at various literary genres and techniques commonly used at the time. These actions will assist in the study of the passage and uncover the levels of meaning behind the words. An authentic interpretation of the Sacred Scriptures is grounded in the Tradition and teachings of the Church. It is carried out "in the light of the same Spirit by whom it was written"[7] (*CCC,* 111).

A thorough exegesis is done with an awareness of the larger truths revealed in *"the content and unity of the whole Scripture"* (*CCC,* 112). In other words a particular biblical text or passage can be fully understood only within the complete picture of both the Old and New Testaments. The Scripture scholar discovers the deeper meaning of Sacred Scripture when she or he takes into account the unity that exists in all truth. This is especially true for the truths of faith. There is coherence between them; understanding one truth helps us to better understand the others. This unity in doctrine is known as the **analogy of faith.**

A Wise Heart

An early Church Father, Saint Fulgence of Ruspe (468–533), stated, "Study your heart in the light of the Holy Scriptures, and you will know therein who you were, who you are, and who you ought to be." Enlightened by the Holy Spirit, biblical scholars must be aware of the author's intention. They must also be conscious of Church Tradition. They need to be attentive to the whole of Revelation written in the Sacred Scriptures. They also need to be mindful of the unity existing in all Church teachings. By doing this, biblical scholars can challenge us to know our past, recognize where we stand today, and envision where we ought to be tomorrow. ✞

21 Literary Forms in the Bible

The Bible is composed of many different types of literature. We must know which types we are reading and realize that each type has its own rules for interpretation.

Key Points

- Forms of literature, also called literary genres, refer to different styles of writing found in the Sacred Scriptures.
- The study of literary forms can give us insight into the "meaning the sacred writers really intended" (*Divine Revelation*, 12).
- The Scriptures are not just another form of literature. They must be read and interpreted in light of the Incarnate Word,

Literary Forms in the Bible		
Type	**Explanation**	**Example**
Creation accounts	Explanations of how something came into existence	Adam and Eve, Noah, Tower of Babel
Psalms	Hymns or songs of prayer that express praise, thanksgiving, petition, lamentation, or a historical memory of God's action on behalf of the Chosen People	Book of Psalms
Prophetic oracles	Counsel and wisdom given by God	Prophetic books
Historical books	Accounts of the saving action of God in human history	1 and 2 Samuel, 1 and 2 Kings
Wisdom literature	Collections of sayings and teachings about how to live a good and wise life, a life pleasing to God	Books of Proverbs, Ecclesiastes, Wisdom
Parables	Brief stories told by Jesus to exemplify moral or religious lessons	Mustard seed, prodigal son
Letters (epistles)	Letters to early Christians to pass on wisdom, correction, and community information	Letters of Paul
Apocalyptic literature	Descriptions of the end times, prophecies of catastrophic upheavals on earth, and promises of a new creation	Books of Daniel, Revelation
Gospels	Accounts of real events and teachings from Jesus' life that give deeper insight into the meaning of his life and mission	Books of Matthew, Mark, Luke, John

exegete
A biblical scholar attempting to interpret the meaning of biblical texts.

Christological
Having to do with the branch of theology called Christology. Christology is the study of the divinity of Jesus Christ, the Son of God and the Second Divine Person of the Trinity, and his earthly ministry and eternal mission.

Jesus Christ, who through the Holy Spirit opens our "minds to understand"[8] (*CCC*, 108) "what God wanted to manifest by means of their [the human authors'] words" (*Divine Revelation*, 12). ☩

22 Senses of the Scriptures

The goals of biblical study are to discover meaning, depth, and truth. It also aims at making sense out of the Sacred Scriptures. **Exegetes** work "toward a better understanding and explanation of the meaning of Sacred Scripture"[9] (*CCC*, 119).

In the *Summa Theologica*, Saint Thomas Aquinas laid the foundation for modern biblical interpretation. He believed the Sacred Scriptures were packed with rich language. The language used held a special meaning in regard to actual events and people, faith, just action, and everlasting life. He maintained, "One can distinguish between two *senses* of Scripture: the literal and the spiritual" (*CCC*, 115). Aquinas uses the word *senses* to refer to different levels of meaning that can be found in the Sacred Scriptures.

The Literal Sense

"The *literal sense* is the meaning conveyed by the words of Scripture and discovered by exegesis" (*CCC*, 116). You might think of this as the obvious meaning of the text. The interpreter examines the actual events being spoken about. The interpreter also examines key characters and various things described in the text. Through cultural and literary exploration, the exegete seeks further understanding of the life, times, and writing styles of God's Chosen People. The literal sense lays the framework for all other senses of the Sacred Scriptures.

The Spiritual Sense

The spiritual sense goes beyond the literal sense of the words to consider what the realities and events of Scripture signify. The spiritual sense can be broken into three categories: allegorical sense, moral sense, and anagogical sense.

The Allegorical Sense

The allegorical sense looks at how the people, events, and things in the literal sense point to the mystery of Christ. In other words, it examines their **Christological** significance.

The Moral Sense

Fundamental to the moral sense of the Sacred Scriptures is the search for what it means to live a just and ethical life. How does a particular passage instruct us to live in right relationship with God, neighbor, self, and the earth?

The Anagogical Sense

The anagogical sense investigates "realities and events in terms of their eternal significance" (*CCC*, 117). In what way does the story lead and direct us toward our future heavenly home?

The View from Every Angle

"The Letter speaks of deeds; Allegory to faith; / The Moral how to act; Anagogy our destiny"[10] (*CCC*, 118). This statement from the *Catechism* quotes a medieval poem. The text

Senses of the Sacred Scriptures in the Exodus Account

Let us apply what we have learned regarding the literal and spiritual senses. We will look at the crossing of the Red Sea in the Book of Exodus (see 14:10–31).

Literal sense: The literal sense tells us God delivered the Israelites by opening the Red Sea. God did this so the Israelites could cross, and then he closed the sea to drown Pharaoh's army.

Allegorical sense: Just as Moses, through God's power, led the Israelites from slavery to freedom, so too are we freed from the slavery of sin, death, and evil by the power of God manifested in Jesus Christ, the New Moses.

Moral sense: Just as God destroyed Pharaoh's sinful power in the Red Sea, so also in the waters of Baptism does Christ "drown" and destroy Original Sin so we may live good and moral lives based on the New Law revealed in the Beatitudes.

Anagogical sense: Just as the Israelites entered the Promised Land through the waters of the Red Sea, so also do we enter the Promised Land, our heavenly home, by passing through the waters of Baptism.

fundamentalist approach

The interpretation of the Bible and Christian doctrine based on the literalist meaning of the Bible's words. The interpretation is made without regard to the historical setting in which the writings or teachings were first developed.

contextualist approach

The interpretation of the Bible that takes into account the various contexts for understanding. These contexts include the senses of Scripture, literacy forms, historical situations, cultural backgrounds, the unity of the whole of the Scriptures, Tradition, and the analogy of faith.

of the poem shows the importance of studying the Sacred Scriptures from every angle. It speaks of the importance of studying the meaning of words and events, the lessons regarding the role of Christ in salvation, the teachings about moral and just living. The poem also speaks about our vocation to be with God always. The literal and spiritual senses open the door to the deeper truth God wants us to know in Sacred Scripture. ✟

23 Relation to Science and History

We live in a time of great inquiry and discovery. We are ever expanding our knowledge and understanding of science, history, and other academic areas. Every day new discoveries challenge how we think or how we view the world. It is easy to presume that faith could conflict with science and history.

Some voices in the world claim that science disproves religious beliefs. The Catholic Church teaches that faith, science, and history can coexist. She also teaches that they can help inform one another. The academic disciplines of math, science, psychology, sociology, history, and literature are wonderful gifts that must be valued and used responsibly. There is a harmony among these academic pursuits and with the truths revealed throughout the whole of the Sacred Scriptures. God instilled in us eager imaginations and inquisitive minds. He created us with the ability to come to a fuller understanding of faith and belief. Our minds were not given to us so we could elevate ourselves or consider ourselves superior to his mysterious ways.

The Whole Picture

In dialogue with the teaching authority of the Church, the wisdom of academic endeavors such as science and history can help us break down the barriers of an overly literalist or **fundamentalist approach** to the Scriptures. It can also free us from an approach that is limited to symbolic understanding. We want to look at the whole picture.

The Church supports a **contextualist approach**. This approach is one where the literal sense of the Scriptures is informed by scientific and historical knowledge. This knowledge informs the spiritual senses of the Scriptures with their deeper symbolic meaning. A contextualist approach simply teaches us how to relate the truths of faith to science. If the Sacred Scriptures are studied in a contextualist manner, "there can never be any real discrepancy between faith and reason"[11] (*CCC,* 159). In other words the truths revealed in the Bible will not conflict with the truths gleaned from science and history.

God acts in and through history, so there is a strong and consistent historic basis for the Old and New Testaments. This is particularly the case with the Gospels. However, the Church does not propose that the Bible's purpose is to present historical and scientific facts. Some of the biblical accounts may not be supported by historical experiences or accurate historical references. But this does not mean the Scriptures are in error or that our scientific explorations are wrong.

A Choir of Truth

In his writings Pope Gregory the Great (540–604) asserts, "Holy Scripture by the manner of its language transcends every science, because in one and the same sentence, while it describes a fact, it reveals a mystery." As human beings we have been trained in the theories of learning and data collecting. Our world has not taught us to deal with human limitations. It has not taught us to deal with truth that is so deep and broad that our limited minds cannot fully comprehend it. This is what Catholics mean by absolute mystery. Science and history, combined with the many other academic disciplines, are avenues for understanding Divine Revelation. However, they have their limitations, which

Catholic Wisdom

Vatican Observatory

Did you know that the Vatican has its own observatory? The purpose of the observatory is to encourage and promote astronomical research. The headquarters of the Vatican Observatory are located at the papal summer residence in Castel Gandolfo, Italy. The Vatican has a second research center located at the University of Arizona in Tucson. The observatory in Tucson is home to the Vatican Observatory Research Group. Learn more at the observatory's Web site.

must be respected and understood. God has given us the minds to pursue these avenues. Therefore all that is unveiled and proven through these avenues will sing in unison with the words of the Sacred Scriptures, leading to the infinite Incarnate Word, Jesus Christ. If science and faith conflict, it means we have an inadequate understanding of one or both of them. ✝

Pope, Monk, Father, and Doctor

Pope Gregory the Great, a canonized saint and Doctor of the Church, was a fervent, holy man. He significantly affected the missionary efforts to Anglo-Saxon kingdoms during the early Middle Ages, laid the groundwork for medieval theology, and influenced our modern liturgical practices. Before being elected to the papacy, Gregory lived the life of a monk. He brought the prayerful and contemplative aspects of the monastery to his role as a religious leader and spiritual guide. As Pope he longed for the solitude of the monastery but felt that the Church, guided by the Holy Spirit, had called him to the Chair of Peter. Thus the Church and world would be his new monastery, his new home.

24 Other Avenues to Understanding the Scriptures

Biblical scholars use many different tools. These tools help them to discover "what meaning the sacred authors really intended, and what God wanted to manifest by means of their words" (*Divine Revelation*, 12). Scholars use traditional approaches to biblical exegesis. They also use other methods of research that often lead to a deeper understanding of the Word of God.

Biblical Archaeology

Should you ever have the opportunity to visit Israel, you will notice that Israeli national parks are different from U.S. national parks. The majority of their national parks are archeological excavations, or digs. The last fifty years have seen a dramatic increase in the number of digs in Israel. The result has been the discovery of many ancient texts, artifacts, and buildings. Archeologists have even found entire cities that date back to the time of Christ and earlier. These discoveries have helped us to understand more clearly what life was like in biblical times.

For example, archeologists have unearthed the ancient Roman city of Sepphoris. This city was rebuilt in the first century AD. It was only about an hour's walk from Jesus' small village of Nazareth. It is entirely possible that Jesus visited Sepphoris as a young man. Maybe he even worked there with Joseph, his foster father. In Sepphoris Jesus would have learned about Greek and Roman culture and witnessed firsthand how "the rulers of the Gentiles lord it over them" (Matthew 20:25).

A particularly important archeological find is the discovery of ancient texts, both biblical and nonbiblical. We do not have an original version of any biblical book. This is why scholars are always searching for the earliest copies. The most important modern discovery of ancient biblical texts is the Dead Sea Scrolls. Also important is the discovery of ancient nonbiblical religious texts like the **Nag Hammadi manuscripts.** They help us to understand the religious beliefs of other nations and peoples during biblical times.

Nag Hammadi manuscripts
Fourth-century writings discovered in 1945 near the village of Nag Hammadi in Upper Egypt, that are invaluable sources of information regarding Gnostic beliefs, practices, and lifestyle. Gnosticism was an early Church heresy claiming that Christ's humanity was an illusion and the human body is evil.

Archaeologists continue to uncover sites across the Holy Land that further our understanding of biblical life and times. College students from around the world volunteer to help in this work.

redact

To select and adapt written material to serve an author's purpose.

Essenes

A group of pious, ultra-conservative Jews who left the Temple of Jerusalem and began a community by the Dead Sea known as Qumran.

Literary Analysis of Scripture

To better understand the meaning the Bible's human authors intended to convey, biblical scholars analyze the Bible as a literary document. They seek to discover other written or oral sources the biblical authors may have known about or even used as they wrote their books. They work to understand how the authors **redacted,** or edited, other writings to create the books we have in the Bible. Scholars examine the books' literary form or genre. They look to see if the book is historical theology or religious fiction. We can then appreciate the authors' true intent. Redactors also look at a book's internal structure. They consider how the author organized the text. They look for clues about the author's purpose and main points. By using these and other forms of literary analysis, biblical interpreters strive to help us "be attentive to what the human authors truly wanted to affirm and to what God wanted to reveal to us by their words"[12] (*CCC*, 109).

To grasp the truth of the Sacred Scriptures, one must look at them from every angle. We must continually dig to reach an authentic knowledge of God's self-revelation. Archaeology and literary analysis aid the Church in understanding God's Revelation in the Scriptures. As a result we can glory in the riches of Divine Wisdom disclosed in the sacred words of the Bible. ✝

The Dead Sea Scrolls

The Dead Sea Scrolls are believed to have been written and preserved by a Jewish religious community, possibly called the **Essenes.** They lived sometime between the first century BC and the first century AD. The Dead Sea Scrolls were discovered in the late 1940s in caves in the Qumran region. The caves are near the northwest shore of the Dead Sea. These documents are important to biblical study because they contain pieces of writing from nearly every book in the Old Testament. The scrolls are perhaps the only surviving copies of biblical documents made before AD 100. They also recount information about the beliefs and customs of the Jewish people of the time.

Review

1. Who has been entrusted with the responsibility of authentically interpreting the Sacred Scriptures?

2. What is biblical exegesis? What should an exegete be attentive to when interpreting the Scriptures?

3. Why is it important to know the literary genres when interpreting a particular book or passage of the Sacred Scriptures?

4. What are the literal and spiritual senses of the Scriptures?

5. Why does the Church teach that there can be no conflict between religious truth and scientific and historical truth?

6. Briefly describe the contextualist approach for interpreting the Bible.

7. What is biblical archaeology and what benefits can it have for understanding the Sacred Scriptures?

Part 3

Overview of the Old and New Testaments

There is a unifying presentation of salvation history woven through the sacred pages of the Old and New Testaments. The Old Testament is called "old" because it relates the teachings and events before the coming of Jesus Christ. It is not an antique of the past but rather a beautiful revelation of God's saving action in the lives of the Israelites. The New Testament, especially the Gospels, records the Good News of Jesus Christ, who is the New Covenant, fulfilling the Old Covenant made between God and the Jewish people. Both Testaments "shed light on each other; both are the true Word of God" (*CCC,* 140). Both are essential in understanding the Incarnation of God's Word.

The articles in this part address the following topics:

25 The Old Testament: *Old* Does Not Mean "Out of Date"

millennium

A period of one thousand years, also referring in modern usage to the transition from the year 1999 to 2000.

How would you define the word *old?* For most of us, the definition would probably include some of the following: *boring, unattractive, lackluster, disposable,* and *out of date.* What we don't always realize is that the old paves the way for the new. We need the old to appreciate and understand the new. The same is true for the Sacred Scriptures. The Old Testament is not out of date or insignificant. Rather it is the foundation of our identity as a people, a family of faith, profoundly touched by the Incarnation of God. The Old Testament contains the Revelation of God, which lays the framework for our Christian faith.

The Old Testament is a sacred text for both Christian and Jewish people. It is also "an indispensable part of Sacred Scripture" (*CCC,* 121). The Old Testament is "a storehouse of sublime teaching on God and of sound wisdom on human life"[13] (122). Contained in the writings of the Old Testament are teachings on the meaning of life, morality, right relationship with God, and the mystery of salvation. We must not discard these writings and teachings. Instead we must read, venerate, and integrate them into our spiritual lives. The Revelation of God in the Old Testament retains "a permanent value"[14] (121). It never loses its worth, and it is always pertinent to the human experience.

The change of the **millennium** was the transition from the year 1999 to 2000. At this time Pope John Paul II challenged us, as a people and Church, to "open wide the doors to Christ" ("15th World Youth Day," 4). In the same spirit, the Old Testament opens wide the doors and windows to the most perfect manifestation of Revelation, Jesus Christ, God's incarnate Son. Embodied within the whole of Jesus' life is the promise made between God and his people in the Old Covenant. Jesus, the New Covenant, who is God himself, fulfills the prophecies of the Old Testament and brings to fruition the hopes and expectations of a broken and sinful people. Even though the books of the Old Testament "contain matters imperfect and provisional"[15] (*CCC,* 122), they bear witness to God's entire plan of loving goodness. The truth is that the Old Testament contains "a storehouse of sublime teaching on God and of sound wisdom on human life, as well as a wonderful treasury of prayers; in them, too, the mystery of our salvation is present in a hidden way"[16] (122). The ancient words of the Old Law, as written in the Old Testament, are not out of date but are instead true "preparation for the Gospel" (1982). The Old Law is the first stage of revealed Law. ✝

Apostle to the Young, Icon of Reconciliation

Pope John Paul II (1920–2005) reigned as Pope of the Catholic Church for nearly twenty-seven years. He spent much of his time as spiritual head of the Church ministering to youth and developing programs to foster their spiritual lives. One of his notable contributions was the launching of World Youth Day. World Youth Day is a celebration of diverse young men and women of faith that takes place internationally every two to three years. John Paul II is also lifted up as a model of reconciliation. He forgave a Turkish gunman who attempted to assassinate him on May 13, 1981. Because His Holiness has been so acclaimed, his cause for canonization was initiated on May 9, 2005.

26 The Old Testament: General Overview

The Old Testament is the account of a loving and communicative relationship between God and the **Hebrew people.** The Hebrew people were also called the Israelites and, later, the Jews. The time frame of the Old Testament spans from the Creation of the world to the Kingdom of the Maccabees. It recounts how God remains faithful, always willing to take sinners back, even when they succumb to the temptations of the world. In the words of the *Catechism:* "The Old Testament is an indispensable part of Sacred Scripture. Its books are divinely inspired and retain a permanent value,[17] for the Old Covenant has never been revoked" (121). The Old Testament contains the Scriptures of the Jewish people (except for a few books), and Christians venerate it as the "true Word of God" (123). Two major centers of culture and life in the ancient Near East, Egypt and Mesopotamia, form the backdrop for the events that take place in the Old Testament.

The Canon

The Catholic Bible is different from the Protestant Bible. The Catholic Bible includes an additional seven Old Testament books called the deuterocanonical (Greek for "second canon") books. The seven books are Tobit, Judith, First and Second Maccabees, Wisdom, Sirach, and Baruch. The decision to include forty-six Old Testament books in the Catholic Bible is part of Apostolic Tradition. All Christians used the Greek translation of the Old Testament, called the Septuagint, which contained the deuterocanonical books. The Protestant reformers rejected the Septuagint as the basis for the Old Testament, so their Bibles do not contain these seven books (although sometimes they are included as an appendix).

The Structure of the Old Testament

The Old Testament can be divided into four categories. These four categories are the books of law, the historical books, the wisdom books, and the prophetic books.

The Books of Law

The name "books of law" refers to the first five books of the Old Testament. These five books teach about Creation and sin and provide inspirational accounts of people of faith and the history, teachings, and laws of the Chosen People of Israel. The books of law are also called the **Torah** (from Hebrew, meaning "law"), the **Pentateuch** (from Greek, meaning "five books"), or the Law of Moses.

The Historical Books

The historical books tell about Jewish history with its many trials and triumphs. They recount the lives of various leaders, including kings, judges, warriors, and prophets. The historical books point to the saving action of God in the lives of the Israelites.

Hebrew people
The descendants of Abraham and Sarah who become known as the Israelites after the Exodus and who later were called Judeans or Jews.

Torah
A Hebrew word meaning "law," referring to the first five books of the Old Testament.

Pentateuch
A Greek word meaning "five books," referring to the first five books of the Old Testament.

Catholic Wisdom

At most Sunday Masses, a reading from the Old Testament is the first reading of the Liturgy of the Word. The Old Testament reading is specifically chosen to correspond to the Gospel reading. This shows the unity and the continuity between the Old and New Testaments.

The Wisdom Books

The wisdom books are characterized by poetry that is steeped in emotion and practical advice on what it means to be wise. They focus on the themes of wisdom, self-control, patience, honesty, diligence, suffering, and respect for elders.

The Prophetic Books

The final section in the Old Testament contains the prophetic books. They proclaim the messages of visionary religious reformers whom God called to challenge the people of Israel to stop their idolatrous practices, to act justly, and to care for the people. These prophets also proclaimed a message of hope and consolation, as well as calling the people to repent of their sins.

A Seamless Garment

The forty-six books of the Old Testament are a seamless garment, each unique in its own way but forming one cloth, one tapestry of God's redeeming and liberating love. Written in its pages are histories, genealogies, laws, customs, rituals, wise sayings, poetry, and prophecies, all grounding us in the Old Covenant made between God and the Jewish people and

Salvation history is filled with accounts of empires' vying for control of the ancient Middle East. How many of the empires on this map have you heard of?

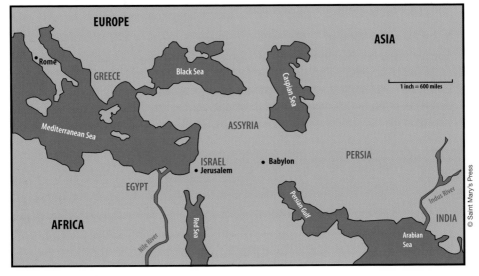

shining a light on the New Covenant Jesus made. The Old Testament is our compass, pointing us in one direction and one direction only—on the pathway to Jesus Christ. ✝

27 The Canon of the Old Testament

Category	Sample Abbreviations	Category	Sample Abbreviations
The Books of Law		**The Wisdom Books (cont.)**	
Genesis	Gn	Proverbs	Prv
Exodus	Ex	Ecclesiastes	Eccl
Leviticus	Lv	Song of Songs	Sg
Numbers	Nm	Wisdom	Wis
Deuteronomy	Dt	Sirach	Si
The Historical Books		**The Prophetic Books**	
Joshua	Jos	Isaiah	Is
Judges	Jgs	Jeremiah	Jer
Ruth	Ru	Lamentations	Lam
1 Samuel	1 Sm	Baruch	Bar
2 Samuel	2 Sm	Ezekiel	Ez
1 Kings	1 Kgs	Daniel	Dn
2 Kings	2 Kgs	Hosea	Hos
1 Chronicles	1 Chr	Joel	Jl
2 Chronicles	2 Chr	Amos	Am
Ezra	Ezr	Obadiah	Ob
Nehemiah	Neh	Jonah	Jon
Tobit	Tb	Micah	Mi
Judith	Jdt	Nahum	Na
Esther	Est	Habakkuk	Hb
1 Maccabees	1 Mc	Zephaniah	Zep
2 Maccabees	2 Mc	Haggai	Hg
		Zechariah	Zec
The Wisdom Books		Malachi	Mal
Job	Jb	✝	
Psalms	Ps		

New Testament

The twenty-seven books of the Bible written in apostolic times, which have the life, teachings, Passion, death, Resurrection, and Ascension of Jesus Christ and the beginnings of the Church as their central theme.

Paschal Mystery

The work of salvation accomplished by Jesus Christ mainly through his Passion, death, Resurrection, and Ascension.

28 The New Testament: Why Is It Called "New"?

The Revelation of Jesus Christ in the **New Testament** is like a beautifully wrapped package waiting to be unwrapped and explored. But unlike with material gifts we get from others, the excitement and newness of Jesus does not wear off. The New Testament is filled with miraculous, captivating, and transforming accounts about Jesus Christ. As the Son of God and God himself, Jesus Christ is the perfect image of God the Father and the fullness of Revelation.

The New Testament is called "new" because God the Father radically broke into the human condition by sending his only Son, Jesus Christ, to initiate a New Covenant with his People. He had never before revealed or manifested himself in such a way. Although God had acted in amazing ways in the Old Testament, his taking on of human nature opened the doors to a new day, a new Revelation, a new freedom.

> The word of God, which is the power of God for the salvation of all who believe (see Rom. 1:16), is set forth and shows its power in a most excellent way in the writings of the New Testament. For when the fullness of time arrived (see Gal. 4:4), the Word was made flesh and dwelt among us in His fullness of grace and truth (see John 1:14).
>
> (*Divine Revelation,* 17)

The Unity of the Old and New

All salvation history written about and reported in the Old Testament "retains its own intrinsic value"[18] (*CCC,* 129) and is necessary to understand the life and mission of Jesus Christ. There is a unity between the Old and New Testaments, two pieces that are necessary to see the big picture of God's gift of grace and redemption. The Old and New Testaments have a reciprocal relationship. They have to be read in light of each other. In other words, "the New Testament lies hidden in the Old and the Old Testament is unveiled in the New"[19] (129). Jesus, as the New Covenant, fulfills all that was promised in the Old Covenant. "Christians therefore read the Old Testament in the light of Christ crucified and risen" (129).

The Heart of All the Scriptures

The Gospels are the "principal witness for the life and teaching of the Incarnate Word" (*Divine Revelation*, 18), Jesus Christ. The Gospels are the heart of the Christian message. In them we find accounts of healing, driving out of demons, and washing of feet. We see the breaking of bread, crucified love, and an empty tomb. When we read about his miracles, his concern for the poor and marginalized, his prayer life, the way he loved others, the way he accepted the Father's will in the garden, his Passion, death, Resurrection, and Ascension, we learn from him. (The saving work of Jesus Christ, accomplished principally through his Passion, death, Resurrection, and Ascension is called the **Paschal Mystery**.) The central object of the Gospels as well as the New Testament as a whole is "Jesus Christ, God's incarnate Son: his acts, teachings, Passion and glorification, and his Church's beginnings under the Spirit's guidance"[20] (*CCC*, 124).

The Sacred Scriptures are truly a gift to all humanity. An integral part of that gift is the Old Testament, which must not be discarded even though we now also have the New Testament. The New Covenant is founded upon the Old, and the Old Covenant illuminates the way to the New. "The unity of the two Testaments proceeds from the unity of God's plan and his Revelation. The Old Testament prepares for the New and the New Testament fulfills the Old; the two shed light on each other; both are true Word of God" (*CCC*, 140). ☩

Pray It!

Matthew, Mark, Luke, and John

One of the best ways to come to know Jesus Christ is to encounter him in the Scriptures. Saint Jerome did the awesome work of translating the Scriptures into Latin, the common language of his time. In some of his writings, he makes references to prayer in relation to the Scriptures. Saint Jerome wrote about the fact that if we don't know the Scriptures then we don't know who Jesus is.

We should pray with the Scriptures as often as possible. The Gospels help us to come to know Jesus and to know about his life, teachings, and message of salvation. So open your Bible, read a portion of one of the Gospels, and take the time to get to know Jesus.

The Color of Stained Glass

Churches are filled with beautiful stained glass depicting images and symbols of Jesus' life, Mary, the saints, and other holy mysteries. Among the images you might find those of a human, lion, ox, and eagle. These colorful images, taken from Ezekiel 1:1–14, symbolize the four Gospels and their opening passages, alluding to the unity of the Old and New Testaments.

The human figure signifies the Gospel of Matthew, because his Gospel opens with a genealogy of Jesus' ancestors. Represented by a lion, Mark's Gospel begins with John the Baptist, the voice of one roaring in the desert. Beginning with Zechariah's offering sacrifice in the Temple, the Gospel of Luke is symbolized by an ox, a sacrificial animal. John's Gospel speaks of Christ's coming from Heaven. As a result an eagle was selected because of its ability to soar through the clouds, the heavenly dome.

© Adam Woolfitt/CORBIS

29 The New Testament: General Overview

The New Testament centers on the words and actions of Jesus Christ and all that he accomplished for the sake of our salvation through his Passion, death, Resurrection, and Ascension and on how early Christian communities received and applied his teachings. It covers the time period from approximately 4 BC to AD 100. The New Testament's twenty-seven books tell about God's fullest Revelation through the Incarnation.

Jesus' life and mission took place in Palestine, also called the Holy Land. In New Testament times, Palestine was divided into three major provinces: Judea, Samaria, and Galilee. Jesus was born in Judea, ministered in Galilee, and invited the "unclean" of Samaria into the circle of salvation. Through his actions Jesus spread his message of hope and reconciliation to all of Palestine.

Politics and Religion

The society Jesus and the early Christian communities lived in was extremely diverse in religious practices. It was governed by Roman rule and also profoundly affected by **Hellenism,** a term for the acceptance of Greek culture. There were many religious groups, or sects, within the Jewish community alone. These included the Pharisees, Sadducees, Essenes, Herodians and Zealots. Each group emphasized a different way of living the Jewish faith. The Pharisees were the educated interpreters of the **Law of Moses.** The Sadducees strictly adhered to the Torah and preserved the sanctity of the Temple. In preparation for the coming of God, the Essenes withdrew to a life of solitude and prayer. The Herodians were the political leaders

Hellenism
The acceptance of Greek culture, language, and traditions.

Law of Moses
The first five books of the Old Testament, which are also called the books of the Law or the Torah. God gave Moses the tablets containing the Law (see Exodus 31:18), which is why it is also called the Law of Moses, or the Mosaic Law.

Live It!

If Necessary, Use Words

The spread of the Christian faith is the result of early Christians' listening to the call to go out and spread the Good News of Jesus Christ. In many cases they shared the Gospel with people who had never even heard of Jesus. Are you aware that the call to spread the Good News is part of your Christian vocation? You may think that most of the people you come in contact with have already heard of Jesus, but that does not mean your work is done.

We are called to preach the Gospel to everyone at all times. This does not mean you have to go out on the street corner and preach to strangers. The manner in which you act can witness your faith to others. Saint Francis is claimed to have said, "Preach the Gospel at all times; when necessary, use words." With this in mind, strive to do every act with great care, knowing that it can be a witness to someone of your love for Jesus Christ.

Parousia

The second coming of Christ at the end of time, fully realizing God's plan and the glorification of humanity.

collaborating with the Roman Empire. The Zealots were a revolutionary group concerned with the restoration of Jewish independence. Nearly 90 percent of the Jewish population did not belong to one of these sects. Collectively they are known as the great majority. Jesus ministered to all Jews but focused much of his time and energy on the great majority.

The Canon of the New Testament

The twenty-seven books in the New Testament, each unique, can be broken down into the following five categories: the Gospels, the Acts of the Apostles, the Pauline letters, the non-Pauline letters, and the Book of Revelation. The Gospels tell about the life, ministry, teachings, Passion, death, Resurrection, and Ascension of Jesus Christ. The Acts of the Apostles, written by Luke, tells about Pentecost, when the Holy Spirit descended on the Apostles, with Mary present among them. Acts also tells about the early Christian community under the leadership of Saint Peter and Saint Paul, guided by the Holy Spirit. Paul and his disciples wrote the Pauline letters to early Christian communities he helped form. The letters offer empowering advice, teaching, community news, and pastoral encouragement and support.

Jesus spent his entire earthly life in a relatively small geographic area. Use the scale on this map to estimate how many miles north to south and east to west he walked.

THE MINISTRY OF JESUS

(1,742) Elevation, in feet
? Exact location questionable

0   30 miles
0   30 kilometers

Sidon

Damascus

Zarephath
MT. LEBANON (11,000)
MT. HERMON (9,200)

Iturea

Tyre
Phoenicia
Panias (Caesarea Philippi)

Trachonitis

Galilee
Ptolemais   Chorazin   Bethsaida?   Feeds five thousand (Lk 9:10–17)
Capernaum
Heals centurion's servant (Mt 8:5–13) and a paralytic (Mt 9:2–8), and raises Jairus's daughter (Mt 9:18–26)
MT. CARMEL (1,742)   Cana   Magdala   Sea of Galilee   Gergesa
Tiberias
Calms the storm (Mk 4:35–41); walks on water (Mt 14:22–33)
Performs wedding feast miracle (Jn 2:1–11)
Nazareth
River Yarmuk
Gadara?
MT. TABOR (1,843)
Transfiguration? (Mt 17:1–13)
Grows up in Nazareth (Lk 2:39–40)
Nain
Esdraelon
River Jezreel
Caesarea
Scythopolis
The Great Sea (Mediterranean Sea)
Raises widow's son (Lk 7:11–17)
MT. GILBOA (1,696?)
Decapolis
Samaria
Talks to Samaritan woman (Jn 4:1–42)
Samaria
Sychar
Gerasa
MT. GERIZIM (2,890)
River Jordan
River Jabbok
Antipatris
Perea
Joppa
Arimathea
Gadara?
Ephraim
Philadelphia
Lydda
Crucifixion and Resurrection
Jericho
Heals Bartimaeus (Mk 10:46–52); calls Zacchaeus (Lk 19:1–10)
Appears to two disciples after Resurrection (Lk 24:13–35)
Emmaus
Jesus' baptism? (Mk 1:9–11)
Azotus
Kirjath Jearim
Jerusalem
Bethabara
Beth Haccerem
Bethany
Qumran
Ashkelon
Bethlehem
Raises Lazarus (Jn 11:1–44)
Medeba
Herodium
Judea
Jesus' birth (Lk 2:1–7)
Machaerus
Gaza
Hebron
Dead Sea (Salt Sea) (–1,300)
River Arnon
Masada
Idumea
Beersheba

The non-Pauline letters serve the same function as the letters Paul wrote, but other authors wrote them, including James, Peter, John, and Jude. The Book of Revelation, written by a Jewish-Christian prophet named John and most likely composed for late–first-century Christians, offers words of support to those enduring persecution because of their Christian beliefs. John speaks of the second coming of Christ at the end of time, known as the **Parousia.**

To fully comprehend all that the books of the New Testament tell us, it is helpful to understand the context in which they were written, from the history and political divisions of the time period to the culture and religious practices of its people. We must know this time and place if we want to truly understand all that was written in the books of the New Testament and revealed in Jesus Christ, the fulfillment of all God's promises of salvation. ✝

30 The Canon of the New Testament

Category	Sample Abbreviations	Category	Sample Abbreviations
Gospels		**Pauline Letters (cont.)**	
Matthew	Mt	1 Timothy	1 Tim
Mark	Mk	2 Timothy	2 Tim
Luke	Lk	Titus	Ti
John	Jn	Philemon	Philem
Acts		**Non-Pauline Letters**	
Acts of the Apostles	Acts	Hebrews	Heb
		James	Jas
		1 Peter	1 Pet
Pauline Letters		2 Peter	2 Pet
Romans	Rom	1 John	1 Jn
1 Corinthians	1 Cor	2 John	2 Jn
2 Corinthians	2 Cor	3 John	3 Jn
Galatians	Gal	Jude	Jude
Ephesians	Eph		
Philippians	Phil	**Revelation**	
Colossians	Col	Book of Revelation	Rev
1 Thessalonians	1 Thess	✝	
2 Thessalonians	2 Thess		

Review

1. What is the proper understanding of the word *old* in "Old Testament"?

2. How are the Catholic Bible and the Protestant Bible different?

3. List the seven deuterocanonical books.

4. What are the four categories of books found in the Old Testament? Briefly explain the type of books in each category.

5. What is the "big picture" painted by both the Old Testament and New Testament together?

6. What is the Paschal Mystery?

7. Name four Jewish groups (sects) present in the New Testament and describe something unique about each group.

8. What are the five categories of New Testament books? What role did they play in spreading the message of Jesus Christ?

Revelation in the Old Testament

Part 1

The Book of Genesis

The Book of Genesis starts with the Creation of the universe and concludes with God's faithfulness to the patriarchs and holy women of the Covenant. Genesis explains our beginning as people of faith. Genesis covers the social and historical circumstances of the Near East in the early part of the second millennium BC, roughly 2000 to 1500 BC. It is not meant to be read as a detailed, chronological account of history but rather as an account steeped in truth and meaning.

Genesis, along with the other four books in the Pentateuch, illustrates God as the source of all creation. It explains the role of humans in the origin of sin and its many devastating effects. It shows God's desire to be in communion with his People and emphasizes the lasting effect of the Covenant God formed with Abraham. God is a God of history who is always faithful to his promise of covenantal love.

The articles in this part address the following topics:

- Creation: In the Beginning (page 91)

- Sin and God's Response (page 94)

- Abraham (page 97)

- Isaac, Jacob, and Joseph (page 100)

31 Creation: In the Beginning

We believe in one God,
  the Father, the Almighty,
  maker of heaven and earth,
  of all that is, seen and unseen.
                    (*CCC*, page 49)

The above words are from the Nicene **Creed.** This Creed is professed every Sunday at Mass. It expresses the belief that God is the principle source of all creation. It is founded on the words of the Sacred Scriptures, most important from the Book of Genesis. The beginning of Genesis tells about how God created the world and all its inhabitants in seven figurative days. Contained in this account of Creation is God's infinite wisdom, his plan of loving goodness, "which finds its goal in the new creation in Christ" (*CCC*, 315). God's creative action in and through the natural order is oriented toward and fulfilled in the Incarnation.

Salvation History Begins

The accounts of Creation, along with the accounts of Adam and Eve, Cain and Abel, Noah and the Flood, and the Tower of Babel (see Genesis, chapters 1–11), are known as **primeval history.** The term refers to the time before the invention of writing and the recording of historical data. Through the

creed
A short summary statement or profession of faith. The Nicene and Apostles' Creeds are the Church's most familiar and important creeds.

primeval history
The time before the invention of writing and recording of historical data.

Notice the energy and the sense of purpose implied by the movement of the animals in this painting. What do you think the artist was saying about creation?

© Alinari / Art Resource, NY

inspiration of the Holy Spirit, these accounts were written long after the events they portray are said to have occurred. They are inerrant because they were written under the guidance of the Holy Spirit.

Thus, when reading the accounts of Creation and the other narratives in Genesis, chapters 1–11, we must seek the meaning the Holy Spirit wished to convey through the words and language of human authors.

Genesis begins with two accounts of Creation. The first account (1:1—2:4a) is a very orderly account of God's creative activity, structured in a seven-day week. The second account (2:4b–25) tells of the creation of the first man, Adam, and the first woman, Eve. These two accounts probably came from different Israelite religious traditions and, under the guidance of the Holy Spirit, were combined by the final author of Genesis. The two accounts complement each other in revealing the nature of God, the holiness of Creation, and human nature and purpose.

The two Creation accounts are not meant to convey historical or scientific fact. They present in figurative or symbolic language the beginning of salvation history. The seven magnificent days of Creation in the first account show that the universe was created out of love and has an inherent goodness, beauty, and order that reflect God's own nature. Several times throughout this account, God looks upon what he has created and sees how good it is. This teaches us that the world is fundamentally good, not flawed or evil. This understanding of Creation is very important for God's people because it shows that God created the universe out of love. This account also shows the awesome creative power of God, who only has to speak and whatever he says becomes reality.

The second account of Creation focuses on the nature and destiny of the human person. It begins with the creation

Catholic Wisdom

Saint Francis of Assisi regularly praised God for his glorious creation. Francis would address aspects of creation as "brother" or as "sister" because we all have the same Creator and Father. One of his prayers is called the Canticle of the Sun. It has the works of creation praising God through their uniqueness: "Be praised, my Lord, through Brother Fire, through whom you brighten the night."

We Believe

The Nicene Creed was developed at the Council at Nicaea in AD 325 and later modified at the Council of Constantinople in 381. It was originally formulated to refute the heresy of Arianism, which denied that Jesus is fully God. Used by many Churches in both the East and West, the Nicene Creed summarizes Christian belief. The Creed consists of three sections pertaining to the Trinity and four statements contradicting the primary tenets of Arianism. Profession of the Nicene Creed is incorporated into the liturgical, sacramental, and prayer life of the Church.

of Adam, whom God formed from the dirt and breathed life into (see 2:7). The description of God breathing life into Adam is a figurative way of saying that human beings participate in God's own divine life. God created a beautiful garden for the man to live in and care for, and God himself walked in the garden (see 3:8). This symbolizes that God created human beings for a life of beauty, peace, and joy, living in full communion with him. God also created a suitable partner for the man, Eve, a woman made from the man's own flesh. This teaches us that God created men and women as loving partners for each other, and that the two sexes are meant to complement and fulfill each other.

Both Creation accounts teach us about the unique dignity that human beings enjoy. In the first Creation account, we read that "God created man in his image; \ in the divine image he created him; \ male and female he created them" (1:27). The human person is created in God's image, which means that only we, out of all his creatures, have moral freedom, intellect, and an eternal soul. We have already mentioned how in the second Creation account God shared his own breath in giving human beings life—a sign of our sharing in divine life. But God also gave Adam the responsibility for caring for the garden and allowed him to name all the animals. This symbolizes that human beings are called in a unique way to participate in God's creative work, especially in caring for his Creation.

Doctor of the Church

A title officially bestowed by the Church on those saints who are highly esteemed for their theological writings, as well as their personal holiness.

Although "the work of creation is attributed to the Father in particular, it is equally a truth of faith that the Father, Son, and Holy Spirit together are the one, indivisible principle of creation" (*CCC,* 316), a truth the two Creation accounts point to. The *Catechism* further states: "God alone created the universe freely, directly, and without any help" (317).

Saint Bonaventure (1221–1274) was a Franciscan theologian and **Doctor of the Church**. He was noted for saying, "In everything, whether it is a thing sensed or a thing known, God himself is hidden within." The two Creation accounts proclaim that light, darkness, sea, sun, living creatures, human beings, and all of creation bear the mark of our God. The glory of God lies within each of these creations. Sometimes God's glory is visible and at other times it is invisible. Creation was not an accident. God orchestrated it. God is the originator, sustainer, and redeemer of all creation. ✝

32 Sin and God's Response

Missing the mark, falling short, brokenness, wrongdoing, misdeeds, an offense against truth: these are all ways of describing the reality of sin. We are created to live according to God's precepts and laws. In other words, we are created to be in right relationship with God and others. Unfortunately our selfish wants and desires get in the way of this right relationship. Sin is "an utterance, a deed, or a desire contrary to the eternal law (St. Augustine, *Faust* 22: PL 42, 418)" (*CCC,* 1871). It is illustrated in the account of the first humans, Adam and Eve (see Genesis 3:1–24), who disobey God by eating forbidden fruit. Their choice to give in to the Devil's temptation and disobey God marks the first sin in salvation history. Their sin is called Original Sin and is often referred to as "the Fall." By Original Sin the first humans disobeyed God and thereby lost their original holiness and became subject to death. Original Sin also describes the *"fallen state"*[1] (*CCC,* 404) in which all the descendants of Adam and Eve, with the exception of Jesus and his mother, Mary, are deprived of original holiness and justice.

The Lasting Influence of Original Sin

Cain and Abel were the sons of Adam and Eve. Cain and Abel are portrayed as having a tumultuous relationship characterized by sibling rivalry and jealousy (see Genesis 4:1–15). One of the religious practices during Old Testament times was to offer sacrifices to God. Because much of life revolved around the land, including raising animals and growing crops, people sacrificed their best animals and produce to God as a sign of their love and fidelity. Abel offers his best animal to God, while Cain presents some meager produce. God is pleased with Abel's offering. This angers Cain. Cain then murders his brother in a spirit of resentment and jealousy. Following in the footsteps of his parents and affected by Original Sin, Cain freely chooses to act contrary to God's law.

The cycle of sin continues. In the account of Noah and the Flood (see Genesis, chapters 6–9), human beings fall prey to the sinful and evil ways. God is saddened by this reality, so he decides to cleanse his creation through a great Flood lasting forty days and nights. Out of love God gives Noah, a good and righteous man, instructions on how to build an ark that will save him and his family. In faith Noah follows the instructions of God and is saved, along with the others on his ark, from the mighty waters of the Flood. Following the Flood a rainbow appears as a sign of God's Covenant with Noah and all living beings. God's Covenant with Noah is an "everlasting covenant" that "will remain in force as long as the world lasts" (*CCC*, 71).

© Cameraphoto Arte, Venice / Art Resource, NY

Like many Bible stories, the account of Cain and Abel is not about just the distant past but is also about us. Jealousy provokes Cain to murder his brother Abel. How has jealousy led to violent words and actions in your life and in the world today?

As Noah's descendants grow in number and settle in different places, the influence of sin takes deeper root in the lives and actions of the people. In the account of the Tower of Babel (see Genesis 11:1–9), power-hungry people attempt to build a tower that will reach the heavens. Longing to be like God, lured by the hope to be famous, and forgetting about their covenantal relationship with God, nothing will stop the people from building a self-serving tower of greed—nothing except the hand of God. God stops the people from building the tower by confusing their speech, making it impossible for them to communicate and effectively carry out their plan.

God's Protection

Beyond the witness of God in creation, he manifested himself to Adam and Eve and "invited them to intimate communion with himself" (*CCC*, 54). Despite their sin and fall, God still "promised them salvation (cf. *Genesis* 3:15) and offered them his covenant" (70). God punishes his children justly but continues to love and protect them. After banning Adam and Eve from the garden, he spares them humiliation by giving them clothes to wear. As Cain is forced to wander the earth, God marks him so no one will harm him. To save the

The Gravity of Sin

There are two kinds of sins: venial and mortal. Sin is considered venial when it is less serious and reparable by charity. It damages our relationship with God but does not destroy it., Mortal sin is a grave offense against God. It is called "mortal," meaning "deadly," because it separates us from God's grace. There are three conditions that must be met for a sin to be mortal: It must be a grave matter; the person committing it must have full knowledge of the evil of the act; it must be freely and deliberately committed. Mortal sin destroys within us the virtue of charity, which helps us love God and our neighbor. Without repentance a mortal sin leads to eternal death. But through the Sacrament of Penance and Reconciliation, a person who has committed mortal sin can receive God's mercy and forgiveness and return to a right relationship with him.

righteous, God gives Noah instructions on how to build the ark. God confuses human speech at the Tower of Babel but creates a diverse people who can survive language barriers.

One act of disobedience, one assertion of pride, one Original Sin led to sins too numerous to count. Each offense against God breeds another offense. According to Saint John of God (1495–1550), patron saint of hospitals and the sick: "Just as water extinguishes fire, so love wipes away sin." God's love, as revealed in Jesus Christ, is the only way to end the cycle of sin and evil. Jesus Christ redeemed humanity and broke the bonds of Original Sin. Through the waters of Baptism, we are united with Christ, and we are cleansed of Original Sin. ✝

Semitic

A term referring to Semites, a number of peoples of the ancient Near East, from whom the Israelites descended.

Near East

In biblical times, the region commonly known today as the Middle East, including the modern countries of Iraq, Iran, Syria, Lebanon, Israel, and Jordan.

33 Abraham

For Christianity, Judaism, and Islam, one of the great models of faith in God is Abraham. Abraham was first known as Abram. Abram experiences many hardships, but through an act of faith, he enters into a covenant relationship with God that changes everything for him and his descendants. Abram and his wife, Sarai, are **Semitic** nomads wandering the highlands of the **Near East.** God asks Abram to leave everything behind and set out for an unknown territory. God promises Abram:

> "I will make of you a great nation,
>   and I will bless you;
> I will make your name great,
>   so that you will be a blessing.
> I will bless those who bless you
>   and curse those who curse you.
> All the communities of the earth
>   shall find blessing in you."
>   (Genesis 12:2–3)

This is the first mention of God's promise to the people of Israel. Abram takes Sarai, his nephew Lot, and all of their possessions and leaves for a strange land, Canaan, not knowing where God is leading them.

"Stars of the Sky"

For many years Abram and Sarai travel in Canaan and other lands. They have no children, and Sarai is past child-bearing age. In Semitic culture children were seen as a sign of prestige and blessing from God. In reassurance God speaks to Abram: "Look up at the sky and count the stars, if you can. Just so . . . shall your descendants be" (Genesis 15:5). Despite this promise from God, Sarai continues to be childless. Sarai finally offers her servant Hagar to Abram so he might father a child by her and have an heir. Abram relents to Sarai's plan and fathers a son, Ishmael, by Hagar.

When Abram is ninety-nine years old, God again speaks with him and establishes his Covenant with Abram and his descendants:

> "My covenant with you is this: you are to become the father of a host of nations. No longer shall you be called Abram; your name shall be Abraham, for I am making you the father of a host of nations. I will render you exceedingly fertile; I will make nations of you; kings shall stem from you. I will maintain my covenant with you and your descendants after you throughout the ages as an everlasting pact, to be your God and the God of your descendants after you."
>
> (Genesis 17:3–7)

Pray It!

Faith in God

Abraham is known for his tremendous faith in God. He was willing to surrender everything and to trust God completely. It's not easy to give up something that God is calling us to let go of. Abraham was asked to leave his homeland and go to a different place. He was asked to trust that God would give him a child born of a wife who had been unable to have children. Abraham was later asked to sacrifice his son. These things were not easy for Abraham. Sometimes the things that God is asking of us aren't easy to do. Abraham's faith in God got him through these difficult situations.

Faith in God will help us to get through our difficult situations. What is God calling you to give up or sacrifice in your life? If you are struggling with surrendering to God's will for you, turn to God in prayer and ask him for the courage to let go and the faith to trust him.

God also tells Abraham that Sarai's new name is Sarah and that God will bless her with a son. God fulfills this promise, and Sarah bears Abraham a son, named Isaac. Through Abraham God chooses to make his Covenant, through which he forms his People. Through this Covenant God later reveals his law to his People through Moses.

Several years after the birth of his son Isaac by Sarah, Abraham's faith is tested again. Abraham believes God wants him to sacrifice his most prized gift and sign of the Covenant, Isaac. Filled with sadness and great distress but trusting the God who fulfills his promises, Abraham prepares to sacrifice his son. Seeing Abraham's amazing faith, God intervenes and stops the sacrifice.

What incredible faith Abraham has. He leaves behind his past, journeys with his wife to a new land, accepts a new identity, and more, is willing to offer God the son he longed and waited for. This is true faith—a faith that risks all for the love of God. Because of Abraham's faithfulness and complete trust in God, he and Sarah are blessed with countless descendants. ☩

Sarah overhears God telling Abraham that she will conceive and bear a child in her old age. Sarah laughs at this prediction, but she does indeed give birth to Isaac, whose name means "laughter."

© Erich Lessing / Art Resource, NY

Hagar

Before the Covenant between God and Abram is formed, Sarai continues to be childless. She finally proposes that Abram take her Egyptian maid, Hagar, as a concubine and father a child by her. The child will legally belong to Sarai. This idea works but not without a lot of bad feelings between the two women. At one point the pregnant Hagar runs away from the harshness of her mistress. In the wilderness a messenger of God appears to her. At his command she returns to submit to Sarai, fortified by the promise that her unborn son, Ishmael, will grow to manhood wild and free.

34 Isaac, Jacob, and Joseph

God continues his Covenant with Abraham's descendants, Isaac, Jacob, and Joseph, who are known as the patriarchs. These men lead their tribal families and, together with their wives, rule a great number of children, servants, and livestock. The Scriptures show how challenging life was during this time, and they emphasize God's saving power to rescue the patriarchs and their families from dangers of all kinds.

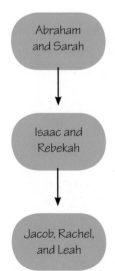

After the death of Abraham, his son Isaac assumes the role of patriarch. Isaac and his wife, Rebekah are the parents of two feuding and imperfect twin sons. Esau symbolizes Abraham's descendants who will not live directly under the Covenant. Jacob represents God's plan to create a people more numerous than the "stars of the sky" (Genesis 22:17). From the moment of their birth, Esau and Jacob contend with each other. This rivalry culminates in Jacob's theft from Esau of Isaac's dying blessing.

Jacob, having supplanted his brother Esau by stealing the blessing, becomes the patriarch at the death of Isaac. Though at times an ambitious schemer, Jacob proves to be a repentant brother, good father, and successful herder. With his two wives, Rachel and Leah, and their maidservants, he fathers twelve sons. God speaks to Jacob in a dream and renews the Covenant promise he made to Abraham. In another dream God changes Jacob's name to Israel. Thus all Jacob's descendants are known as Israelites.

Among Jacob's twelve sons is his favorite, Joseph. This favoritism, combined with Joseph's ability to interpret dreams, causes great jealousy among the eleven other brothers. The brothers conspire and sell Joseph as a slave to a passing merchant. He ends up in Egypt. There he rises to power and becomes the second in command to Pharaoh. Years later Joseph's brothers come to Egypt looking for food. After testing them, Joseph forgives them, and Joseph and his brothers are reconciled. The brothers bring their father, Jacob, and their families to Egypt to live. In this way the Israelites settle in Egypt, where Pharaoh eventually enslaves them.

God transcends the brokenness of humanity so all may know his promise of reconciliation and peace. From the account of an old and barren couple (Abraham and Sarah) to the tale of trickery and deception between two brothers over birthright (Jacob and Esau) to an account of Joseph, the favored son of Jacob, sold into slavery by his eleven jealous brothers, nothing stands in the way of the fulfillment of God's covenantal promises. Jacob's family becomes a large tribe, and his large tribe will become twelve even larger tribes. God's promise to Abraham of numerous descendants is becoming fulfilled. Despite the intentional and unintentional obstacles humans create, God will still guide us, like a parent, to the **Promised Land.**

Promised Land
The land (Canaan) God promised to the children of Abraham.

Live It!

All Is Possible for God

Have you noticed that the people God picks for his work aren't necessarily the best qualified for the task? Sometimes the people he picks are physically unable to do what God is asking of them. For example, the woman God selected to be the mother of his Chosen People was elderly and barren. Sarah had issues with her being picked for this task. She even laughed at it! Yet, in the end, her condition didn't get in the way of God's will. He is able to use any person or situation to manifest his power. We have all been chosen by God. You may feel unworthy and incapable of doing what he asks of you. You may have poor grades and be worried about getting into the college you want to attend. You might be unpopular or the worst player on the team. It does not matter. You have been chosen. Pray and seek his will, and when he makes it known to you, know he will give you the grace to accomplish it.

The Twelve Tribes of Israel

When someone refers to the Twelve Tribes of Israel, they are talking about a confederation of twelve Hebrew tribes, groups, or clans of faithful people who traced their origin to the patriarch Jacob. After Jacob's first eleven sons were born, God renamed Jacob Israel (see Genesis 32:29). Thus the descendants of Israel's sons (Reuben, Simeon, Levi, Judah, Issachar, Zebulun, Joseph, Benjamin, Dan, Naphtali, Gad, and Asher) became the Israelites, God's Chosen People. Their names came to symbolize the Twelve Tribes that settled in the Promised Land. Jesus chose Twelve Apostles in honor of the tribes and as a symbol of the restoration of the People of God.

The Continuing Role of Patriarchs

The vocation of mother and father to a people in faith was portrayed in the lives of the Old Testament patriarchs and holy women. This vocation was continued in the Christian era with the call of the Twelve Apostles and the early Church Fathers. The leaders in both the Old and New Covenants were channels for God's plan of loving goodness. God entrusts these people with spiritual leadership. Even when these leaders make mistakes, God transforms their mistakes into stepping-stones toward the Reign of Heaven. What is so amazing is that the spiritual fathers and mothers of the past, who embody both the beauty and darkness of humanity, fanned the flame of God's promise of eternal joy. ✝

Review

1. What truth can we learn from Genesis about Creation?

2. What is Original Sin?

3. What did God offer Adam and Eve despite their sin?

4. What is the difference between a venial sin and a mortal sin?

5. What were the terms of the Covenant between God and Abraham?

6. What is a patriarch? Name four of the patriarchs in the Old Testament.

7. What are the Twelve Tribes of Israel and what is their origin?

Part 2

The Book of Exodus

The Book of Exodus is a captivating account of slavery, liberation, and trust. The Book of Exodus covers the period from about 1500 to 1250 BC. It tells of a people, the Israelites, who are enslaved to the Egyptian dynasty. God responds to the Israelites' cries for freedom by calling Moses, a holy and courageous man. Moses answers God's call and challenges the forces of the Pharaoh and leads the Israelites through the waters of the Red Sea. The Israelites follow Moses only to experience the hardships of the wilderness on their journey to the Promised Land.

Having endured persecution and facing the obstacles of travel in the desert, the Israelites become a people, a holy nation, governed by God's law at the foot of Mount Sinai. When presented with the Ten Commandments, they form an identity as the Chosen People of God. Exodus, which means "to go out," sings of a God who will save his People from the snares of the world. It speaks of a compassionate God who sustains even in the most difficult situations, a God who longs to be in a covenant relationship with his children.

The articles in this part address the following topics:

35 A People Enslaved

pharaoh
A ruler of ancient Egypt.

"I have witnessed the affliction of my people in Egypt and have heard their cry. . . . I know well what they are suffering" (Exodus 3:7). The Lord spoke these words to Moses when his People, the Israelites, were enslaved. There is no record of the enslavement of the Israelites in Egyptian historical documents. However, slavery and persecution were part of the experience of the Israelites in Egypt, and are recounted in the Book of Exodus.

The Roots of Persecution

To understand the Exodus, it is important to know the situation of the Israelites in Egypt. After a period of welcome and peace in Egypt, the **pharaoh** begins to see the growing number Israelites as a threat. Pharaoh orders the Israelites to be enslaved. The Egyptian leadership, including Pharaoh and his great military leaders, force the Israelite people into harsh and inhumane work. At some point Pharaoh orders the deaths of all male Israelite babies. This action eventually resulted in the unexpected adoption and hidden identity of Moses in the courts of Pharaoh.

Pharaoh's order to kill all the Hebrew male babies failed because of courageous and resourceful women: the midwives, Moses' mother and sister, and even Pharaoh's daughter.

Young Moses

To save her infant son, Moses' mother places him in a basket and floats him down the Nile River. He is discovered by Pharaoh's daughter. She enlists Moses' mother, not knowing she is the baby's mother, to care for and help raise the infant Moses. Thus Pharaoh's daughter adopts Moses, and he grows up in the house of Pharaoh.

After Moses reaches adulthood, he sees an Egyptian striking an Israelite slave. In defense of the slave, Moses kills the Egyptian and hides the body in the sand.

© Trolley Dodger/Corbis

When it becomes known what Moses has done, he fears for his life and flees to the land of Midian. There he encounters the daughters of Reuel, a priest of Midian. Moses stays with Reuel and marries his daughter Zipporah.

From imminent death, to life as a prince of Egypt, to murder, to a new life in Midian, the beginning of Moses' life

The Martyrs of Compiègne

Catholic tradition has a long history of men and women who have endured suffering and persecution because of their faith. Among these many men and women are the Martyrs of Compiègne. These martyrs were a group of sixteen Carmelite nuns who were killed by guillotine during the French Revolution (1789–1799). The French Revolution ended with a period known as the Reign of Terror. It got this name because Robespierre, a political leader and opponent of the traditional God of Christianity, ordered the deaths of anyone opposing his political or religious ideals. The Carmelites of Compiègne, along with many other holy men and women, faced death because they would not denounce their God. Several books recount the story of the Martyrs of Compiègne, as does a famous opera titled *Dialogues of the Carmelites*.

Pray It!

Send Someone Else!

The Bible is full of people whom God called to do his will. Moses is an example of a person God called to be a prophet and to speak God's Word. However, Moses lacked confidence, and he said to the Lord: "If you please, Lord, send someone else!" (Exodus 4:13).

Like Moses we may not feel worthy or capable of responding to God's will for us. It is a challenge and will call us beyond our comfort zone. We just need to trust God enough and allow him to work through us. God provided Moses what he needed to accomplish his will (Aaron's support), and he will provide what you need too. Pray and ask God to make his will known to you.

Father,
Help me to know what your will is for me.
Give me good judgment to know what you are calling me to do
and the grace necessary to accomplish your will.
Amen.

reveals the mysterious and glorious work of God. God takes
an infant and leads him on a journey that will bring him to
a personal encounter with God and a commission to be an
instrument of God's will. ✝

Yahweh
The most sacred of
the Old Testament
names for God,
which he revealed to
Moses. It is frequently
translated as "I AM" or
"I am who am."

36 The Exodus

God hears the cries of his children enslaved in Egypt. In
response he saved them from persecution and led them out
of slavery under the leadership of Moses. Moses is almost
a victim of Pharaoh's decree that all Hebrew male babies
should be killed. He witnesses the persecution of his people
as he grows up in the palace of Pharaoh and flees his life of
privilege after killing an abusive Egyptian. Calling out to
Moses from the burning bush, God reveals his sacred, divine
name, **Yahweh,** which is often translated as "I am who am."
He calls Moses to be his voice of truth and arm of justice. As
a humble and a courageous man, Moses embodies the hopes
and aspirations of God's Holy People to live no longer under
the darkness of Pharaoh's reign but rather to walk freely in
the light of God's Reign.

Conflict and Contradiction

Sent by God and assisted by Aaron, his brother, Moses
stands up to Pharaoh by exclaiming, "Let my people
go!"(Exodus 5:1). Pharaoh, whom Egyptian culture considered to be divine, cannot give in to another of God's
demands. He is angry and orders even harsher treatment of
the enslaved Israelites. Again at the command of God, Moses
and Aaron confront Pharaoh and his idolatrous and abusive
ways. Again he does not heed their message. Even though
through these two holy men God works the wonder of
turning a staff into a snake, Pharaoh will not back down. He
cannot let his own perceived divine status be challenged.

To show who the true God is, God unleashes ten plagues
on Pharaoh and Egypt. These are meant to dismantle the
authoritative patterns of the Egyptian Empire and lead to
the freedom of the Israelites. God, "who is always there,
present to his people in order to save them" (*CCC*, 207), will
not allow the arrogance of one man to direct the fate of a

Passover
The night the Lord passed over the houses of the Israelites marked by the blood of the lamb, and spared the firstborn sons from death. It also is the feast that celebrates the deliverance of the Chosen People from bondage in Egypt and the Exodus from Egypt to the Promised Land.

good and righteous people. Beginning with water turning to blood, the first plague, God exerts his identity as the one true God, demanding that his People be set free. Pharaoh manages to endure the first nine plagues and still refuses to free the Israelites.

After the ninth plague, God says to Moses: "One more plague will I bring upon Pharaoh and upon Egypt. After that he will let you depart. In fact, he will not merely let you go; he will drive you away" (Exodus 11:1). In the tenth plague, the life of all firstborn males, human and animal—including the firstborn son of Pharaoh—is taken. This particular event is known as the **Passover,** during which the Lord passes over all houses marked with the blood of the sacrificial lamb but enters the houses not marked with this sign of faith to kill the firstborn children and animals.

The Saving Act

Pharaoh is grief stricken over the loss of his son, the symbol of his prosperity and power. He finally relents and begs Moses and the Israelites to leave Egypt. In a spirit of vengeance, however, Pharaoh changes his mind and sends his chariots to pursue the Israelites. Trapped between the Red Sea and the wrath of Pharaoh, the Israelites cry out to Moses, "Were there no burial places in Egypt that you had to bring us out here to die in the desert?" (Exodus 14:11). Moses responds, "The LORD himself will fight for you; you have only to keep still" (verse 14). Moses stretches his arms over the sea, "and the Lord swept the sea with a strong east wind throughout the night and so turned it into dry land" (verse 21). The Israelites are able to cross the sea on dry land to safety. In a

Catholic Wisdom

Exodus at the Easter Vigil

Seven Old Testament and two New Testament readings are assigned to the Easter Vigil, the special Mass celebrated after sunset on the night before Easter Sunday. The *Lectionary* explains that is it permissible to read fewer than the assigned nine but stresses that the reading from Exodus (see 14:15—15:1), which tells the account of the Israelites' escape through the Red Sea, should never be omitted.

final act of destruction on Egypt, the sea flows back into place as the Egyptians attempt to cross in pursuit.

The account of the Israelites' escape from Egypt in the Book of Exodus tells of the saving power of God. God keeps his promises to his People, even when a situation appears hopeless and impossible. His offer of liberating love and sanctifying grace remains steadfast and will never be subject to the designs of a world constructed on the humiliation of the human spirit. ✝

Passover

On the night of the tenth plague, God directed the Israelites to slaughter a one-year-old male lamb (called the Passover, or Paschal, lamb) and place some of the lamb's blood on the two doorposts of the house where the Israelites gathered. They were to roast the lamb and eat it with unleavened bread (bread made without yeast) and bitter herbs. On that night the Lord would descend on Egypt and strike down every firstborn human and beast, "but the blood will mark the houses where you are. Seeing the blood, I will pass over you." (Exodus 12:13). The Israelites are commanded to celebrate the Passover meal every year to remind them of their escape from slavery through God's power.

Centuries later, on or near the feast of Passover, on the night before he died, Jesus shared the Last Supper with the disciples. He broke the bread and said, "Take and eat; this is my body." He then took the cup and said, "Drink from it, all of you." (See Matthew 26:26–27.) Although the sacrifice of the original Passover lamb saved the Israelites from physical death, Jesus' sacrifice saves all who put their faith in him from eternal death, and gives us the gift of eternal life with God. Jesus is the new Paschal Lamb.

manna

Little flakes the Israelites collected and boiled or baked into a breadlike substance, symbolizing God as the sole sustainer of life.

37 Building Trust in God

Liberation from Egyptian slavery and the crossing of the Red Sea are just the start of the journey of the Israelites. On the way to the Promised Land, the Israelites have to cross a vast wilderness. They enter a land where their fate seems uncertain, food and water are scarce, and the natives are unwelcoming. Encountering these less-than-ideal conditions, the Israelites immediately forget God's liberating action as demonstrated in their Exodus from slavery, and they also forget his promise to protect them even in the darkest times.

Disgruntled by the harsh conditions of the desert and disillusioned by the leadership of Moses, the people question, "Is the LORD in our midst or not?" (Exodus 17:7). They complain and begin idealizing their previous life in Egypt, failing to remember the harsh treatment of Pharaoh, forgetting the God who listens to their cries, and discounting the courage of Moses in accepting the call to lead them to freedom. Yet God does not forget his promises. When the people are hungry, God rains down **manna,** little flakes that the people collect and then boil or bake into a breadlike substance. When the people are thirsty, God draws water from a rock. When they are afraid, God protects them. The manna from Heaven, a bread of life, is sent to satiate their powerful hunger. Still they question the presence of God.

Traveling through the desert forced the Israelites to rely on God for survival. How does life today make it easy for us to forget that we also need to rely on God?

© Gejra / shutterstock.com

An Identity Formed

In all their struggles and complaints, the Israelites are forced not only to work together but also to build a community based on trust in God's saving power. Some people are called to assist Moses by becoming leaders. Part of their role as leaders is to help the people recall God's wondrous deeds in the Exodus and to recognize God's saving presence in their midst. They empower the people, a forgetful people, to move forward with a sense of trust and hope in the ways of the Lord. They remind the people of a God who never forsakes his promises.

The people are traveling an unclear road with many twists and turns. Yet God never leaves them. God draws them together as a family and gives them a new identity. They become a people brought from the depths of slavery and called to a new land so they can be the Chosen People who sing of God's greatness. ✞

The Bread of Life

The manna symbolizes God as the sole sustainer of life and foreshadows the Eucharist, which is the "fount and apex of the whole Christian life" (*Dogmatic Constitution on the Church*, 11). In the Eucharist Christ is fully present—body, blood, soul, and divinity. While Jesus traveled on the earth, he fed people not only with food but also with his presence and words. Jesus instituted the Sacrament of the Eucharist at the Last Supper with the intent that people of all times and places would be able to feed on his presence and word. Jesus is our Bread of Life and Cup of Salvation.

38 The Ten Commandments

Slavery, freedom, desert wandering. Now it becomes time for God to "seal" the Israelites' identity. In all their experiences, God gradually works to create a people with a new identity and sense of mission. The finishing touches on this new identity take place at the foot of Mount Sinai. Mount Sinai is the sacred ground where God forms a Covenant

Ten Commandments

Sometimes called the Decalogue, the list of ten norms, or rules of moral behavior, that God gave Moses and that are the basis of ethical conduct.

Sinai Covenant

The Covenant established with the Israelites at Mount Sinai that renewed God's Covenant with Abraham's descendants. It establishes the Israelites as God's Chosen People.

with his Chosen People. Contained within this Covenant are laws and obligations, known as the **Ten Commandments.** They will govern the people's relationship with God and with one another.

From Liberation to Covenant

When the Israelites were enslaved, they were stripped of their identity and lived under the law of Pharaoh. Brought through the waters of the Red Sea and led to Mount Sinai, the Israelites enter a Covenant with God. At Mount Sinai Moses climbs the mountain. There God directs him to tell the Israelites that God has brought them safely to this place and if they keep the Covenant, they will be the Lord's holy nation.

Moses returns to the people and shares the LORD's offer of his Covenant. Within the framework of this **Sinai Covenant,** God declares himself to be their God, a God of fidelity, love, and justice. Harking back to the Covenant between God and Abraham, God promises that the Israelites will be his "special possession, dearer to [him] than all other people" (Exodus 19:5). The Israelites will be a "kingdom of priests, a holy nation" (verse 6). In return they must be a righteous, moral people who live according to his law. By agreeing to the terms of the Covenant, the Israelites will dwell in the Promised Land, or as it is described in Exodus, "the land flowing with milk and honey" (33:3), and will know a God whose "mercy is from age to age" (Luke 1:50).

Live It!

Loving Limitations

Whenever someone says we are not allowed to do something, we often immediately want to go out and do it. We tend to dislike having limitations put on us. The problem is that sometimes what we want is not always what is good. Some limitations are necessary and even the most loving thing one can provide.

For example, a mother tells her child not to leave the yard and run into the street. Why? Is it because she wants to keep her son or daughter from having a good time? Of course not! She makes this rule because she loves her child and does not want the child to get hurt. In a similar way, God gives commandments to guide us, not to restrain us. He does this because he loves us. Pick one of the Ten Commandments that seems restrictive to you and write down the positive things that come from following it.

The Ten Commandments

On the third day at Mount Sinai, God again summons Moses
to the mountaintop and gives him the Ten Commandments.
Delivered to the Israelites by Moses but written "with God's
own finger" (Exodus 31:18), the Ten Commandments are the
first stage of revealed law, conveying God's expectations of
his People. In this sense the Ten Commandments express the
Israelites' covenant relationship with God. These ten norms

The Ten Commandments

1. I am the LORD your God: you shall not have strange Gods before me.
2. You shall not take the name of the LORD your God in vain.
3. Remember to keep holy the LORD's day.
4. Honor your father and your mother.
5. You shall not kill.
6. You shall not commit adultery.
7. You shall not steal.
8. You shall not bear false witness against your neighbor.
9. You shall not covet your neighbor's wife.
10. You shall not covet your neighbor's goods.

(*CCC*, pages 496–497)

summarize the law of God in the Torah. They are concerned with how people lead their lives. The Ten Commandments lay the framework for building a more just society, and they teach people how to live in right relationship with God, expressing "the implications of belonging to God through the establishment of the covenant" (*CCC*, 2062).

The heart of the Ten Commandments is reverence and love for God and love of neighbor. In receiving the Commandments from God, the Israelites' identity as the people of God is sealed.

The Old Law given to Moses is a preparation for the Gospel revealed through Jesus Christ. Jesus Christ fulfills the Old Covenant and Law. He affirms the Old Law received by Moses (see Matthew 5:17) and brings it to perfection. Like Moses he delivers the law from a mountain in the Sermon on the Mount. Like the Old Law, the New Law is based in love of God and love of our neighbor. It is a law of grace because the Holy Spirit gives us the strength to live it out through faith and the Sacraments. And it is a law of freedom because it is not guided only by guidelines and rituals but calls us to freely share God's love in acts of charity and justice. ✟

Review

1. What caused the enslavement of the Israelites?

2. How did God respond to the enslavement of his People?

3. Why did the tenth plague convince Pharaoh to release the Israelites?

4. What was the attitude of the people of Israel toward God while they were in the midst of the desert? Why did they feel like this?

5. What is manna? What is it a sign of?

6. What is at the heart of the Ten Commandments?

Part 3

The Historical Books

One of the four major sections of the Old Testament is called the historical books. However, the historical books in the Bible are not like the history books you read in school. The authors of the historical books were not concerned primarily with historical data. Instead they intended to write a sacred history that reveals God's plan of salvation. The historical books recount Israelite history from around 1250 BC to 100 BC. They focus on the settlement of the Promised Land and the unification of the kingdom under David. They discuss the eventual division of the united kingdom into northern and southern kingdoms. They also portray the destruction of the two kingdoms and the rebuilding of a nation after exile. The following articles focus on the first two realities: settlement and unification.

Joshua, the judges, and the first three kings of Israel—Saul, David, and Solomon—are major characters in the historical books. God calls each for a special mission grounded in his holy will. These characters are flawed and sinful human beings through whom God performs amazing acts of love and mercy. The historical books place God at the center of human experience, giving meaning to the struggles of everyday life. These unique books lift up people being blessed when they live in right relationship with God.

The articles in this part address the following topics:

39 Joshua: God Is on Our Side

"So prepare to cross the Jordan here, with all the people, into the land I will give the Israelites. As I promised Moses, I will deliver to you every place where you set foot" (Joshua 1:2–3). These words represent the calling of Joshua, the successor to Moses. Joshua leads the Israelites into Canaan. After the death of Moses, the Israelites need a strong leader to guide their path toward the Promised Land. God commissions the heroic and faithful Joshua, who had served Moses as a trusted leader. Joshua's and Moses' stories are similar. Both Joshua and Moses experience God in miraculous ways, both part a body of water, and both hear trumpets when they accomplish God's covenantal plan. Most important, both heed God's call, saying yes with their entire beings to participate in the history of salvation.

A Foreign Land

Pope John Paul II prays for peace at Mount Nebo, the traditional site where God showed Moses the Promised Land.

Under the leadership of Joshua, the Israelites enter the land of Canaan, a land God promised to Abraham and his descendants. The Israelites find Canaan to be hostile because of the **polytheistic beliefs** of the Canaanites, including the worship of the god **Baal** and his consort, the goddess **Asherah**. It is also hostile because the native peoples refuse to hand

© Gianni Giansanti/Sygma/Corbis

over their land. Regardless of the obstacles, Joshua and the Israelite army swiftly conquer the land of Canaan. One of the pivotal moments in their conquest is the fall of a small town on the West Bank known as Jericho. The place is notable because the Israelites meet the prostitute Rahab and other outcasts from the unjust system of governance in Canaanite society. Rahab aids the Israelites in their conquest both for her own self-preservation and for the creation of a Canaan based on equality and justice. To reward Rahab for her help, the Israelites spare her and her family during the destruction of Jericho. Rahab can be seen as a symbol of oppressed individuals governed by the selfish laws of humanity, not the Law of Moses, which protects the rights of all people under God's promise of peace and prosperity.

polytheistic beliefs
Beliefs in many gods and goddesses.

Baal . . . Asherah
Two Canaanite gods of earth and fertility that the Israelites worshipped when they fell away from the one true God.

Warrior and Faithful Leader

In the accounts of battles and conquest in the Book of Joshua, God is presented as a warrior waging a holy war. How can a God of love wage such a savage and brutal war? Can the image of warrior be reconciled with the image of a compassionate and merciful God? It is important to remember that the words in the Sacred Scriptures are conditioned by the language and culture of the Israelites. The Israelites believed God was on their side. The metaphor of warrior provided the Israelites with a sense of security. Their warrior God freed them from the clutches of Pharaoh and would lead them into battle for the Promised Land. For the Israelites, war was a holy act to fulfill the promise God made to their fathers and mothers in faith by protecting them from

Catholic Wisdom

We Will Serve the Lord

"As for me and my household, we will serve the LORD" (Joshua 24:15) This well-known verse can be found on coffee mugs and plaques. These are the words Joshua spoke to the Israelites before his death. Joshua faced many obstacles while leading the Israelites into the land of Canaan, but he believed God was always with him and his people. This quotation should serve as a reminder that God is on our side, especially when we face difficult situations.

the influences of cultures hostile to their religious beliefs and practices.

One aspect of Joshua that may be overlooked among the stories of the battles is his undying devotion to God. Joshua not only serves as a strong military leader for the Israelites but also models a true commitment to the Covenant with God. Even when God provides odd-seeming directions to Joshua, Joshua remains true to them. In fact, at the time of his death, Joshua says to the Israelites: "If it does not please you to serve the LORD, decide today whom you will serve, the gods your fathers served beyond the River or the gods of the Amorites in whose country you are dwelling. As for me and my household, we will serve the LORD" (Joshua 24:15). In remaining faithful to God, Joshua demonstrates to the Israelites that when they remain true to the Covenant, God will abundantly bless them.

From a contemporary approach, we can interpret that God, as both just warrior and loving Covenant maker, does not seek brutality and savagery but instead longs for a world founded on the words he spoke to Abraham, the Law he gave to Moses, and the truth he revealed in the heart of Joshua. We need to remember that God is always on the side of what is right and good. In Joshua, whose name means "salvation of God," God stands firm against the wicked ways of the world, challenges the people who lack trust, and last but not least, fulfills the promise he made to Abraham. (The name Jesus is another pronunciation of the Hebrew name Joshua.) ✞

Rahab

Rahab is mentioned not only in the Book of Joshua but also in the New Testament. The Letter to the Hebrews says, "By faith Rahab the harlot did not perish with the disobedient" (11:31), and the Letter of James says, "Was not Rahab the harlot also justified by works when she welcomed the messengers and sent them out by a different route?" (2:25). Rahab is recognized by the authors of the New Testament as playing a role in God's plan. She is an example of how God can work through anyone, even the most unlikely, to bring salvation to his People.

40 Judges: The Book of Deliverers

After the Israelites settle the Promised Land and enter a time of peace, there is less of a need for strong leaders like Moses and Joshua. Yet over time both the people's faithlessness to the Covenant and foreign invasions require new leaders. Thus Israelite history from around 1200 to 1000 BC is marked by the leadership of twelve heroic, yet flawed, individuals known as the **judges.** Their role was different from that of our judges today. These leaders settled disputes within their own tribe or between tribes. The judges also led the military defense against outside invaders. Most important they challenged Israel to remain faithful to God.

The Book of Judges does not attempt to give a chronological account of the time between the settlement of Canaan and the rise of the monarchy. Rather it is a series of short accounts about human leaders' accomplishing God's will. After the death of Joshua, the Israelites fall into a cycle of sin. This cycle includes sin, calamity, repentance, and deliverance. The judges emerge when the Israelites begin to fall away from their core religious identity by worshipping false gods. Two of the main gods the Israelites were worshipping were Baal and Asherah. When Israel forgets its Covenant commitments, the people become selfish and timid and end up being dominated by idol-worshipping neighbors. However, each time this happens, the Israelites eventually repent, and God brings a hero, a judge, who leads the people from destruction.

Though some judges are faithful to the Covenant, others are not. Even though the fidelity of some judges wavers, God's will is still accomplished. God transcends the frailty of the human condition so his plan may be fulfilled in the lives of the Chosen People. On not quite the same scale as Moses and Joshua, the judges, in all their strengths and weaknesses, are key figures in God's fortifying plan of redemption and eternal happiness.

Three Notable Judges

The twelve judges, as leaders of the Twelve Tribes of Israel, are important in their own ways, but three distinguished judges are worth discussing in greater detail: Deborah,

Gideon, and Samson. Deborah, the fourth judge of Israel, is a strong, confident woman, commanded by God to launch a war against the Canaanites, their king, Jabin, and his general Sisera, because of their aggressive attack and pillage of Israel. After leading the Israelite army to victory, Deborah breaks into song, praising God and his many servants. She sings, "May all your enemies perish thus, O LORD! / but your friends be as the sun rising in its might!" (Judges 5:31).

© Stefano Bianchetti/Corbis

It takes an angel's appearance to cause the judge, Gideon, to be committed to the true God. Who is God using to help you in your relationship with God?

Before his conversion, Gideon was an **idolatrous** man. Encountering "the angel of the LORD" (Judges 6:11), he quits worshipping foreign gods and pledges his allegiance to the one true God of Israel. Because of this conversion, Gideon makes it his mission to destroy the altars of false gods. The story of Gideon demonstrates how one person's faith, or lack of it, can unite or divide a people. When Gideon's faith is strong, he brings the tribes together. When it is weak—practically nonexistent— he leads them into idolatry.

Live It!

Priorities

Worshipping false gods may seem like a strange idea to you. Perhaps in your mind, there is no question that the Father, Son, and Holy Spirit was, is, and will forever be the only God. However, idolatry is essentially letting something other than God take his place in your life. So idolatry can be the unconscious belief that you need something other than God to make you truly happy and fulfilled. This can manifest itself in subtle ways. An inordinate desire for money, sex, clothing, or popularity can all be forms of idolatry.

It was a subtle form of idolatry that led the judge Samson astray. His desire to be with Delilah overtook his faith in God and paved the path for his downfall. Being aware of your priorities in life is essential. Write them down and evaluate them. Are your priorities consistent with all that Jesus taught and the Church professes? Do any of your priorities indicate that deep down you feel the need to have something besides God to be truly happy?

© CORBIS

God blesses Samson with superhuman strength, but Samson also has many character flaws. His story teaches us that God works through imperfect people.

Samson is a strong, passionate man who has trouble keeping his religious commitments. Samson accomplishes amazing feats for God, including the legendary acts of tearing a lion apart with his bare hands and killing a thousand Philistines with the jawbone of an animal. His character flaws lead to his capture, torture, and debasement at the hands of the Philistines. However, because of a final act of trust in God, Samson is able to deliver Israel from the Philistines.

idolatrous
Worshipping false gods.

Deborah, Gideon, and Samson, along with the other nine judges, point out that Yahweh is the king of all people, deserving of all our trust and reverence. The judges act as a conscience for the Israelites, continually calling and reminding them to be faithful to their Covenant with God, for in God all things can be accomplished. Without him all action is meaningless and stands in the way of truth. ✝

Eight Enliveners of Faith

The pages of Church history contain the lives of holy men and women, like the judges, called by God to enliven the faith of his People. From founding religious communities to building hospitals and educational institutions that serve the poor, they worked to make God's covenantal promise of love known. The Church gives these people the title saint. Nine holy people whose vocation took root in the United States are officially recognized as saints: Saint Rene Goupil (1607–1642), Saint Isaac Jogues (1607–1646), Saint Rose Philippine Duchesne (1769–1852), Saint Elizabeth Ann Seton (1774–1821), Saint Mother Theodore Guerin (1798–1856), Saint John Neumann (1811–1860), Saint Damien of Molokai (1840–1889), Saint Frances Xavier Cabrini (1850–1917), and Saint Katharine Drexel (1858–1955).

monarchy

A government or a state headed by a single person, like a king or queen. As a biblical term, it refers to the period of time when the Israelites existed as an independent nation.

theocracy

A nation ruled by God.

41 From Saul to Solomon: The Desire for Unity

Following the time of the judges, the Israelites demanded a centralized form of leadership under a king, a form known as a **monarchy.** They were concerned about the growing divisions among the Twelve Tribes and the increased power of other nations. Because the Israelites were separated by tribal allegiance and disjointed under the leadership of the judges, they experienced the consequences of division and sin. We see this in the horrible accounts of violence against innocent people in the second half of the Book of Judges. The Israelites longed for someone to bring them together, helping them to gather their many resources and talents to become a cohesive people, a powerful nation-state directed by God's holy will.

Samuel, the last judge and a prophet of Israel, resisted the idea of monarchy out of fear that the Israelites were replacing the ruler of all creation, God, with the human authority of a king. Samuel wanted a **theocracy,** a nation ruled by God, not a monarchy ruled by a king. Samuel warned the people of the danger of kings. Nonetheless, God, honoring the Israelites' request, directed Samuel to anoint a king. The Lord said to Samuel, "Grant their request and appoint a king to rule them" (1 Samuel 8:22). Thus a monarchy was established. With the institution of monarchy came three wise, yet flawed, kings: Saul, David, and Solomon.

Three Men of Interest

The Book of First Samuel recounts the life of Israel's first king, Saul (1020–1000 BC). From the Tribe of Benjamin and anointed king by Samuel, Saul commits his reign to freeing the Israelites from their enemies. However, after Saul is anointed king, he twice disobeys God's Law. First, he himself offers a prebattle sacrifice instead of waiting for Samuel to do so. (Only priests are allowed to offer sacrifices.) Then following another battle, he takes the enemy king and livestock as spoils of war rather than destroying them as God wants.

Saul also faces a problem in the person of David, who eventually dethrones and replaces Saul as king. As David becomes popular, Saul becomes increasingly envious of him and eventually tries to kill him. Saul's reign as king ends tragically, and he fails in his many attempts to form a centralized nation. Mortally injured in battle, he kills himself by falling on his sword.

King David (1000–961 BC) is a successful military leader, savvy politician, gifted musician, and lover of God. David struggles with his lust for power. But he accomplishes what he sets out to do when he follows the will of God.

Many stories surround David. One of them occurs before he is king. This is the young David's encounter with the dreaded Philistine giant, Goliath, when he manages to kill Goliath with a slingshot. Remembered for uniting all Twelve Tribes under one ruler and expanding the kingdom to include most of Palestine, David is both a visionary leader and repentant sinner.

In the Book of First Kings, we hear about Solomon (975–922 BC), the son of King David. Solomon is the third king of Israel. He is noted for building the Temple of the Lord in honor of his father, for strengthening and modernizing the Israelite army, and for creating trade alliances with other nations. Not only does he build the Temple, but also he constructs a magnificent palace and enlarges Jerusalem, now the capital city of Israel. He is a man of great wisdom and judgment, as well as an ambitious ruler who imposes steep taxes and forced labor on the Israelites.

A man of seven hundred wives and three hundred concubines (symbolic numbers indicating a great and perfect number of wives and concubines), Solomon allows his foreign wives to practice their idolatrous ways. He eventually follows these practices himself. In response to his idolatry, God tells Solomon, "Since this is what you want, and you have not kept my covenant and my statues which I enjoined on you, I will deprive you of the kingdom and give it to your servant" (1 Kings 11:11).

All three kings demonstrate the need to live in right relationship with God. When each man remains true to God's plan, he is able to accomplish great things and create a unifying bond among the Chosen People. When each is lured away from God by his own ego and self-interest, he stands in the way of what is good and holy. Whether or not human beings and their leaders remain faithful to God's Covenant, God is always there. From Saul to David to Solomon, God built a glorious kingdom rich in mercy that faltered only because of the weakness and sin of human beings. ✝

The First Temple

King Solomon built the First Temple in honor of King David, his father. Solomon designed the Temple, financing it by taxes on the people of Israel. It took seven years to build. When finished it was an amazing building complete with cedar paneling, gold overlay, intricate carvings, statues, and ivory-paneled doors. The Temple served both as a testament to the political power of the monarchy and as a symbol of the presence of God. The First Temple, however, was completely destroyed by the Babylonian King Nebuchadnezzar (also known as Darius) in 586 BC.

The Israelites' worship at the Jerusalem Temple foreshadows our worship of Jesus Christ. The Israelites worshipped the glory of God in their Temple. Now we worship Jesus Christ in his resurrected glory. The Israelites worshipped God through animal sacrifice, and now we worship Christ and his saving sacrifice, the fulfillment of the hopes of the Israelite people. Jesus even compares himself to the Temple (see John 2:19).

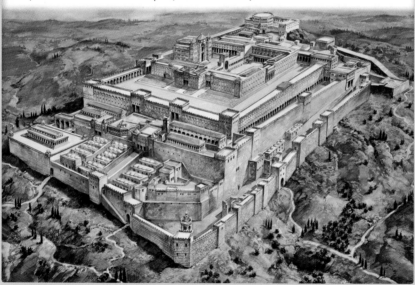

© DeA Picture Library / Art Resource, NY

42 David: Recognizing a Servant

Repentant heart, vengeful spirit, faithful companion, lover of God, lustful ruler, skilled musician, handsome hunk, jealous ego, military leader, passionate dancer, and visionary king!

These characteristics fit the great monarch King David, who united the northern and southern tribes. David is an intriguing character in the Old Testament. His life is full of contradictions. One moment he commits his entire being to the establishment of God's Covenant on earth. The next moment an adulterous affair ensnares him, leading to murder. The story of King David shows the experience of being caught in the tension between a life enamored of the empty promises of the world and a life committed solely to the will of God. David falls prey to the ways of sin but always returns to the Lord with a repentant heart.

Ark of the Covenant

A sacred chest that housed the tablets of the Ten Commandments. It was placed within the sanctuary where God would come and dwell.

Deep Friendship

One of the less known stories about David is his friendship with Jonathan, son of King Saul. David and Jonathan love each other with undying loyalty. Their relationship is volatile at times, but they would do anything for each other, including Jonathan's willingness to risk his life to protect David from Saul. Reconciliation and sacrifice mark David and Jonathan's deep bond. When Jonathan dies David experiences an immense sense of loss. This story is significant because it demonstrates the tender, compassionate side of David—a man of enormous depth called by God to build life-giving relationships, leading to a fuller understanding of God's Covenant with his People.

David and the Israelites worshipped the presence of God in the Ark of the Covenant. We adore God's presence in the Body and Blood of Jesus Christ.

God's Servant

Another memorable story about David centers on his free-spirited celebration of the arrival in Jerusalem of the **Ark of the Covenant,** a sacred chest that housed the tablets of the Ten Commandments. For the Israelites the Ark was an ancient symbol of God's holy protection. At its arrival, "David, girt with a linen apron, came dancing

© Arte & Immagini srl/CORBIS

servant leadership

A type of leadership based on humble service to all God's people.

before the Lᴏʀᴅ with abandon" (2 Samuel 6:14). David leaps and offers burnt offerings, because God's presence is in the people's midst. David decides to build a house for the Lord, but the prophet Nathan tells David not to do so. God has another plan. God will instead build a house for David, but this house will not be a building. It will be a royal dynasty, a line of descendants that will endure forever. This promise from God to David is known as the Davidic Covenant. We see this promise fulfilled with the birth of Jesus Christ, who is David's descendant.

A Paradigm of Service

Although David accomplishes much for God, he allows his human desires to blind him to God's saving action. Whether it is his lust for women, especially his future wife Bathsheba, or his longing for power and fame, David's sinful ways sometimes hinder him in seeing or promoting the will of God.

Unique about David is that he always returns to the Lord begging for mercy and promising to change. He recognizes his need for God's strength if he is to serve the Chosen People and the unfolding Covenant. David models **servant leadership.** Despite all his sins and faults, he beckons to God to raise him from the abyss of despair so he may rule with a just heart and a serving hand. Servant leaders recognize their need for forgiveness and reconciliation. In return they can extend mercy and compassion to all in need. Even in all his brokenness, King David journeys through life serving the teachings of the Covenant, leading the Israelites toward the

Pray It!

Psalm 51

We all sin and fall short of the love we have for God. Our struggle with sin is no different from that of some great figures of the Bible. Throughout his life David committed grave sins against our Lord. At one point he committed adultery with Bathsheba while her husband was away at battle. Then Bathsheba became pregnant. To cover up his sin, David arranged for Uriah, Bathsheba's husband, to be killed in battle.

Even though he was guilty of serious sin, David repented and asked God for forgiveness. Psalm 51 is his plea to God for mercy and forgiveness. It is a reminder to us that if we are truly repentant, God will forgive us. The next time you face temptation or sin, read Psalm 51 and ask for God's help and mercy.

horizon of eternal peace, and heralding the hope of a king
yet unborn. ✝

A King Yet Unborn

"I will raise up your heir after you, sprung from your loins, and I will make his kingdom firm. It is he who shall build a house for my name. And I will make his royal throne firm forever" (2 Samuel 7:12–13). Spoken to David by the Lord, these words laid the foundation for the Jewish expectation of a messiah, a descendant of David. This prophecy is fulfilled in Jesus Christ, the King of Glory. The genealogies contained in the Gospels of Matthew and Luke trace Jesus' ancestry through David. Many people of Jesus' time did not acknowledge him as a fulfillment of this Old Testament prophecy because he did not fit the traditional image of a king. He denounced the trappings of royal leadership and wealth by taking on the humility of a man, eventually resulting in his death on a cross.

Review

1. Who was Moses' successor? What was to be his task?

2. List the similarities between Moses and his successor.

3. What important function did the judges serve in the lives of the Israelites?

4. List the three judges mentioned in this section and briefly describe their accomplishments.

5. Why did the Israelites want a king?

6. What were the accomplishments of Saul, David, and Solomon? What were their personal weaknesses?

7. How is David a model of servant leadership?

Part 4

The Prophetic Books

The prophetic books cover hundreds of years of Israelite history. The Israelite kingdom had been unified under the reigns of Saul, David, and Solomon. After Solomon died Israel split into two kingdoms: the northern kingdom, which was still called Israel, and the southern kingdom, which was called Judah. These two kingdoms were ruled by different kings. As in the time of the judges, the people turned away from God and his holy Commandments. From the eighth to the fourth centuries BC, God called prophets to speak to the people on his behalf. They reminded the people that God would hold them accountable for their idolatrous and unjust practices. When the people were in crisis, the prophets reminded them of God's saving love. The prophetic message was essentially threefold: act justly toward one another, return to God with faithful hearts, and hope in God's deliverance—which culminated in the expectation of a messiah.

The articles in this part address the following topics:

43 The Prophets: A Radical Redemption

The course of salvation history is a journey of many peaks and valleys, highs and lows. In the Old Testament, the high points of this journey show a unified, holy people living in right relationship with God and making the promise of the Covenant known in word and action. The low points happen because human beings are weak and forgetful. They often lose sight of their Covenant relationship with God. They become absorbed in the sinful ways of the world. When the Israelites lose their way, they need someone to call them back to the source of all life and hope, God. They need a prophet. A *prophet,* a word coming from the Hebrew *nabi,* probably meaning "spokesperson" or "one who is called," refers to a person chosen by God to communicate a message of salvation. The prophet communicates a message on behalf of God. This message, or **prophecy,** usually offers divine direction or consolation.

The Bible mentions many prophets. Seventeen prophets have books in the Bible named after them. The words and lives of many other prophets, such as Moses, Nathan, Elijah, and Anna, are recorded in other books. The messages of the prophets with books named after them fall into two categories. First are the prophets who lived before and during the **Babylonian Exile** of the Israelites. They generally delivered messages of warning. Second are the prophets who lived during and after the Babylonian Exile (which ended in 539 BC) who generally delivered messages of comfort and hope.

prophecy
A message communicated by prophets on behalf of God, usually a message of divine direction or consolation for the prophet's own time. Because some prophetic messages include divine direction, their fulfillment may be in the future.

Babylonian Exile
In 587 BC, the Babylonians pillaged Judah, destroyed the Temple and the city of Jerusalem, and banished the people in chains to serve as slaves in Babylon. The Exile lasted until 539 BC.

Awake, O Sleeper

"Wake up! Are you aware of what is going on around you? Why do you sleep when there is so much pain and division? When will you return to the Lord?" Many prophets writing before the Babylonian Exile speak these words to people lying dormant. The people are unaware that their lives and hearts are moving further away from the will of God. As herald of God's salvation, the prophets act as the conscience of a people who have been lulled into complacency and sinfulness. They assure the people that God has not abandoned them and that they need to repent of their sins to find joy again. They challenge the complacency of the Israelites.

They direct the Israelites' attention and open their eyes to the many obstacles standing in the way of a meaningful relationship with God and others.

Sleep No Longer, the Time Is at Hand

Through the prophets God declares to the Israelites that now is the time "to do right and to love goodness, and to walk humbly with your God" (Micah 6:8). The prophets challenge people not only to look at their own lives but also to reflect and respond in a spirit of hope to the unjust practices of the world. At other times the prophets provide solace and comfort to a hurting and oppressed people. Whether calling for a change of heart or offering hope to a distressed people, the prophets' message is often not received well. The message challenges the existing way of life. Prophets were often ostracized, silenced, and sometimes killed for their messages of warning, reformation, and consolation.

A Universal Call and Message

The vocation to prophecy never dies. Every generation needs men and women to challenge it to remain faithful to God in good times and bad. Sin, injustice, and despair affect every time and place. Therefore a saving message of love must be proclaimed. Beginning with the biblical prophets and con-

Pray It!

No Special Skills Required

Did you know that God calls people from all walks of life to be prophets? No special skills are required. All that is needed is an open heart willing to do his work. Look up these Scripture passages to learn more about the prophets chosen by God:

- He called Miriam, a slave. (Exodus 15:20–21)
- He chose Amos, a shepherd. (Amos 7:14)
- He chose Elisha, a farmer. (1 Kings 19:19)
- He chose Ezekiel, a priest. (Ezekiel 1:3)

Then take a moment to pray and ask God to help you discern your vocation in life. Are you being called to the priesthood or to consecrated life? Do you feel called to ministry in your parish community? Are you being called to be a witness of faith as an athlete, student, or worker? God is calling you. Take a moment to be quiet and listen to his gentle voice.

tinuing to our world today and beyond, God raises up holy prophets to "proclaim a radical redemption of the People of God, purification from all their infidelities, a salvation which will include all the nations"[2] (*CCC*, 64). Those who hear and heed the messages of the prophets are no longer enslaved to the darkness of infidelity and sin. They are free to revel in the redeeming love of God. ✝

A Modern Prophet of Hope and Justice

Archbishop Oscar Romero (1917–1980) was a man of great conviction and an avid defender of human rights. As Archbishop of El Salvador, Romero witnessed the severe persecution and oppression of the poor by the Salvadoran political and social regime. Within the Archdiocese of El Salvador, numerous priests, brothers, nuns, and lay missionaries were being assassinated for providing educational opportunities for the poor and speaking out against the unjust ways of the government. Romero strongly believed that the Church must be united with the poor, and he advocated for the rights of the marginalized and oppressed. While Romero was celebrating Mass on March 24, 1980, a political group opposed to his teachings assassinated him. A couple weeks before his assassination, he was quoted as saying: "If God accepts the sacrifice of my life, may my death be for the freedom of my people. . . . A bishop will die, but the Church of God, which is the people, will never perish" (*Longhorn Catholic*, May 2008).

44 Major and Minor Prophets

The Sacred Scriptures are filled with numerous accounts about the lives of prophets, their prophecies, and their role in salvation history. Seventeen books in the Old Testament are named for specific prophets, known as the writing, or canonical, prophets. The writing prophets are divided into two groups: the major prophets and the minor prophets. The classifications of major or minor are not based on how important the prophets and their messages were but rather on the length of their writings. The size of the book determines whether it is major or minor. There are also two books in the prophets section of the Old Testament that are not, strictly speaking, collections of prophetic speeches. ✝

Prophets			
Major Prophets	**Minor Prophets**		**Writings Related to the Prophets**
Isaiah	Hosea	Joel	Baruch
Jeremiah	Amos	Obadiah	Lamentations
Ezekiel	Jonah	Micah	
Daniel	Nahum	Habakkuk	
	Zephaniah	Haggai	

45 Ezekiel: Challenging Idolatry and Injustice

"Son of man, eat what is before you; eat this scroll, then go, speak to the house of Israel" (Ezekiel 3:1). God's call of Ezekiel to be a prophet was unique: God invites him to dine on his holy Word, his righteous law. At tasting the truth of God, Ezekiel proclaims it to be "as sweet as honey" (verse 3). Ezekiel begins his prophetic ministry in 593 BC in Babylon and concludes it in 573 BC. He is part of the first group of Israelites forced to relocate during the Babylonian Exile.

Ezekiel is sent to be a "watchman" for Israel. He is called to speak on behalf of God to a divided people—some still in Jerusalem and others who have been relocated to Babylon—whom God is punishing for their sinful ways. The Israelites are not only unfaithful and idolatrous but also unjust toward the poor and lowly in society. The Israelites have become comfortable with treating one another poorly and with their dehumanizing attitudes toward the lowly. Ezekiel, more than any other biblical prophet, uses symbolic actions to enhance his prophetic messages. Some actions include lying on his left side for 390 days and on his right side for forty days (see Ezekiel 4:1–6), shaving his head and using his hair to deliver a message (see chapter 5), and packing his baggage and acting out escaping from captivity (see 12:1–16). After each symbolic act, God tells Ezekiel how to explain its meaning to the Israelites.

Led Astray

Some of Ezekiel's major themes include the presence of the Lord in the Temple, the awesomeness of God, personal responsibility for one's life and faith, and oracles against the enemies of Israel. Ezekiel delivers particularly hard warnings to the leaders of Israel. He compares the leaders of Israel to shepherds' failing to lead their sheep on the path of righteousness. Because the Israelite leaders are too busy taking care of themselves, they do not "strengthen the weak nor heal the sick nor bind up the injured" (Ezekiel 34:4). Consumed with selfish wants and misplaced loyalty, the shepherds allow their sheep to scatter, wander, and fall prey to the wild beasts. The wild beasts symbolize the foolish and idolatrous beliefs (worship of false gods) of the surrounding cultures. The leaders do not lead with the justice and fairness of good shepherds. They are personally responsible for the eventual destruction of a people.

Live It!

Called to Be a Prophet

We are all called to be prophets who speak the Word of God with both our words and actions. However, being a prophet is difficult. Prophets point out wrongdoing. They call people to respect God and one another. Perhaps, like some of the biblical prophets God called to do his work, we can feel inadequate to the task. Or we might be afraid of being made fun of like many of the prophets were.

We should take courage by looking at our modern-day prophets. Blessed Mother Teresa called us all to serve the poor. Bishop Oscar Romero called for political reforms in his home of El Salvador. You may even know a prophet in your school who calls others to do the right thing. How will you live out your role as a prophet?

herald
To proclaim or announce a saving message.

Ezekiel is a powerful voice crying out against the abuses of the Israelite leaders and their followers. The Israelites have forgotten the Covenant and have turned to idolatrous practices. The Israelites have also failed to remember the dignity and worth of each human. By not caring for the needs of one another and the vulnerable, they disrespect God's plan of loving goodness.

Dry Bones

One of the most famous and bizarre prophecies in the Book of Ezekiel is his vision of dry bones. Ezekiel has a vision of a field filled with bones. God directs Ezekiel to "prophesy over these bones, and say to them: Dry bones, hear the word of the LORD" (37:4). When God gives this direction to Ezekiel, he is talking about the lifeless, unjust lives of the Israelites. God commands Ezekiel to **herald** a time when God will breathe new life into their dead faith. Even though the Israelites have chosen the ways of the wicked, God will transform them into a new people, cleansing them from all their iniquities. God is a God of justice and faithfulness. He will not let their bones, their hearts, remain dry and lifeless. Nothing will stand in the way of his promise of salvation. God is an awesome God, drawing life from the unlikeliest places.

Ezekiel is a guardian of the Covenant, protector of the truth, and prophet of justice. It is fitting that Ezekiel's name means "God will strengthen," because his prophecies proclaim the might and power of God to turn a pile of dry bones into a "vast army" (37:10) of the Covenant. He announces the establishment of a new House of Israel, built on fidelity to God, respect for the dignity of all God's children, and true worship in a new Temple. This prophecy will be brought to fulfillment by Jesus Christ. Christ came so that we would not remain lifeless but have abundant life (see

Ezekiel's vision of dry bones coming to life is a wonderful metaphor for how God can work in our lives. God's power can bring new life to our relationships, our work, and our spirituality.

© Fridmar Damm/Corbis

John 10:10). Jesus Christ is the Word of God who prepares the way and brings about our resurrection from death to new life. ✝

The Cardinal Virtues

A virtue is a habit that creates in us a kind of inner readiness or attraction to move toward or accomplish moral good. The four Cardinal Virtues are the key virtues on which the other virtues depend. They are intimately connected to the messages of the prophets. The Cardinal Virtues are justice, prudence, temperance, and fortitude.

- **justice:** The fair and equitable distribution of life's necessities. The biblical idea of justice is based on the truth that all humans have innate dignity and worth as children of God.
- **prudence:** An approach to problems and situations using a degree of caution and a discerning heart.
- **temperance:** A balanced life characterized by moderation and self-control.
- **fortitude:** Individual strength and courage to overcome obstacles to a moral life.

46 Jeremiah: Success in the Lord

> Before I formed you in the womb I knew you,
>   before you were born I dedicated you,
>   a prophet to the nations I appointed you.
>   (Jeremiah 1:5)

Embodied in these powerful words is the call of both a reluctant and courageous prophet by the name of Jeremiah. Jeremiah is born of a priestly family in 645 BC. As a priest and prophet of the southern kingdom of Judah, Jeremiah struggles at times with God and his call to be a prophet. Nonetheless, Jeremiah remains true to his prophetic mission, even when he is plagued with doubt and fear. Covering the time period of 626–583 BC, the writings and prophecies of Jeremiah are situated in the events leading up to and occurring during the Babylonian Exile. A central theme of

Jeremiah's prophecies is the need for the unfaithful Israelites to repent and return to the Lord.

Unfaithful Israel

The Book of Jeremiah describes how, once again, the Israelites fall into the idolatrous practices of the surrounding nations. They fail to live up to the terms of the Covenant. Jeremiah warns the Israelites that their idolatrous customs are "dumb and senseless" (Jeremiah 10:8). Using vivid words like *desolation, destruction, sorrow, corruption,* and *horror,* Jeremiah prophesies that if the people do not repent of their sinful ways, punishment is inevitable. Jeremiah pleads for the Israelites' **fidelity.** He attempts to describe the destruction the Israelites will experience if they do not denounce their false and lying prophets. Jeremiah draws on the familiar analogy of a potter and clay. He compares God to a potter and Israel to one of the objects he molds.

God is disgruntled because the object the Potter is making (Israel) "turned out badly" (18:4). God crushes it to create something new and more beautiful. Further on in the analogy, Jeremiah proclaims that God will not crush the people if they are sorry and become a renewed people bound by the Covenant.

Jeremiah confronts a people so taken with the empty promises of the world that they do not seem to fear punishment. He describes the punishment from God as the cup of judgment from which "they shall drink, and be convulsed, and go mad" (25:16). Although his message seems harsh and vengeful, Jeremiah ultimately tries to motivate a stubbornly disloyal people to change. Jeremiah suffers greatly for his prophetic ministry. He is imprisoned, beaten, and thrown into a well to die. Despite all this, Jeremiah continues to be faithful to his call. Sadly, he sees many of his prophecies come to fruition when he witnesses the destruction of Jerusalem and the Temple at the hands of the Babylonians.

Following the destruction of Jerusalem, Jeremiah's prophecies become hopeful. He prophesies that the enemies of Israel will be destroyed and that a **remnant,** a portion of individuals remaining faithful to God, will be safe from the wrath of God. He refers to this portion of faithful believers

© Adam Woolfitt/CORBIS

After reading about Jeremiah's life and prophecies, think about what emotion the sculptor was trying to capture in this statue.

as "good figs" (Jeremiah 24:5). Jeremiah promises the remnant that when the Israelites are delivered from exile, God will make a new Covenant with them, a law that will be written on their hearts. This prophecy is fulfilled in Jesus Christ. Christ is the New Covenant. Through the power of the Holy Spirit, the separation caused by Original Sin has been erased and Christ lives in our hearts. Through him salvation is extended beyond the people of Israel to include all people.

The whole of Jeremiah's message is one of faithfulness. Blessed Mother Teresa of Calcutta (1910–1997), a nun and servant of the poor, said, "I do not pray for success, I ask for faithfulness." Unlike Teresa the Israelites lost sight of what was important. They were no longer a faithful and trustworthy people. Jeremiah beckoned them back to the source of absolute truth and steadfast love: God. Jeremiah heralded a success that could not be measured by the standards of the world but only by one's fidelity to God's plan of salvation. ✝

fidelity
Faithfulness to obligation, duty, or commitment.

remnant
A prophetic term for the small portion of people who will be saved because of their faithfulness to God.

Sorrow, Repentance, and Reconciliation

Jeremiah preached a message of repentance. Today we still need to repent when we sin. As Catholics we are blessed with the Sacrament of Penance and Reconciliation. This Sacrament, one of the Seven Sacraments, provides an opportunity to express sorrow for our sin and be reconciled with both God and the Church. Essential to receiving the Sacrament is a contrite heart. Our contrite heart is a heart with a hatred for a sin and our commitment not to sin again.

47 Isaiah: The Long-Awaited One

The Book of Isaiah probably covers three different periods during the years 742 to 500 BC: before the Babylonian Exile, during the Exile, and after the Exile. In each period the voice of a prophet bearing the name Isaiah arises to speak about the issues at hand. In the events leading up to the Babylonian Exile in the eighth century, the original Isaiah, sometimes called First Isaiah, challenges the Israelites in Jerusalem to place their trust in God alone and eliminate the injustices of the rich against the poor. First Isaiah also foretells the arrival

messianic hope
The Jewish belief and expectation that a messiah would come to protect, unite, and lead Israel to freedom.

Immanuel
A Hebrew word meaning "God is with us."

stump of Jesse
A phrase taken from Isaiah 11:1 that traces Jesus' lineage to Jesse's son, King David.

of *Immanuel*, a Hebrew word that means "God is with us." First Isaiah delivers a message of impending disaster at the hands of Babylon and of hope for a kingdom where God's justice and peace reign supreme.

Second Isaiah, prophesying during the Babylonian Exile, offers words of hope and encouragement to an exiled and captive people. Chapters 40–55 in the Book of Isaiah are Second Isaiah's prophecies. Second Isaiah foretells the fall of Babylon and the eventual liberation of the Israelites. Second Isaiah also contains the "suffering servant" poems, which are the foundation for the people's **messianic hope.** These poems have amazing parallels to the Passion of Christ (see Isaiah 42:1–4, 50:4–9, 52:13—53:12). The poems of the "suffering servant" portray a servant of God who will encounter great suffering and end in glorification. This prophecy is fulfilled in Jesus Christ who suffers his Passion and death and is glorified in the Resurrection and Ascension.

After the Exile, Third Isaiah (chapters 56–66) cries out against the Israelites' return to unjust and idolatrous practices. He demands they become a respectful community of equals. Third Isaiah challenges the people to work for justice as they rebuild their lives after the Exile. He tells the people that if they learn the ways of justice, God will lift up Israel as a glorious nation.

God with Us

The Book of Isaiah sings of messianic hope. This hope is summarized in Isaiah 7:14: "The virgin shall be with child, and bear a son, and shall name him **Immanuel.**" *Immanuel* comes from a Hebrew word meaning "God is with us." Christians came to see that the promise of Immanuel was fulfilled in Jesus Christ. Christ is with us in the struggles of everyday

Catholic Wisdom

Option for the Poor

The Prophet Isaiah delivered a message to the people that called for just and fair treatment of the poor. Following the example of the prophets and Christ, the Church has a special concern for the poor and the vulnerable. This is one of the themes of Catholic social teaching. It is this theme that is at the root of activities such as Operation Rice Bowl, which many Catholic school students participate in.

life, conquering all that enslaves and divides the family of
God. In the words of Isaiah, this Immanuel, the Promised
One, will be known as "Wonderful-Counselor, God-Hero,
Father-Forever, Prince of Peace" (9:5). These titles reveal that
the Messiah to come will be wisdom incarnate, a defender of
his People, a faithful parent, and an agent of peace.

New Heavens, New Earth

Isaiah prophesies that Immanuel will inaugurate a peaceful
kingdom where even "the wolf shall be a guest of the lamb,
/ and the leopard shall lie down with the kid" (Isaiah 11:6).
With the arrival of the Promised One, all things will change
under the heavens and on the earth. A new king from the
stump of Jesse and throne of David will judge with righteousness. The old order of infidelity and injustice will be
replaced with a new order of trust, reconciliation, and equity.
The long-awaited Messiah will be a "morning star, son of the
dawn" (14:12), shedding the light of his knowledge on the

A Season of Expectation

The writings of Isaiah are read mainly during the liturgical season of Advent.
Advent, meaning "to arrive," is the time of year when Christians prepare their
hearts and lives for the coming of Christ at Christmas and the eventual
second coming of Christ in glory. The season of Advent marks the beginning of
the liturgical year. One Christian practice in this season is to mark the passing of the four weeks of Advent by
lighting the candles of an Advent
wreath. Another practice is
the praying of the "O" Antiphons from December 17 to
23 during evening prayer. The
O Antiphons refer to Isaiah's
prophecy of a coming messiah.
They highlight the Messiah's
titles. The O Antiphons are "O
Wisdom," "O Sacred Lord," "O
Flower of Jesse's Stem," "O Key
of David," "O Radiant Dawn," "O
King," and "O Emmanuel."

darkest recesses of the earth. The earth and the heavens will no longer be ruled by the wicked and sinful ways of humanity. They will be ruled by a Savior who lifts up the lowly and sends the rich away empty.

Isaiah invites the people of the Covenant to prepare their hearts and lives for the dawn of a new day, a day where all creation bows before Immanuel, "God is with us." With the advent of Immanuel, the heavens and earth will be made new. They will become a place where all can draw water joyfully "at the fountain of salvation" (Isaiah 12:3). The prophecy of Isaiah embodies the hopes and aspirations of a people longing for the moment when a savior will set them free. The Book of Isaiah heralds an event that will change the course of salvation: the arrival of the Word of God made flesh. ✝

Review

1. What role do prophets play in salvation history?

2. What was the general message of the prophets before the Babylonian Exile? How did that message change after the Exile?

3. What is the difference between major and minor prophets?

4. Why is Ezekiel called a prophet of justice?

5. What were some of Ezekiel's symbolic actions, and why did he perform them?

6. How does Jeremiah respond to the idolatrous practices of the Israelites?

7. What message was Jeremiah preaching with his analogy of God the potter?

8. What is the major theme of Jeremiah's message?

9. What is messianic hope, and how is it related to the prophecies of Isaiah?

Part 5

Wisdom Literature

Many inspirational biblical quotations you may hear come from a section of the Bible known as wisdom literature. Wisdom literature is distinct from other sections in the Old Testament. It expresses minimal interest in the history of Israel and rarely refers to the Law. Instead it focuses on everyday life. Through poetry and other literary devices, the wisdom books draw universal truth and meaning from the mysteries of life. By exploring suffering and death, the fate of the righteous and foolish, and the splendor of love, these books offer advice on finding balance and harmony. They support the person of faith in the quest to glean wisdom from human emotion and struggle. God, the source of wisdom, is at the center of all experience.

For the most part, the authors of the wisdom books are unknown. Much of their content, however, is attributed to great leaders like King Solomon and King David. Attributing the writings to the kings served as a way to convey the authority of what is written and taught. The following books comprise wisdom literature: Job, Psalms, Proverbs, Ecclesiastes, Song of Songs (or Song of Solomon), Wisdom (or Wisdom of Solomon), and Sirach (or Ecclesiasticus).

The articles in this part address the following topics:

141

48 Job: Understanding Suffering

"Why do good people suffer?" Most people ask this question in an attempt to find meaning in undeserved suffering and pain. The Book of Job tells of a "blameless and upright" man (1:8) by the name of Job, who endures the tragic loss of family, land, home, and health. Written somewhere between the seventh and fifth centuries BC, the book recounts one human being's struggle to make sense out of what seems to be unnecessary and undeserved suffering. Job's experience questions the core belief of its time, that God rewards the righteous and punishes the unjust. The author of Job asks a question we still ponder today: Why do good people suffer and wicked people prosper? The author of Job wrestled with that question and wrote a poetic debate of a virtuous and successful man named Job who loses everything. Despite this loss his trust and faith in God never waver.

It's not fair! Job debates with his friends, maintaining that his suffering is not the result of any personal sin. Where have you witnessed people suffering unfairly?

© Chris Hellier/CORBIS

God Does Not Cause Suffering

From the start it is clear that God allows Satan to test Job through a series of losses, but God does not cause his suffering. The presence of Satan in the Book of Job shows that God never initiates human suffering. God allowed the suffering, knowing Job can withstand any trial because of his deep and abiding faith. Unlike Satan, God does not question the goodness of Job. He is on Job's side.

Even though Job's friends insist he is being punished for his actions, Job maintains his innocence and turns to God for answers. Job never blames God for his misfortunes. He does demand an audience with God to gain insight into his present situation. God appears before Job and overwhelms him with questions he cannot answer. Then Job realizes God is so great and complex that the human mind can never fully grasp his ways. Bowing in humility and trust before the awesomeness of God, Job states:

"I know that you can do all things,
  and that no purpose of yours can be hindered.
I have dealt with great things I do not understand;
  things too wonderful for me, which I cannot know."

(Job 42:2–3)

Job's suffering ultimately strengthens his faith.

Lessons Learned

We can glean many lessons from the life of Job about suffering, righteous anger, patience, and the glory of God. First, suffering is not always the result of personal sin and should not be viewed as a punishment from God. Although we human beings are limited in our understanding of suffering, it can also strengthen our faith. In times of suffering, we

Pray It!

Prayer of Serenity

Have you ever been faced with a situation that seemed unbearable? Like Job we will be faced with obstacles and challenges in our lives. When this happens it is important to remember that God is always with us and that we can ask him for the acceptance, courage, and wisdom to overcome these challenges. The next time you feel overwhelmed by life or are facing a particular challenge, pray the Prayer of Serenity and ask God for help.

God, grant me the serenity
to accept the things I cannot change,
courage to change the things I can,
and wisdom to know the difference.
Living one day at a time,
enjoying one moment at a time,
accepting hardship as a pathway to peace,
taking, as Jesus did,
this sinful world as it is,
not as I would have it,
trusting that You will make all things right
if I surrender to Your will,
so that I may be reasonably happy in this life
and supremely happy in the next.
Amen.

(Attributed to Reinhold Niebuhr)

can either blame God or turn to God. Second, God does not want his People to suffer. When we cry out in distress, God hears our cries. Third, the life of faith takes root in a patient heart. Patience in our sufferings and struggles is essential if we want to grow in our relationship with God. Our fourth and final lesson centers on God's deserving our love and respect even when life takes a turn for the worse. Though we may question God, we are called to realize that God's ways are too immense and wondrous for the human mind to grasp.

In the poetic words of Saint John Vianney, the sufferings we encounter "on the road to heaven are like a fine stone bridge on which you can cross a river. Christians who don't suffer cross this river on a shaky bridge that's always in danger of giving way under their feet." Like Job we have to navigate suffering with faith and trust so our bridge to Heaven is firm. ♱

Saint John Vianney: The Patron Saint of Parish Priests

Saint John Vianney (1786–1859) was known as the Curé d'Ars, or the parish priest of the French village of Ars. He grew up during the French Revolution and witnessed the persecution of the Church, especially its clergy. From a young age, he looked up to the priests who remained committed to their vocations during the revolution, even though they faced possible persecution and death. John answered God's call to be a priest and devoted his life to filling the needs of Church leaders, young nuns, the sick, and sinners. Many miracles are associated with him, and numerous seminaries and churches bear his name.

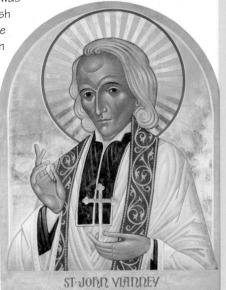

ST·JOHN VIANNEY

49 The Psalms: Learning to Pray

The Book of Psalms, also known as the **Psalter,** was written by different authors spanning many generations. Although the authors of the majority of the **Psalms** are unknown, many Psalms are attributed to King David because of his reputation as a gifted writer and musician. In Hebrew the Psalms are called the *Tehillim*, meaning "praises" or "hymns of praise to God." When translated from the Greek word *psalmos*, the word *psalms* refers to songs accompanied by stringed instruments. The 150 Psalms tell of Israel's relationship with God. The Psalms reflect Israel's experiences of both the joys and sorrows of the journey of faith.

The Psalms are classified according to three types of **hymns:** lament, thanksgiving, and praise. A **lament** is an outcry for God's intervention in difficult situations. People wrote hymns of lament when they felt disconnected from God or when they felt an absence of God during the harsh realities of life. Underlying this experience of absence was a confidence in God's ability to draw life from the darkest circumstances. People composed hymns of **thanksgiving** to thank God for his amazing action in their lives. Thanksgivings were usually responses to amazing acts of vindication or deliverance on the part of God for his Chosen People. Hymns of **praise** extol God as Creator of the earth and author of history. This type of hymn sings of the majestic, faithful, and saving name of God.

Mirror of the Soul

Saint Athanasius of Alexandria, a Church Father and a defender of the faith, made the following statement about the Psalms: "It seems to me that these words of the Psalms become like a mirror to the person singing them, so that he might see himself and the emotions of his soul." The emotions contained in the Psalms not only mirror the experience of a particular people in time but also reflect the whole history of salvation. The words of the Psalms were central to the teachings and prayers of Jesus. From the cross Jesus invoked the poetic words of Psalm 22:1: "My God, my God, why have you abandoned me?" At his death he said, "Into your hands I commend my spirit" (31:6). The early

Psalter
The Book of Psalms of the Old Testament, which contains 150 Psalms.

Psalms
Hymns or songs of prayer to God that express praise, thanksgiving, or lament.

hymns
Poetic song lyrics written to honor God.

lament
A Psalm that conveys mourning and petitioning of God in times of need (see, for example, Psalm 38).

thanksgiving
A prayer of gratitude for the gift of life and the gifts of life (see, for example, Psalm 47).

praise
A prayer of acknowledgment that God is God, giving God glory not for what he does, but simply because he is (see, for example, Psalms 113 and 114).

Church Fathers wrote extensively about the meaning of the Psalms. The saints proclaimed their importance in learning how to pray. The Church continues to incorporate them into her sacramental and liturgical practices.

For the People of God, the Psalms are a voice of hope in despair, truth amid misunderstanding, and interconnection in the face of isolation. In Psalm 130:1 we hear: "Out of the depths I call to you, LORD." The Psalms rise from the depths of the human heart, grounding people in the past, giving direction to the present, and pointing to a future beyond human imagination. The Psalms are filled with wisdom that empowers individuals to express their inner longing for God: to be a people of prayer. ✝

Lament, Thanksgiving, Praise

Lament: Psalm 55:2–4

Listen, God, to my prayer;
  do not hide from my pleading;
  hear me and give answer.
I rock with grief; I groan
  at the uproar of the enemy,
  the clamor of the wicked.

Thanksgiving: Psalm 116:1,17–18

I love the LORD, who listened
  to my voice in supplication,
who turned an ear to me
  on the day I called. . . .
I will offer a sacrifice of thanksgiving
  and call on the name of the LORD.
I will pay my vows to the LORD
  in the presence of all his people.

Praise: Psalm 19:2–3

The heavens declare the glory of God;
  the sky proclaims its builder's craft.
One day to the next conveys that message;
  one night to the next imparts that knowledge.

50 Ecclesiastes: The Ongoing Search for Meaning

"For in much wisdom there is much sorrow, / and he who stores up knowledge stores up grief" (Ecclesiastes 1:18). This statement summarizes the overall perspective of the author of the Book of Ecclesiastes. At first glance it seems pessimistic, but it actually is grounded in a sense of realism. The author, known as the Teacher or **Qoheleth,** is perplexed by the mystery of God's ways. Having acquired great wisdom, the Teacher realizes there is much more he does not understand about life and God. Life is one big riddle. At the heart of the riddle is a God who transcends human intellect. Because our understanding of God is always changing, there are no easy answers to the difficult questions of life. The Book of Ecclesiastes, written in the third or fourth century BC, challenges readers to see things in a different light by providing practical advice about the journey of faith.

Qoheleth

A Hebrew word for *Ecclesiastes,* meaning "preacher" or "one who convokes an assembly."

A Time for Everything

The heart of true wisdom is the acknowledgment that "there is an appointed time for everything, / and a time for every affair under the heavens" (Ecclesiastes 3:1). From life to death, tears to laughter, love to hate, we must bow before the infinite wisdom of God. "From beginning to end" (verse

Live It!

Making Life Meaningful

Have you ever been asked, What is the meaning of life? This question is often asked by someone who is troubled about something. Perhaps the person experienced a death in the family or is puzzled by all of the injustice and suffering in the world. The Book of Ecclesiastes addresses matters like these, but it does not provide easy answers. Many of the answers to questions about life, death, pain, and suffering are mysteries known by God only.

There is a similar question that you *can* answer though: How can *you* make life meaningful? We are all called to love and serve one another as Christ did, but we are given unique gifts and talents to carry it out in our own particular way. No two people are the same. You will find many ways to make life meaningful, and these ways will change as you grow older. How can you help to make your life and the lives of those around you meaningful right now?

11), God is author of all that is, was, and will ever be. The Teacher proclaims that God's ways are not our ways, nor is his timeline ours. Therefore the wise heart embraces the unknown, realizing that "whatever God does will endure forever; there is no adding to it, or taking from it" (verse 14). The closer one draws to God, the more one is willing to trust in his care. Letting go of the need to control and know everything paves the way for God's plan of salvation.

Carpe Diem: "Seize the Day"

The author of Ecclesiastes exclaims that "All things are vanity!" (1:2). This means that life lacks permanence and we don't know its meaning. This is not intended to put a damper on living. The author advises people to respond to the vanity of life by making the most of all of God's gifts. The author encourages everyone to to eat, drink, and enjoy the fruits of their labors, all of which are gifts from God. Living every day with great energy and joy does not mean ceasing to seek wisdom. However limited our wisdom may be, it guides the searching heart toward God. We are told, "Words

Ecclesiastes 3:1–8: A Time for Everything

There is an appointed time for everything,
　　and a time for every affair under the heavens.
A time to be born, and a time to die;
　　a time to plant, and a time to uproot the plant.
A time to kill, and a time to heal;
　　a time to tear down, and a time to build.
A time to weep, and a time to laugh;
　　a time to mourn, and a time to dance.
A time to scatter stones, and a time to gather them;
　　a time to embrace, and a time to be far from embraces.
A time to seek, and a time to lose;
　　a time to keep, and a time to cast away.
A time to rend, and a time to sew;
　　a time to be silent, and a time to speak.
A time to love, and a time to hate;
　　a time of war, and a time of peace.

from the wise man's mouth win favor, / but the fool's lips consume him" (10:12).

Ecclesiastes helps human beings to find meaning in the chaos and ambiguity of life. It supports believers in the quest for wisdom, even a wisdom that can never fully grasp God's ways. In regard to finding answers to the riddles of human existence, Saint Clare of Assisi (1194–1253) said we need to "place [our] mind before the mirror of eternity, . . . place [our] soul in the brilliance of glory." God is the mirror of eternity and brilliance of glory. To find meaning one must chase after wisdom, always living according to God's timeline, seizing every opportunity of beauty, and recognizing the limits of human understanding. ✝

51 Song of Songs: The Beauty of Love

Song of Songs, also called the Song of Solomon, was written by an unknown author sometime after the Jews' return from the Babylonian Exile in 539 BC. Contrary to popular belief, King Solomon did not write the book. It may have been originally attributed to him due to his authoritative name. Although short, Song of Songs is composed of rich poetry with vivid imagery describing the beauty of love. Taken literally it is a collection of love poems that affirm the goodness of human sexuality and love. It lifts up the sanctity of human love and passion as gifts from God. Interpreted from an allegorical perspective, the relationship between the lover and the beloved in Song of Songs symbolizes the relationship between God and Israel or Jesus and the Church.

Ideal Human Love

What is love? According to Saint Bernard of Clairvaux, "Love is an affection of the soul. . . . It is spontaneous in its origin and impulse; and true love is its own satisfaction." Authentic love cannot be forced, nor should it be self-seeking. Ideal human love flows from the depths of the soul. Because it is spontaneous, it finds joy in mutuality, honesty, trust, and sacrifice. Love is powerful. In Song of Songs we hear, "You have ravished my heart, my sister, my bride; / you have ravished my heart with one glance of

© Andrew Duany / shutterstock.com

The faithful love between a husband and wife is an allegory of God's love for the Israelites and also for Christ's love for the Church. How would you describe an ideal marriage?

your eyes" (4:9). Later we are told, "Deep waters cannot quench this love, / nor floods sweep it away" (8:7). These poetic lines attest to the intensity and strength of the love between a lover and beloved. Through the use of bridal imagery, the author of Song of Songs demonstrates the beauty and splendor of love. The love between a bridegroom and his bride is described as a seal on the heart worth more than all the riches in the world.

Creator and Creature

As an allegory for God's relation- ship with the Israelites, Song of Songs paints a picture of God as a faithful lover of his beloved People. God has called his Chosen People, his bride, to a spiritual union of perfect love. As an allegory for Christ's relationship with the Church, the *Catechism* asserts that the Church is "the spotless spouse of the spotless lamb. It is she whom Christ 'loved and for whom he delivered himself that he might sanctify her'"[3] (757). Christ formed an "unbreakable alliance"[4] (757) with his beloved bride, the Church, whom he nourishes and sustains with saving love.

Taking it a step further, Bernard examines Song of Songs as an allegory for the relationship between God and the individual. Bernard states: "Of all the movements, sensa- tions and feelings of the soul, love is the only one in which the creature can respond to the Creator and make some sort of return however unequal though it be." No matter how imperfect our love may be, God desires the affection and love of each of his beloved children.

Song of Songs is a hidden treasure in the Old Testa- ment. Many people are unaware of its existence, and those who have heard of it do not realize its great worth. Whether viewed literally or allegorically, Song of Songs emphasizes the centrality of ideal love in the quest for God. ✞

Saint Bernard of Clairvaux

From a young age, Saint Bernard had a profound love for Jesus Christ and a special devotion to the Virgin Mary. Longing to serve the Lord as a monk, he entered the Cistercian order at the Abbey of Citeaux in 1112 because of the Cistercians' simple and austere lifestyle. Early in his vocation to the monastic life, Bernard began a new abbey in Clairvaux, French for the "valley of light." As abbot of this new foundation, he cared for the souls of several hundred monks. During his thirty-eight years as abbot, he helped establish sixty-five Cistercian monasteries. Along with his charismatic leadership, Bernard was known for his sound theological writings and sermons on Song of Songs and the role of Mary in God's plan for the salvation of humanity. He was canonized a saint in 1174 and declared a Doctor of the Church in 1830.

© Summerfield Press/Corbis

52 Wisdom: Seeking Truth

During the first century BC, Jewish leaders were concerned about preserving the Jewish heritage and faith. As the Jewish people settled in new lands and were removed farther from their homeland of Judah, they feared they were losing sight of their ancestors' accomplishments. One of the Jewish leaders, whose name remains unknown, wrote the Book of Wisdom to encourage the Jews to remain faithful to the wisdom revealed in their history and tradition. The author of the Book of Wisdom proclaims that authentic wisdom has guided the Jewish people since the beginning of time.

personification

A literary technique that uses human characteristics to describe nonhuman realities.

There are three main divisions of the Book of Wisdom. The first addresses the reward of justice, the second praises wisdom, and the third reflects on the Exodus events. The wisdom of the past must be remembered and incorporated into the present. The same wisdom that guided their ancestors passes "into holy souls from age to age," producing "friends of God and prophets" (Wisdom 7:27).

Wisdom Personified

One of the notable characteristics of the Book of Wisdom is its use of **personification.** This literary technique uses human characteristics to describe something nonhuman. Wisdom, also called *Sophia* in Greek and *Sapientia* in Latin, is God's wisdom. In the Book of Wisdom, wisdom is personified as a female. The use of the pronouns *her* and *she* emphasizes a feminine nature of wisdom. The book tells us:

> She is the aura of the might of God
> . . . a pure effusion of the glory of the Almighty;
> . . . refulgence of eternal light, . . .
> spotless mirror of the power of God.
>
> (7:25–26)

Why do you think the Wisdom Books of the Bible personify God's wisdom as a woman?

The ultimate embodiment of God the Father's wisdom is realized in Jesus Christ, the only Son of God. In First Corinthians, Paul calls Jesus the Wisdom of God (see 1:24).

Teacher, Counselor, and Preserver

The Book of Wisdom presents wisdom as a manifestation of the creative Spirit of God. We must seek wisdom if we want to know and understand God. Wisdom is called an "instructress" (Wisdom 8:4) in the ways of God. If we long to learn, wisdom will teach us about moderation, prudence, justice, and fortitude. For the author of the Book of Wisdom, wisdom is the ancient knowledge of the past and the awareness of what lies ahead. As counselor wisdom speaks to the inner heart, the inner soul. She directs the heart toward right judgment. When all is well, she counsels the heart in ways of righteousness. In times of grief, she infuses the soul with the healing knowledge of God.

In the Book of Wisdom, Wisdom preserves the history of salvation by reminding the Jewish community of both God's creation of the world and his salvation of Israel in the Exodus. Wisdom reminds the people that God is both Creator and rescuer. Wisdom acts throughout salvation history by lifting up the sinner, giving courage to the fearful, delivering the enslaved, sheltering the lost, and opening "the mouths of the dumb" (Wisdom 10:21). She continues dancing in the hearts of God's People. From the beginning of creation to its culmination, wisdom connects human beings to the stories of the past, unifies the family of today, and sings of that which has yet to be spoken. ☦

Catholic Wisdom

Our Lady, Seat of Wisdom

One of the devotional titles given to the Blessed Virgin Mary is Our Lady, Seat of Wisdom. In the Old Testament, Solomon was known as the wise king seated upon his throne. Jesus Christ, the Wisdom of God, became incarnate in the womb of the Virgin Mary. Mary is likened to Solomon's throne. She is the throne, or the seat, of the Wisdom of God, Jesus Christ.

Two More Voices on Wisdom

There are two other important pieces of wisdom literature: the Book of Proverbs and the Book of Sirach. Each book contributes to the human understanding of wisdom. The Book of Proverbs collects poems and wise sayings representing the wisdom from generations of Israelite history. Just like Song of Songs, Proverbs personifies God's wisdom as a woman. Proverbs tells us where to find wisdom: in the streets, the marketplace, and the city. The Book of Sirach, also known as Ecclesiasticus, was written around 180 BC by Jesus Ben Sira. Sirach is organized around one central theme: "All wisdom comes from the LORD and with him it remains forever" (1:1). In support of this theme, Sirach praises the wisdom revealed in the heroes of Jewish faith.

Review

1. What is recounted in the Book of Job?

2. What lessons can we learn from Job's suffering?

3. Describe the three types of hymns found in the Book of Psalms.

4. How are the Psalms important for the People of God, the Church?

5. What are some of the main themes in the Book of Ecclesiastes?

6. What is the main literary genre found in Song of Songs?

7. How is Song of Songs an allegory?

8. Why is wisdom important according to the Book of Wisdom?

9. How is wisdom personified in the Wisdom of Solomon?

Revelation in the New Testament

Part 1

The Gospels

God's saving work did not end with the words of the prophets. In fact, the Covenants, the Law, and the prophets of old prepared the way for one of the most important events in salvation history: the Incarnation. The divine Son of God assumed a human nature and became man for the sake of our salvation. The New Testament announces the Good News of Jesus Christ, the only Son of God, who is true God and true man.

The four Gospels are the very heart of the Scriptures. The Gospels According to Matthew, Mark, Luke, and John herald the Good News that God came to earth to fulfill the promises made to our ancestors, to form a Covenant with all people, and to overcome the slavery of sin and the darkness of death. They are our primary source for all that was revealed in the life and teachings of our Savior and Messiah. The Gospels are not identical. Each presents Jesus' life and teachings from a different perspective. Yet in harmony and without error, they announce the truth that Jesus is the one and only way to the Father. All who believe "will not walk in darkness, but will have the light of life" (John 8:12).

The articles in this part address the following topics:

53 The Central Place of the Gospels

The *Catechism* states: "The *Gospels* are the heart of all the Scriptures 'because they are our principal source for the life and teaching of the Incarnate Word, our Savior'"[1] (125). All of the Sacred Scriptures are essential in understanding God's saving plan, but the four **Gospels** teach us about God's most definitive and perfect Revelation—his Son, Jesus Christ, who is true God and true man. The word *Gospel* literally means "good news." The Gospels of Matthew, Mark, Luke, and John tell the Good News that God sent his only Son to save his people from sin. They contain accounts of Jesus' teachings and actions and the events of the Paschal Mystery, his Passion, death, Resurrection, and Ascension. No other story or text could ever compare to the revelatory truth contained in the Gospels. In the words of Saint Caesaria the Younger, "There is no doctrine which could be better, more precious and more splendid than the text of the Gospel"[2] (*CCC*, 127).

Gospels
Translated from a Greek word meaning "good news," referring to the four books attributed to Matthew, Mark, Luke, and John, "the principal source for the life and teaching of the Incarnate Word"[3] (*CCC*, 125) Jesus Christ.

Pray It!

We Are Called to Be Disciples

Lord,
You have chosen me
 and humbly I respond to your invitation.
Like the first disciples,
I too, must be willing to trust you completely.

Help me to reach out to those most in need,
to have compassion for the poor,
and to live a just life.

You have taught me to turn the other cheek;
may I show mercy through forgiveness,
and pray for those who have harmed me.

Help me to generously share with others
all that you have given me.
Thank you for the gift of salvation
and the freedom, joy, and inner peace that comes with it.
Amen.

venerated
Respected and given
devotion.

In all of Scripture, the Gospels "occupy a central place because Christ Jesus is their center" (*CCC*, 139). Salvation history is like a circle with Jesus as its center. Our primary sources for information about Jesus Christ, the axis and center of salvation history, are the Gospels. They recount the amazing and miraculous action of God. Building on themes from the Old Testament, the four Gospels point to Jesus as the New Covenant. Although the Gospels are not historical biographies like those one might read today, they contain the redeeming truth of the long-awaited fulfillment of God's promises. We would err if we approached the Gospels as strict historical biographies of the life of Jesus. However, all four Gospels tell about real historical events that occurred in the life and mission of Jesus Christ. Though the four Gospels differ from one another, they harmoniously and without error, announce the Good News of Jesus Christ. Therefore they must be read, **venerated,** and studied.

An Invitation to Faith

"But these are written that you may believe that Jesus is the Messiah, the Son of God, and that through this belief you may have life in his name" (John 20:31). This line from the Gospel of John summarizes the overall intent of the Gospel writers. The Gospels foster faith in Jesus Christ as the divine Son of God who assumed a human nature for the sake of our salvation. The healings, exorcisms, and miracles they recount point to Jesus' divinity. Jesus' perfect obedience to his Father, his sinlessness, his sacrificial death, and his glorious Resurrection and Ascension reveal his saving work. Realizing that generations of people would not have the opportunity to hear and see Jesus' words and works firsthand, the Gospel writers wrote all this down so people would have abundant faith.

The Gospels call us to the light of God's truth revealed in and through the Incarnation. They invite us to accept Jesus into our hearts and be baptized, becoming a part of the Body of Christ, the Church. They call us to participate in the sacramental life of the Church. The Gospels challenge us to follow Jesus and to apply his teachings to our everyday lives. The choice to follow Jesus Christ involves a decision to become a person of just action. Matthew, Mark, Luke, and John are clear in the conviction that faith in Jesus requires

The Mass

Mass is another name for the Sacrament of the Eucharist. It is based on the Latin word *missa*, meaning "to be sent." The word *mass* refers to the dismissal at the end of the Eucharistic celebration, at which worshippers are told "to go in peace to love and serve the Lord" (*The Roman Missal*, page 567). The Mass is divided into two parts: the Liturgy of the Word and the Liturgy of the Eucharist. The Liturgy of the Word involves readings, a homily, and general intercessions. Central to the Liturgy of the Word is the proclamation of a passage from the Gospels. The Liturgy of the Eucharist makes present Christ's saving work accomplished mainly through his Passion, death, Resurrection, and Ascension. The Liturgy of the Eucharist includes the Eucharistic Prayer and the Communion Rite.

In the first part of the Mass, we "feast" on God's Holy Word, followed by the banquet of Jesus' Body and Blood. In the words of the Church, "the liturgy of the Word and liturgy of the Eucharist together form 'one single act of worship'[5]; the Eucharistic table set for us is the table both of the Word of God and of the Body of the Lord"[6] (*CCC*, 1346).

© P Deliss/Godong/Corbis

a response—a change in attitude and habit. As "principal source"[4] (*CCC*, 125) of God's Word made flesh, the Gospels invite all people to know and understand the Lord. ✞

54 Three Stages in Gospel Formation

A comprehensive study of the Gospels must take into account the ways they were developed and formed. The Gospels were not written overnight. They resulted from an experience that was passed on in spoken word and eventually preserved in writing. Biblical scholarship has defined three parts in the formation of the Gospels: the life and teachings of Jesus, oral tradition, and the written Gospels (see *CCC*, 126).

The Life and Teachings of Jesus

The Incarnate Son of God lived in a particular time and place. Because he became man and lived, died, was resurrected, and ascended to Heaven within a historical context, our ancestors in faith had the amazing opportunity to witness God in the flesh. They were able to touch him, hear his holy Word, and witness his saving actions. They heard him teach and witnessed his miracles and signs pointing to him as the true Son of God. In his Passion, death, Resurrection, and Ascension, human beings saw the divine Word of Life. The awaited Messiah dwelt among them.

Oral Tradition

"What we have seen and heard / we proclaim now to you, / so that you too may have fellowship with us" (1 John 1:3). After the Ascension and outpouring of the Holy Spirit at Pentecost, the teachings and actions of Jesus and events of his Passion, death, Resurrection, and Ascension were transmitted by word

Catholic Wisdom

An Itinerant Preacher

An itinerant preacher is a person who travels from place to place preaching the Word of God. Jesus was an itinerant preacher, as were the Apostles. This was how they spread the message of salvation. Some religious orders began as traveling preachers and continue this mission today. One of those orders is the Dominicans, which is also known as the Order of Preachers. This is why the abbreviation for the Dominican order is *OP*.

of mouth. Aided by the Holy Spirit, the Apostles and early disciples "handed on to their hearers"[7] (*CCC*, 126) the Good News that God came to earth to save his People and inaugurate his holy Reign. Oral proclamation helped spread the vitally important message of salvation offered to all through Jesus Christ. This message is known as the **kerygma**. The recounting of Jesus' Good News and all he had done for the sake of our salvation fostered faith and converted hearts.

The Written Gospels

After some time the early Church became concerned about preserving authentic records and testimonies about Jesus. There was a growing fear that the Good News of Christ's saving work could be distorted or interpreted incorrectly if they were not preserved more formally. This may have been especially needed because many of the eyewitnesses to Jesus' life were dying or being killed. As a result the oral accounts were written down in various communities of believers. The Gospel writers synthesized into writing what "had been handed on"[8] with the goal of sustaining the "honest truth about Jesus"[9] (*CCC*, 126). ✝

Life and Teaching → Oral Tradition → The Written Gospels

55 Why Four Gospels?

God manifested his wondrous power by creating a diverse world. Since the creation of humans, people have differed not only in race and gender but also in their community affiliations and experiences. This was true as well for the early Christian communities. Although their belief in Jesus Christ, the Incarnate Son of God, unified them, they were separated by different concerns and challenges. In responding to the specific needs of their communities, the **Evangelists**—the Gospel writers of Matthew, Mark, Luke, and John—composed four accounts of Jesus' life and teachings. The four Gospel writers proclaimed the Paschal Mystery in

kerygma

A Greek word meaning "proclamation" or "preaching," referring to the announcement of the Gospel or the Good News of divine salvation offered to all through Jesus Christ. *Kerygma* has two senses. It is both an event of proclamation and a message proclaimed.

Evangelists

Based on a word for "good news," in general, anyone who actively works to spread the Gospel of Jesus; more commonly and specifically, the persons traditionally recognized as the authors of the four Gospels, Matthew, Mark, Luke, and John.

synoptic Gospels

From the Greek for "seeing the whole together," the name given to the Gospels of Matthew, Mark, and Luke, because they are similar in style and content.

Quelle

Also called the Q Source, a theoretical collection of ancient documents of the teachings of Jesus shared among the early followers of Christianity.

Paschal Lamb

In the Old Testament, the sacrificial lamb shared at the seder meal of the Passover on the night the Israelites escaped from Egypt; in the New Testament, the Paschal Lamb is Jesus, the Incarnate Son of God who dies on a cross to take away "the sin of the world" (John 1:29).

unique and varied ways to the communities to which they belonged.

Faith Portraits

The Gospels are a unique form or genre of literature. You might think of them as religious or theological biographies of Jesus Christ. They are based in the actual teaching of Christ and the historical events of his life. Guided by the Holy Spirit, the Evangelists focused on aspects of Jesus' life and teachings that were most meaningful to their Christian communities. What one community valued or needed to learn may not have been the same for another community. The Evangelists could tell the same story in slightly different ways to emphasize the religious truth their communities needed.

Matthew, Mark, and Luke are called **synoptic Gospels** (from a Greek word meaning "seeing the whole together"). These Gospels are similar in style and share much of the same content. This is because Luke and Matthew probably used Mark, as well as the **Quelle,** or the Q Source, when compiling their Gospels. Even though they are similar in style and content, the synoptic Gospels present slightly different images of Jesus that were meaningful to their community members. The Gospel of John was written much later than the synoptic Gospels. It used more symbolic language to express the true identity of Jesus.

Live It!

Images of Jesus

There are many different images of Jesus in the Gospels. You will find Jesus telling about the Father's love and mercy, but you will also find him warning people of the consequences of sin. He washes the feet of his disciples and he also drives the money changers out of the Temple area with a whip. He loves sinners unconditionally, but he also challenges them to live in accordance with God's law.

Which images of Jesus speak to you and your life today? Compile a list of Gospel passages that speak to your life right now. And do not pick only the easy ones! Which parts challenge you to change yourself to be more Christlike? Keep the list handy and refer to it regularly in prayer.

The Same Truth

Four Gospels, four portraits of the same Jesus. What does it all mean? All four Gospels are necessary in understanding and comprehending God's saving love revealed in his Incarnate Son. As "the heart of all the Scriptures" and "principal source for the life and teaching"[10] of our Savior (*CCC*, 125), the Gospels reflect the mystery of Christ. The Holy Spirit guided the Gospel writers to foster and enliven the faith

Four Images of Jesus

We might say that woven throughout each Gospel is a prevailing image or portrait of Jesus. Each image reveals an aspect of Jesus' role in salvation history.

Gospel of Mark: *The Suffering Servant of God:* Jesus is the **Paschal Lamb,** who, in his self-sacrifice on the cross, redeems the human family.

Gospel of Matthew: *Teacher and Prophet:* Jesus teaches and proclaims the radical redemption of God.

Gospel of Luke: *Compassionate Healer:* Jesus restores humanity to right relationship with God.

Gospel of John: *Incarnate Word of God:* Jesus is the Word of God in the flesh, present since the beginning of time, "who takes away the sin of the world" (John 1:29).

These unique images complement the names and titles of Jesus Christ that are common to all the Gospels: Jesus (literally meaning "God saves"), Christ or Messiah (meaning "Anointed One"), Lord, and Son of God.

of human beings from different backgrounds with varying needs. The Gospels may diverge in some details but will never contradict one another in meaning. The Gospels point to the one and absolute truth—Jesus Christ is the divine Son of God and the Lord of all creation! ✝

Review

1. Why are the Gospels the heart of all the Scriptures?

2. How were the Gospels developed and formed?

3. Why do the Gospels present four different portraits of Jesus?

4. What is the primary difference between the synoptic Gospels and the Gospel of John?

5. What is the overall message of the Gospels?

Part 2

Revelation in and through Jesus in the Synoptic Gospels

The Gospels of Matthew, Mark, and Luke are known as the synoptic Gospels. They follow a similar pattern in both their overall structures and their individual narratives. Their accounts present similar views of the life and work of Jesus. However some of the shared accounts contain differing details. The synoptic Evangelists, especially Matthew, point to Jesus as the Son of the Father and, as Son, the perfect teacher of God's saving message. They announce Jesus' role as Compassionate Savior who has a special concern for the sick, the poor, and those generally considered unimportant by the people of his time. This is especially visible in the Gospel of Luke. All the synoptic Gospels emphasize the Paschal Mystery, asserting that Jesus is the Suffering Servant who must die to ransom and save all humanity.

The articles in this part address the following topics:

56 The Gospel of Matthew

The Gospel According to Matthew is the first Gospel in the New Testament. Its placement indicates the high esteem the Gospel held in the early Church. Composed by AD 85, the Gospel of Matthew addresses a mixed community of Jewish Christians and **Gentiles** (non-Jewish people). The community had diverse social groups, ethnic identities, and financial means. The **Matthean** community probably experienced rejection and even some persecution by Jewish leaders as a result of their belief in Jesus. Many Jews did not accept the truth of Jesus. He did not fit their image of the expected Messiah. They were expecting a royal king who rules from a throne and abides by the laws of the past.

Matthew's community was caught in the tension between the old and the new. They were being pulled in two directions. The first was their desire to remain true to their Jewish roots. The second was their ardent belief that Jesus was the long-awaited Messiah. Because of this tension and because many Jews did not accept the divinity of Jesus,

© Gianni Dagli Orti/CORBIS

the Gospel of Matthew highlights Jesus as the fulfillment of many Old Testament hopes and prophecies. Matthew wanted his Jewish Christian readers to know that believing in Jesus was not a break with their tradition; he wanted them to see it as a continuation of their tradition. Matthew begins his Gospel by listing Jesus' genealogy. Through the genealogy Matthew connects Jesus to Abraham, the father of Judaism, and to David, Israel's greatest king. By showing an ancestral connection between Jesus and these two great leaders

The Gospel of Matthew connects the Jewish faith and Scriptures with the words and life of Jesus Christ. What traditional symbol for the Gospel is contained in this image (see page 84)?

of faith, Matthew proclaims that there is continuity "between Israel of old and the new thing that God has done in Christ" (*The Collegeville Bible Commentary,* page 861). Matthew validates the community's link to the covenantal promises of the past. At the same time, he justifies these Christians' new devotion to Christ and his mission.

The Supreme Teacher

In the Gospel of Matthew, Jesus is often portrayed as frequently conflicting with Jewish leaders. His conflicts are especially with the Pharisees and **scribes.** The conflicts center on the proper interpretation of the law. The Pharisees and scribes felt as if Jesus was doing away with the Law as presented by Moses. Jesus clarifies that he did not come to get rid of the Law of Moses. He came to fulfill it (see Matthew 5:17). He challenges certain Jewish beliefs that were too narrowly interpreted. These particular beliefs were overly concerned with the letter, rather than the spirit, of the Law. In the Sermon on the Mount (see Matthew 5:1—7:29), Jesus gave a new interpretation of the Law. He declared that he is "the supreme and definitive teacher of a higher form of righteousness that surpasses that practiced" (*Saint Mary's Press® College Study Bible,* page 1419) by Jewish leaders. To further emphasize the role of Jesus as teacher, Matthew structures his Gospel around five major discourses, or speeches. In these discourses Jesus radically redefines Jewish Law and proclaims the saving love of God. The Law given to Moses in the Old Testament finds its fulfillment in the life and teachings of Jesus Christ.

Salvation for All

The Gospel of Matthew includes several titles for Jesus, including Son of God, Son of David, and Son of Man. These titles emphasize the true identity of Jesus. Each title points to Jesus as the teacher and Savior of all people, including non-Jews. In fact, the Gospel of Matthew tells about amazing people of faith who are not Jews: the Magi (see 2:1–12), a Roman centurion (see 8:5–13) and a Canaanite woman (see 15:21–28). Matthew portrays Jesus as the master teacher, or **rabbi,** who defines as the Chosen People all who hear and accept the Good News of salvation. ✝

Gentiles
Non-Jewish people.

Matthean
Related to the author of the first Gospel.

scribes
People associated with the Pharisees or Sadducees who were skilled copyists, professional letter writers, and interpreters and teachers of the Law.

rabbi
An honored teacher in the Jewish tradition.

Different Jewish Groups During Jesus' Time

Society during the time of Jesus and early Christianity was diverse in culture, economic status, religious beliefs, and political thought. Several different Jewish groups existed during this period, the most prominent being Pharisees, Sadducees, Herodians, Essenes, and Zealots.

- **Pharisees:** A Jewish religious group that strictly observed and taught the Law of Moses.
- **Sadducees:** A group of powerful and often wealthy Jews who were connected to the Temple priests and often disagreed with the Pharisees.
- **Herodians:** A group of Jewish leaders, including the Temple high priests and Jewish royal families, who collaborated with the Roman governors.
- **Essenes:** A group of pious, ultraconservative Jews who left the Temple of Jerusalem and began a community beside the Dead Sea, known as Qumran.
- **Zealots:** People who banded together during the time of Christ to violently resist Roman occupation.

57 The Gospel of Mark

The Gospel of Mark is the shortest of the four Gospels. Its length, however, does not determine its value. In sixteen chapters the Evangelist Mark manages to capture the essence of who Jesus is and what it means to be a disciple. The original author of this Gospel is uncertain. There is a tradition that the author was John Mark, a companion of Saint Peter mentioned in Acts of the Apostles 12:12. Whomever the author was, he was most likely a Gentile Christian who may have been a disciple of Peter. Mark was the first Gospel written, approximately between AD 65 and AD 70. It seems to be directed at a community of non-Jewish Christians experiencing persecution, possibly at the hands of the Roman emperor Nero. Mark constructs a narrative of Jesus' life that helps his community to make sense of their suffering and persecution.

Mark's Christology

The Gospel of Mark carries an aura of secrecy around the identity of Jesus. This atmosphere is known as the **messianic secret.** More than any Gospel, Mark emphasizes the humanity of Jesus. Jesus is portrayed as experiencing a full range of human emotions, including anguish and pain. Central to Mark's Christology is the image of Jesus as the Suffering Servant. This is in contrast to some Jews' expectation of a victorious messianic king. Mark presents a Messiah who suffers to do the will of God his Father. Jesus' Passion and death are necessary for God's saving plan to be realized.

Adding to Mark's portrayal of Jesus' humanity, Mark never portrays Jesus as referring to himself as the Messiah or by any other synonymous titles, such as Son of God, Savior, or Son of David. There is only one exception. This is when the high priest asks Jesus if he is the Messiah, and Jesus responds "I am" (14:62). Other people in the Gospel of Mark, however, do identify Jesus as the Messiah. In Mark 8:29 Jesus asks his disciples, "Who do you say that I am?" Peter replies, "You are the Messiah." In another encounter, Jesus is identified as the son of David by a blind man named Bartimaeus (see Mark 10:46–52). Throughout this Gospel the only other characters consistently portrayed as naming the true identity of Jesus are the demons he casts out.

messianic secret
A theme in the Gospel of Mark that portrays the disciples and others as recognizing Jesus' identity as the Messiah. However, Jesus directed them not to tell anyone else.

The Gospel of Mark emphasizes Jesus' humanity and his suffering for our salvation. What traditional symbol for the Gospel is contained in this image (see page 84)?

© The Gallery Collection/Corbis

Syrophoenician
A person from the Phoenician cities of Tyre and Sidon. Jews considered Syrophoenicians "outsiders" because of their idolatrous practices.

Golgotha
A Hebrew word meaning "place of the skull," referring to the place where Jesus was crucified.

Discipleship

At the start of Mark's Gospel, the disciples are lifted up as models of faith. They are the ones who leave everything behind to follow Jesus. As the Gospel continues, Mark sometimes portrays the disciples unfavorably. Mark depicts the disciples as lacking trust and faith. They are unable to comprehend Jesus' teachings, and are disloyal in Jesus' darkest hour. Unique to Mark is the favorable representation of less-known characters. We hear about a poor widow giving all she has to the Temple treasury (see Mark 13:41–44). We journey with a **Syrophoenician** woman who humbles herself before Jesus for the sake of her daughter's health (see 7:24–30). We read about Simon the Cyrenian, who carries Jesus' cross on the road to **Golgotha** (see 15:21). Through the shortcomings of the disciples and the strong faith of minor characters, Mark's Gospel teaches that true discipleship must imitate Jesus in both his ministry and his suffering. The call to be a disciple is the call to remain faithful to Jesus' message even in times of great difficulty and persecution. ✝

The Persecution of the Early Church

During the first three centuries of the Church, Christians experienced periodic persecution at the hands of the Roman emperors and governors. Christians were suspect because they denied the divine origin of the Roman Empire and instead proclaimed the divinity of Jesus Christ and their faith in the alternative Reign he preached. In AD 64 a great fire broke out in Rome. It destroyed large portions of the city and caused major economic hardship for many Roman people. Capitalizing on the already existing prejudice toward Christians, the Emperor Nero (AD 37–68) blamed them for the fire. Nero unleashed the first documented cases of Christian persecution. The Roman Empire burned Christians and crucified them and fed them to lions. Saint Peter and Saint Paul were martyred during the reign of Nero. Other emperors, including Domitian, Trajan, and Marcus Aurelius, continued Nero's persecution of Christians when it suited their needs.

58 The Gospel of Luke

The author of the Gospel of Luke seems to have been a Gentile convert to Christianity. There is a tradition that the author may have been Luke, "the beloved physician" (Colossians 4:14). Luke had been a companion of Saint Paul. The author wrote not only the Gospel of Luke but also another book in the New Testament called Acts of the Apostles (or simply Acts). The Gospel of Luke and Acts of the Apostles are a two-volume work on the life and mission of Christ and the life in the early Church. They are best understood when read together and interpreted as a whole. Luke had to rely on information from eyewitnesses to Jesus' life and ministry because he did not personally know Jesus. Biblical scholars believe the Gospel of Luke to have been written by AD 80–90. The audience of both the Gospel of Luke and Acts of the Apostles is identified by the title Theophilus. This term means "lover of God." It refers to Gentile Christians in Antioch of Syria or Achaia in Greece. Luke's Gospel is structured around the question, Who is welcome in the Kingdom of God?

Samaritan

An inhabitant of Samaria. The Samaritans rejected the Jerusalem Temple and worshipped instead at Mount Gerizim. The New Testament mentions the Jewish rejection of Samaritans in both the parable of the Good Samaritan (see Luke 10:29–37) and the account of Jesus' speaking with the Samaritan woman at the well (see John 4:1–42).

anawim

A Hebrew word for the poor and marginalized.

Who's "In" and Who's "Out"?

Luke makes clear that Jesus is the compassionate Savior who welcomes all. In several ways he emphasizes that Jesus is a friend to those who are poor and those who are outsiders. First, through the faith of a Gentile centurion (see Luke 7:1–10) and of a **Samaritan** (see 10:25–37), Luke demonstrates that both the Gentiles and Jews are part of God's saving plan.

Second, much of Jesus' ministry and preaching is directed toward the plight of the *anawim*. *Anawim* is the Hebrew word for the poor and marginalized. An example of this is visible in the **Canticle** of Mary which is also

© Gianni Dagli Orti/CORBIS

The Gospel of Luke emphasizes Christ's compassion for outcasts and the poor. It also makes clear that both Jews and Gentiles are welcome in the Kingdom of God. What traditional symbol for the Gospel is contained in this image (see page 84)?

canticle

From the Latin *canti-cum,* meaning "song." It usually refers to biblical hymns (other than the Psalms), such as those found in Song of Solomon in the Old Testament and the hymns of Mary (see Luke 1:46–55) and Zechariah (see 1:68–79) in the New Testament. By extension, *canticle* is sometimes used to describe other hymns in the liturgy.

called the **Magnificat** (a Latin term that means "[my soul] praises"). In the canticle Mary sings of a God who lifts up the lowly, fills the hungry with "good things," and sends the rich away empty (see Luke 1:46–55). The parable of the rich man and Lazarus (see 16:19–31) points to a future when the poor will dine in the Kingdom of Heaven and the rich will be shut out because of their neglect of the poor.

Third, Luke emphasizes the presence of women in the ministry of Jesus. The Gospel of Luke includes many accounts about women, including Mary's visit to her cousin Elizabeth before the births of their sons, Jesus and John the Baptist (see Luke 1:39–66). Others, like the widow's son (see 7:11–17), the sinful woman (see versus 36–50), and Mary and Martha (see 10:38–42), highlight the significance of women in the Reign of God. The final groups given special attention in the Gospel of Luke are the sick and sinners. During Jesus' time sickness was thought to be a sign of evil or a punishment from God for a sinful life. Dispelling this myth Jesus travels throughout Galilee healing people possessed by demons, those with leprosy, and those who are paralyzed. He offers forgiveness to sinners.

Jesus comes as a Savior to all. His message of salvation is not confined to a particular religious or social group. Rather, it is for all who willingly hear and heed the Good News. Jesus fulfills the hopes of ancient Israel. At the same time, Jesus demonstrates God's fidelity to all humanity, including the lowly and marginalized. Jesus is the universal Savior, healing, redeeming, and reconciling all creation. ✝

Two Important Prayers

The Gospel of Luke includes the Canticle of Mary (the *Magnificat*) and the Canticle of Zechariah. These are two important prayers in the life of the Church. In the *Magnificat* Mary sings of God's salvation for all: the humble, the poor, the hungry, and the descendants of Abraham. The Canticle of Zechariah is also referred to as the *Benedictus,* a Latin term meaning "blessed." Zechariah thanks God for sending a Savior from the line of David. He sings of a Savior who brings salvation through forgiveness of sins and who will "guide our feet into the path of peace" (1:79). We recite the *Benedictus* during morning prayer and the *Magnificat* during evening prayer in the Liturgy of the Hours. The Liturgy of the Hours or Divine Office is the official daily liturgical prayer of the Church, which involves praying at various hours throughout the day.

59 The Central Accounts in the Synoptic Gospels

The synoptic Gospels contain similar accounts about the defining moments in Jesus' life. Among these moments are the birth of Jesus, the Baptism of Jesus, the temptation of Jesus, and the Sermon on the Mount (or Sermon on the Plain in the Gospel of Luke). By reading and studying how each Gospel tells these accounts, we are led further into the truth of God's saving plan as manifested in his most definitive Revelation, the Incarnate Word.

A Savior Has Been Born

The Gospels of Matthew and Luke provide accounts of Jesus' birth, called the **Infancy Narratives**. The narratives in these two Gospels have many similarities to each other but also major differences. For example, in Matthew, the **Annunciation** of Jesus' birth takes place with Joseph. The angel of the Lord tells Joseph to not be fearful of taking Mary into his home. The angel also lets Joseph know that Mary will conceive through the Holy Spirit. In the Gospel of Luke, the Annunciation of Jesus' birth takes place with Mary. The Archangel Gabriel tells Mary that the Holy Spirit will descend upon her and she will conceive a child while still remaining a virgin (see sidebar on page 44 for more about Mary). The angel also tells her that her child shall be called "the Son of the Most High" (Luke 1:32). In God's divine timeline, the Holy Spirit completes in Mary all the preparations for Christ's coming. By the action of the Holy Spirit, the Father gives the world his Son as foretold by the prophet Isaiah: "The virgin shall be with child, and bear a son, and shall name him Immanuel" (Isaiah 7:14).

By the power of the Holy Spirit, Mary conceived Jesus, the divine Son of God and the Second Person of the Trinity. She remained a virgin in conceiving him and giving him birth, and for all eternity. Because she is the mother of the Son of God, who is also God himself, we call Mary the Mother of God. By accepting God's will at the Annunciation and agreeing to her role in the Incarnation, Mary was already collaborating in the work Jesus was to accomplish.

Magnificat
This is the first Latin word (from *magnus,* meaning "great," and *facere,* meaning "to make") of the prayer of Mary in response to the Annunciation of the birth of Jesus in the Gospel of Luke (see Luke 1:46–55).

Infancy Narratives
The accounts of Jesus' birth and early childhood.

Annunciation
The event in which the Archangel Gabriel came to Mary to announce that she had found favor with God and would become the mother of the Messiah.

© Burstein Collection/CORBIS

By studying these differences, we come to understand the focus of each Gospel. The authors use the Infancy Narratives as a prologue to help readers see his central theme. Matthew and Luke place the conception and birth of Jesus, the Incarnation, in the context of a humble family. This points out that salvation comes in the form of an ordinary child. The Messiah will not take on the trappings of power and wealth but will instead be clothed in humility and service. The Christmas mystery proclaims that "we must humble ourselves and become little" (*CCC*, 526) if we want to enter the Reign of God. The Infancy Narratives also highlight that particular groups of people, like the shepherds and the **Magi,** recognize Jesus as the Messiah and that others, such as Jewish leaders like King Herod, do not.

You Are My Beloved Son

The Baptism of Jesus manifests his identity as the "Messiah of Israel and Son of God" (*CCC*, 535). The Holy Spirit comes upon Jesus in the form of a dove, and the Father's voice declares that Jesus is his Beloved Son. Jesus' Baptism inaugurates his mission and ministry in the world. Jesus begins a new chapter in salvation history by obeying the will of his Father to proclaim the Reign of God. He says yes to the whole of God's plan, which culminates in his death on a cross "for the remission of our sins"[11] (*CCC*, 536).

© Keith McIntyre / shutterstock.com

Just as Jesus anticipates his own death and Resurrection in the waters of Baptism, we do likewise in our own Baptism. We are dipped into the waters of Baptism to rise with Jesus, being reborn of the Spirit so we "live in the newness of life" (Romans 6:4).

Get Away, Satan

The Scriptures tell us that Jesus was led into the desert by the Holy Spirit where he would encounter temptation. Mirroring the temptations of Adam in the Garden of Eden and of the Israelites in the desert, Satan tempts Jesus in the desert. In contrast to Adam and the Israelites, Jesus remains faithful and totally obedient to his Father's will. Jesus is the New Adam, who conquers sin and evil. In the words of the *Catechism*, "Jesus' victory over the tempter in the desert anticipates victory at the Passion" (539).

Feed Them Yourselves

A miracle that is present in all three synoptic Gospels as well as the Gospel of John is the multiplication of the loaves. In this miracle Jesus blesses a few loaves of bread that miraculously become enough to feed thousands of people. The multiplication of the loaves calls to mind the miracle of the manna in the Book of Exodus. The account of the multiplication of loaves carries Eucharistic significance. In the institution of the Eucharist, Jesus takes bread, lifts it, blesses it, and gives it to those around him. He satisfies our spiritual hunger with his own flesh and blood.

Your Reward Will Be Great

In the Gospels, Jesus proclaims a New Law. The New Law is the grace of the Holy Spirit, which we receive through faith in Christ and the Sacraments. The New Law finds its clearest expression in Matthew's Sermon on the Mount and Luke's Sermon on the Plain. The **Beatitudes** (see Matthew 5:3–10 and Luke 6:20–26) capture the heart of the New Law. These blessings fulfill the divine promises of the Old Law by orienting us toward their true meaning and goal: the establishment of the Kingdom of Heaven.

Magi
Wise men of the East who followed a new star that directed them to the birth of Jesus.

Beatitudes
The teachings of Jesus that begin with the Sermon on the Mount and that summarize the New Law of Christ. The Beatitudes describe the actions and attitudes by which one can discover genuine happiness and they teach us the final end to which God calls us: full communion with him in the Kingdom of Heaven.

The difference between Matthew's and Luke's proclamations of the Beatitudes is that Matthew focuses more on spiritual reality ("Blessed are the poor in spirit" [5:3]), whereas Luke centers more on material reality ("Blessed are the poor" [6:20]). Although there are slight differences between the two, they have the same message.

The Beatitudes tell us our goal. They show us the end God is calling us to: communion with him in the Kingdom of Heaven where we will see him face to face. There we will find our rest in him and live eternally. They call for a reversal of the world's value system and a total conversion of the heart. The Beatitudes respond to our heart's innermost desire for happiness. This response is contained in the Beatitudes, because they fulfill God's promises to Abraham and direct our lives towards Heaven. The Beatitudes also contain the message that "*everyone* is called to enter the kingdom" (*CCC*, 543). The Reign of God belongs to all who accept it with humble hearts. ✞

© David Barnet/Illustration Works/Corbis

All four Gospels tell of the multiplication of the loaves and fish, signifying the importance of this event. How would you describe the meaning of this miracle to someone who was unfamiliar with it?

Live It!

Turning It All Upside Down

"**B**lessed are the poor in spirit . . . they who mourn . . . the meek." These don't really seem to be blessings in our culture, which too often gives us the message that to be happy, we need every desire satisfied right now! The ancient Jewish people also lived in a culture that thought of someone who was prosperous, happy, and healthy as being "blessed." In the Beatitudes, Jesus turns it all upside down.

The humbling situations of those in mourning or in poverty can make one ripe for the Kingdom of Heaven, because it is then that one reaches out to God. Consider your own life. When have you cried out to God? In the good times, or when you were in need? In the Beatitudes, Jesus teaches us that living for others is the way to the Kingdom of Heaven. Being meek and merciful peacemakers puts others ahead of ourselves, which is the way Jesus lived. How do the Beatitudes turn the way we think today upside down?

The Origins of the Nativity Scene

One of the ways Christians celebrate the Advent and Christmas seasons is by placing Nativity scenes in their churches and homes. (The Nativity scene is also called a *crèche*, from the French word meaning "manger.") The origins of the Nativity scene can be traced back to Saint Francis of Assisi (1181–1226), who felt it was important to celebrate Jesus' birth in a humble stable. Francis was one of the first people to create an entire Nativity scene. On Christmas Eve in 1223, Francis and friends gathered in Greccio, Italy, to celebrate Mass and reenact Jesus' birth. Their reenactment involved the use of a manger, straw, and animals.

60 The Parables and Miracles in the Synoptic Gospels

Jesus traveled the land of Galilee, preaching and teaching about the Reign of God. Jesus proclaimed the saving message of God in both word and deed. In presenting the Good News of salvation, Jesus taught in **parables.** They are short stories that use everyday images to communicate "mysteries of the kingdom of heaven" (Matthew 13:11). Coupled with Jesus' use of parables were "mighty deeds, wonders, and signs" (Acts of the Apostles 2:22) known as **miracles.** These are marvelous and unexpected events that manifest the presence and power of God.

parables
Short stories that use everyday images to communicate religious messages.

miracles
Marvelous and unexpected events that manifest the presence and power of God.

Parables

The word *parable* comes from a Greek word meaning "comparison." Parables often present a story in the form of a simile, a literary device in which two different things are compared to illustrate a point. The words *like* or *as* often connect the two things being compared. For example, Jesus says, "The Kingdom of Heaven is like . . ." or "The Reign of God is like . . ." Then he compares it to a mustard seed, a wedding feast, ten virgins, a pearl of great price, and so on.

Parables have characteristic features. First, they teach timeless spiritual and ethical truths. Each parable gives deeper insight into the true meaning of the Reign of God. Second, parables are based on everyday life. The stories

Passion

The sufferings of Jesus during his final days in this life: his agony in the garden at Gethsemane, his trial, and his Crucifixion.

grew out of the common life and cultural experiences of Jesus' audience: family, farming, shepherding, trades, crafts, and religious practices. Third, Jesus usually told parables in response to questions or situations. To understand a parable's message, it helps to see whom or what Jesus was responding to. Fourth, one must have the eyes of faith to understand the truth of the parable. Nonbelievers are confused and perplexed by the story and its larger meaning. Fifth, parables are often filled with surprises. Jesus captured the attention of his listeners by adding a surprising twist or ending to a story. For example, in the parable of the prodigal son (see Luke 15:11–32), the younger son leaves home and squanders his entire inheritance, while the older son remains loyal to his father and fulfills his duties as a son. At the younger son's return home, his father does not greet him with anger nor does he reject him as would have been expected in the culture of his time. Instead the father welcomes the prodigal son with open arms and throws a party, illustrating the boundless and forgiving love of God even when we make mistakes. Parables challenge listeners to implement the Word of God into their everyday lives. Individuals must respond to the message revealed.

Miracles

When Jesus performed miracles, he revealed that the kingdom was "present in him" and attested "that he was the promised Messiah"[12] (*CCC*, 547). The miracles provide credibility to Jesus' words and teachings by concretely demonstrating his power over sin and evil. They reveal the Reign of God as a place where all are welcome, including the outcasts, and a place where suffering and evil are banished. Jesus performs four types of miracles: healings, exorcisms, control

Catholic Wisdom

Parables of Jesus

Jesus used parables to teach spiritual and ethical truths. The parables of Jesus are often referred to in the readings at Mass and in the writings of the popes. When Jesus used parables, he used images the people of his time could relate to. In some ways priests act in a similar way when they relay the truths of the Scriptures to us during the homily by using examples and images that relate to us.

over nature, and restoration of life. In miracles of healing, Jesus cures people with leprosy, fever, blindness, deafness, and paralysis. Miracles of exorcism depict Jesus' driving evil spirits or demons out of people. Nature miracles demonstrate Jesus' control over the forces of nature. Restoration-of-life miracles point to Jesus' power over life and death. ✝

The Four Types of Miracles

Healing Miracles

- **Jesus cleanses a leper:** Matthew 8:1–4, Mark 1:40–45, Luke 5:12–16
- **Jesus heals a paralytic:** Matthew 9:1–8, Mark 2:1–12, Luke 5:17–26

Exorcisms

- **Jesus heals the possessed:** Matthew 8:16, Mark 1:32–34, Luke 4:40–41
- **Jesus heals a boy with a demon:** Matthew 17:14–21, Mark 9:14–29, Luke 9:37–43

Control-of-Nature Miracles

- **Jesus calms the storm:** Matthew 8:23–27, Mark 4:35–41, Luke 8:22–25
- **Jesus walks on water:** Matthew 14:22–33, Mark 6:45–52

Restoration of Life

- **Jesus raises the daughter of Jairus:** Matthew 9:18–19,23–26; Mark 5:21–24,35–43; Luke 8:40–42,49–56
- **Jesus raises the widow's son:** Luke 7:11–17

61 The Paschal Mystery in the Synoptic Gospels

The heart of God's plan of salvation is Christ's work of redemption through Christ's **Passion,** death, Resurrection, and Ascension into glory. Christ's work of redemption, accomplished through these events, is known as the Paschal Mystery. In the words of the Church, "The Paschal mystery of Christ's cross and Resurrection stands at the center of the

**garden at
Gethsemane**

An olive grove near
the Mount of Olives,
where Jesus gathered
with the Apostles to
pray and prepare for
his Crucifixion on
Calvary.

Good News" (*CCC*, 571). In the Paschal Mystery, God's glorious love is revealed in the death of his Son. Jesus willingly hands over his life for the ransom of many—paying the debt for our sins to save us.

The synoptic Gospel writers draw us into the mystery of Christ's Passion, death, Resurrection, and Ascension at the Last Supper. During this event Jesus institutes the Holy Eucharist. The night before Jesus suffers and dies on the cross, he gathers the Twelve Apostles to celebrate the Feast of Passover to remember the Exodus from Egypt. During this meal Jesus identifies himself as the new Paschal Lamb. He will lay down his life so humanity will be liberated from sin. At the Last Supper, Jesus takes ordinary bread and wine and consecrates them. Through Consecration they become his Body and Blood, the Holy Eucharist. He states: "Take and eat; this is my body. . . . This is my blood of the covenant, which will be shed on behalf of many for the forgiveness of sins" (Matthew 26:26,27).

From Passion to Death

The Passion of Christ refers to the sufferings of Jesus during his final days in this life: his agony in the **garden at Gethsemane,** his trial and scourging, and his Crucifixion. From the garden at Gethsemane to Jesus' crucified body on the cross, we encounter the very human side of Jesus. We journey with Jesus as he experiences feelings of fear, betrayal, and abandonment. In the garden Jesus says, "My Father, if it is possible, let this cup pass from me" (Matthew 26:39). He is mocked and ridiculed during his trial. He is cruelly whipped before his journey to Golgotha. While traveling the road to Golgotha, Jesus experiences pain and exhaustion. On the cross he cries out, "My God, my God, why have you forsaken me?" (27:46). Even though Jesus experiences the real emotions of humanity, he remains obedient to his Father's will throughout his entire Passion.

Jesus' death on the cross is the most selfless act of love human beings have ever witnessed or ever will witness. Crucifixion is one of the cruelest and most painful methods of execution, and the Romans reserved it for the lower classes and those who rebelled against Roman authority. By obediently accepting suffering and death on a cross, "Jesus atoned for our faults and made satisfaction for our sins to the

Father"[13] (*CCC*, 615). It was his love for us to the end that gives his sacrifice its redemptive value. His death opens the gates of Heaven for all. Jesus models for us the path of true discipleship. The faithful disciple willingly accepts suffering for the greater glory of God. As Saint Rose of Lima says so eloquently, "Apart from the cross there is no other ladder by which we may get to heaven"[14] (*CCC*, 618).

From Resurrection to Ascension

Only through the Resurrection can we understand the ultimate message of the cross: God loves us so much that he offers his Son as the Paschal Lamb in "reparation for our disobedience"[15] (*CCC*, 614) and as the "definitive redemption of men" (613). Jesus' Resurrection is made evident in the Gospels through the accounts of an empty tomb and Jesus' post-Resurrection appearances around Galilee. The empty tomb and linens signify that "by God's power Christ's body had escaped the bonds of death and corruption" (657). The Resurrection affirms the truth of Jesus' teachings. It heralds that Jesus was and is the Savior of all humanity. Jesus was not just an extraordinary man but also the Messiah who offered new life through his Resurrection. Christ's Resurrection points to our own future resurrection.

Pray It!

Centering Our Prayer

One way of praying is to take a word or a phrase and meditate on it by reciting it over and over. You can do this with the great prayers of the Liturgy. For example, at the Easter Vigil the ancient hymn known as the "Exultet" is proclaimed. It recounts the history of our salvation. It is a song that should fill us with great joy as we gain a deeper awareness of Christ's loving sacrifice. To make this prayer part of your personal prayer life, take a portion of the text of the "Exultet" and meditate on it. Here is a phrase that could be used for this purpose:

Father, how wonderful your care for us!
How boundless your merciful love!
To ransom a slave you gave away your Son.

Take time to sit in prayer and repeat these words of the "Exultet" in your mind and in your heart. Let them fill you with hope and joy.

The final event in the Paschal Mystery is the Ascension, during which Christ is taken up into Heaven to be seated at the right hand of the Father. The Evangelists wanted to emphasize through their accounts of the Ascension that Jesus passed totally into the presence of God and in doing so, moved beyond our experience of space and time. This may seem confusing, but it actually means that Jesus entered

Commemorating the Paschal Mystery

The Easter Triduum refers to the three-day period on the liturgical calendar that commemorates the Last Supper, the Crucifixion, and the Resurrection of Jesus Christ. The Easter Triduum begins on Holy Thursday, with a celebration of the Last Supper. It continues on Good Friday with a memorial of the Crucifixion. On Holy Saturday evening, at the Easter Vigil, the Triduum reaches a high point by celebrating the Resurrection. The Triduum ends with evening prayer on Easter Sunday. The Easter Vigil is the first Easter celebration of the Resurrection of Christ, held sometime between sunset on Holy Saturday and sunrise on Easter Sunday. This first celebration of the Resurrection opens the door to the liturgical season of Easter. After forty days of rejoicing comes the celebration of the Ascension. The Easter season ends on the fiftieth day with the celebration of Pentecost. We commemorate the Paschal Mystery because it is Christ's work of redemption that grants us salvation.

© Bill Wittman

into the Father's presence in Heaven while still keeping his human nature. Just as important Jesus wasn't taken away from us; rather, he is still in our midst. His Ascension allows him to be anywhere at any time. He is the Head of the Church and assures the constant outpouring of the Holy Spirit on all God's People. As the Church prays: "By his birth we are reborn. In his suffering we are freed from sin. By his rising from the dead we rise to everlasting life. In his return to you in glory we enter into your heavenly kingdom" (*The Roman Missal,* page 437). ☩

Review

1. Who was the audience to whom the Gospel of Matthew was written?

2. What was the tension that existed in Matthew's community? How did this affect the manner in which Matthew wrote about Jesus?

3. What is unique about the way Mark presents Jesus in his Gospel?

4. What image of Jesus is prominent in the Gospel of Luke?

5. What is a central question about the Kingdom of God that the Gospel of Luke answers?

6. What three important accounts about Jesus' life are found in all three synoptic Gospels?

7. What role do the parables play in the message of Jesus?

8. How do the miracles performed by Jesus manifest the Father's saving plan?

9. How does Jesus accomplish the redemption of humanity?

10. Describe the central events of the Paschal Mystery.

Part 3

Revelation in and through Jesus in the Gospel of John

The Gospel of John, in unison with the synoptic Gospels, proclaims that Jesus is the Messiah, the true path to salvation. The Evangelist John uses dialogues filled with symbolic language and rich theology. The dialogues present Jesus as the Incarnate Word of God.

The Gospel of John emphasizes the divinity of Jesus. It makes use of signs and allegorical statements to reveal the true identity of Jesus as the eternal Son of God. Lengthy speeches, or discourses, provide the framework for Jesus to teach about his body and Word as bread for the soul and to teach about the intimate connection between discipleship and service. John also contains the most developed teaching on the Holy Spirit, the Divine Third Person of the Trinity. Particular to this Gospel is its distinctive presentation of the Paschal Mystery as a glorious manifestation of God's self-giving love.

The articles in this part address the following topics:

62 The Gospel of John: God Incarnate

The Gospel of John, written approximately AD 90–100, is filled with symbolic imagery, poetic verse, and rich meaning. Many people credit this Gospel to a man named John, "the disciple whom Jesus loved" (John 13:23), but the actual author is unknown. Many believe the author was a member of a Christian community founded by the **Beloved Disciple.** Because the Gospel text went through at least three stages of development, its tradition and teachings represent the whole **Johannine** community rather than just one individual.

The Gospel was written for two main reasons. First, it was composed to evangelize both Gentiles and Jews. Second, the author wanted to strengthen the faith of his local Christian community, as well as that of Christians everywhere.

John's Gospel is divided into two major sections: the Book of Signs (1:19—12:50) and the Book of Glory (13:1—20:31). The focus of the Book of Signs is seven miraculous signs Jesus performed. In contrast to the synoptic Gospels, in John Jesus teaches primarily through signs, not parables. These signs reveal the identity of Jesus as the one sent from the Father in Heaven. Also in the Book of Signs, John gives special attention to our relationship with God and one another. The Book of Glory centers on the Paschal Mystery. It is called the Book of Glory because John describes the Passion, death, Resurrection, and Ascension as a glorification of Jesus according to the Father's plan. Throughout the Book of Glory, John emphasizes the importance of the Holy Spirit in the life of the Church after Jesus' death.

Beloved Disciple
A faithful disciple in the Gospel of John who is present at critical times in Jesus' ministry. The Beloved Disciple may have been the founder of the Johannine community.

Johannine
Related to the author of the fourth Gospel.

Logos
A Greek word meaning "Word." *Logos* is a title of Jesus Christ found in the Gospel of John that illuminates the relationship between the three Persons of the Holy Trinity. (See John 1:1,14.)

John's Christology

While the synoptic Gospels emphasize the humanity of Jesus, the Gospel of John stresses his divinity. In his Prologue, John describes Jesus as the preexistent ***Logos*** (Word), who is God and was with God at the beginning of Creation and takes on flesh to dwell among us. John proclaims that Jesus, the Incarnate Word, is "the light of the human race" (John 1:4). Jesus is the Light that overcomes the darkness and the Light that gives direction to our lives. The themes of light and darkness appear frequently in John. For John light comes from above and darkness comes from below.

Great Men of Faith

The name John is derived from the Hebrew name Yochanan, meaning "Yahweh is gracious." John is an extremely popular name because of two New Testament saints: John the Baptist and the Apostle John. Throughout Church history more than two hundred holy men, including popes, saints, and blesseds, have borne the name John. Among this distinguished group of faith-filled men are the following five notable figures:

- **Saint John Chrysostom** (347–407) was an early Church Father known for his wonderful preaching, contributions to the development of liturgical theology, and avid denunciation of political and Church abuse.

- **Saint John Fischer** (1459–1535) was a Catholic bishop in England during the Protestant Reformation. Along with Saint Thomas More, he was executed by King Henry VIII for refusing to accept the king as the head of the Church of England.

- **Saint John Houghton** (1486–1535) was a Carthusian who refused to accept King Henry VIII as the head of the Church of England, which led to his martyrdom.

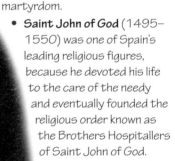

- **Saint John of God** (1495–1550) was one of Spain's leading religious figures, because he devoted his life to the care of the needy and eventually founded the religious order known as the Brothers Hospitallers of Saint John of God.

- **Saint John Baptist de La Salle** (1651–1719) was a French priest who founded the Institute of the Brothers of the Christian Schools (or Christian Brothers) to develop educational methods that meet the needs of all young people.

In declaring Jesus as the Light, the Evangelist asserts the divinity of Jesus. John concludes his Prologue by saying that Jesus is the fulfillment of the Old Law. He further states, "No one has ever seen God" (1:18). Therefore, the only way we can see and know God is through the only Son of God, Jesus Christ. ✞

sign
The Johannine name for a miracle of Jesus.

63 Signs and Miracles

Unique to the Gospel of John is his use of the word *sign* in place of *miracle*. A sign points to a deeper reality and meaning. In calling Jesus' miracles "signs," the Evangelist conveys that these "mighty deeds [and] wonders" (Acts of the Apostles 2:22) point to a larger truth. They move listeners and readers beyond what is witnessed to a deeper level of mystery and understanding. These signs reveal the divinity of Jesus, who is the only Son of God and the Incarnate Word. They confirm that the Father sent Jesus to chart a new course of salvation. The author of the Gospel of John tells his readers that the signs "are written that you may [come to] believe that Jesus is the Messiah, the Son of God, and that through this belief you may have life in his name" (John 20:30).

John's Gospel contains seven signs, or miracles—far fewer than the synoptic Gospels describe. John is intent on

Live It!

Giving Flesh to Your Faith

The word *incarnate* literally means "to become flesh." Because the Father loves us, he sent his Son to redeem us. Notice that the Father did not send his only begotten *idea* to us. He sent his Son in the flesh, who taught, fed, healed, and loved both his friends and enemies.

Jesus does not walk the earth in the same way he did two thousand years ago. We are called to be part of the Body of Christ to, with the help of the Holy Spirit, continue his mission. We are called to give flesh to our faith. Faith is not simply a thought or a belief. It must be lived.

Consider the following questions: Have I given enough time to prayer to discover God's will in my life? In what particular ways is God calling me to live out my faith? What concrete actions can I begin doing now to flesh out God's will in my life? You may be surprised at what you discover.

presenting a smaller number of miracles in greater detail and depth. Four of the seven miracles contained in John are not included in the synoptic Gospels. These four miracles include changing water to wine at Cana (see 2:1–11), curing the paralytic (see 5:2–18), healing the man born blind (see 9:1–7), and raising Lazarus from the dead (see 11:38–44).

The signs are teachable moments. In the synoptic Gospels, Jesus teaches often through parables. In the Gospel of John, Jesus teaches through signs and **allegories.** John

The Seven Signs

Some biblical scholars have drawn a parallel between the seven signs in John and the seven days of Creation. Just as God miraculously created the world in seven days, so too does God in Jesus miraculously perform seven acts of wonder that help bring about a new world order:

- **First Sign:** Jesus changes water into wine at Cana (see 2:1–11).
- **Second Sign:** Jesus restores the health of an official's son (see 4:46–54).
- **Third Sign:** Jesus heals a paralytic (see 5:2–18).
- **Fourth Sign:** Jesus feeds the five thousand (see 6:1–15).
- **Fifth Sign:** Jesus walks on water (see 6:16–21).
- **Sixth Sign:** Jesus restores sight to a man born blind (see 9:1–7).
- **Seventh Sign:** Jesus raises Lazarus to life (see 11:1–44).

© Alinari Archives/CORBIS

does not include any parables in his Gospel, probably to emphasize the meaning behind the seven signs. The signs teach that Jesus, the wonder worker, is God himself and that because of this, he is the fullness of Revelation.

Symbolic Meaning

John's accounts of Jesus' miracles focus on symbolic meaning rather than on the concrete action itself. The physical miracles—signs—symbolize a deeper truth and reality. When Jesus changes water into wine (see John 2:1–11), John foreshadows that Jesus will be the Blood (wine) of the New Covenant. In the account of Jesus' healing of the official's son (see 4:46–54), faith in Jesus leads to wholeness and health. The feeding of the five thousand (see 6:1–15) alludes to Jesus' satisfying of our spiritual hungers. The story of Jesus walking on water (see verses 16–21) demonstrates that Jesus has the power to calm our every fear and rid our hearts of all anxiety. The restoration of sight to the blind man (see 9:1–7) symbolizes spiritual insight into the real identity of Jesus. The blind man has eyes of faith to see the one and only Light—Jesus Christ. Lazarus's resurrection from the dead (see 11:1–44) heralds Christ's power over life and death and shows that Jesus is the path to eternal life. It foreshadows the death and Resurrection of Jesus. ✝

allegory
A literary form in which something is said to be like something else, in an attempt to communicate a hidden or symbolic meaning.

64 The "I Am" Statements

The Gospel of John challenges its hearers to recognize Jesus as the Messiah. Along with performing miraculous signs, Jesus declares his role in salvation history through a series of "I am" sayings. These sayings hearken back to God's revealing himself to Moses in the burning bush. In that encounter God reveals his name as "I am who am" (Exodus 3:14). Through the "I am" sayings, John makes it clear that Jesus is God. The "I am" sayings are statements that use familiar images and symbols to establish Jesus' divinity and to provide several ways of understanding Jesus' mission. Seven "I am" sayings appear in the Gospel of John. The following chart lists these meaningful and rich sayings: ✝

"I am the bread of life" (6:35).
"I am the light of the world" (8:12).
"I am the gate for the sheep" (10:7).
"I am the good shepherd" (10:11).
"I am the resurrection and the life" (11:25).
"I am the way and the truth and the life" (14:6).
"I am the vine, you are the branches" (15:5).

65 The Bread of Life and Last Supper Discourses

A discourse is a long speech Jesus gave to teach about matters of faith and salvation. The heart of Jesus' discourses in the Gospel of John is the revelation that he is God and that his presence is the presence of God. Hearing his words is hearing the Word of God. In the Bread of Life Discourse and the Last Supper Discourse, Jesus teaches about his true identity and reassures his followers of his continued presence. Those who don't believe or understand demand signs to prove his identity as the Son of God. Those who do believe seek assurance that Jesus will always be with them.

Bread from Heaven

In John's Bread of Life Discourse, Jesus declares, "I am the bread of life; whoever comes to me will never hunger, and whoever believes in me will never thirst" (John 6:35). Speaking to a group of people demanding signs of his identity, Jesus asserts that he is Bread from Heaven. He is not the perishable manna their ancestors ate in the desert but rather the "true bread" (verse 32) that "gives life to the world" (verse 33). Unlike the ancestors who ate manna in the desert and died, those who eat the Bread of Jesus will live forever. Jesus is teaching a group of people who are very familiar with the Old Testament tradition, in which Wisdom is depicted as providing nourishment (see Sirach 24:21 and Isaiah 49:10). As the Bread of Life, Jesus is our sole source of nourishment.

He perfects and fulfills the teachings of the Old Law and the Wisdom tradition.

In Johannine theology, the Bread of Life refers to both Jesus' Body and Word. We are to feast on his Body and Blood made present in the Eucharist and assimilate his life-giving Word into our lives. John foreshadows Jesus' death by emphasizing that Jesus will give his "flesh for the life of the world" (John 6:51). His Body will be broken and his Blood will be poured out so all might have life abundantly.

Love and Service

John's account of the Last Supper is different from the synoptic Gospels' accounts. In John it is not a Passover meal, nor does the account describe the preparations for the meal. John points to Jesus as the Paschal Lamb that will be slaughtered for the salvation of all. A defining moment of John's Last Supper is Jesus' humble act of washing the feet of his disciples. Jesus demonstrates that the path of authentic discipleship is humble service and love, from the simple act of serving a meal to the washing of a person's feet as a household servant in Jesus' time would have done. Jesus directs us to give our lives in service to others, just as Jesus gives his self in the breaking of bread and the washing of feet. Our service must be rooted in the "new commandment" to "love one another" (John 13:34). As demonstrated in the

"I am the bread of life; whoever comes to me will never hunger, and whoever believes in me will never thirst" (John 6:35).

The Necessity of Relationship

In the Book of John, the teaching of Jesus emphasizes the relationship between Jesus and the Father and the relationship between us and Jesus. Throughout the Bread of Life and Last Supper Discourses, Jesus constantly teaches that he is the path to the Father. Jesus proclaims, "The Father and I are one" (John 10:30). He also does this through particular "I am" sayings, such as "I am the way and the truth and the life" (14:6). In Jesus' priestly prayer at the end of the Last Supper Discourse, he intercedes for us with his Father. Jesus prays for the protection of the disciples and their continued mission to spread the Good News revealed in the Incarnation.

Though the emphases in the synoptic Gospels and the Gospel of John differ at times, the four Gospels are closely connected and affirm and support one another. Together the four Gospels affirm the importance of the Kingdom of God and being in right relationship with God. For the Kingdom of God to be present, we must be in right relationship with God. With the grace of the Holy Spirit, our faith in Christ restores our relationship with God, making the Kingdom present in our lives.

teaching of Jesus as the true vine, service and love are the fruits of those who remain in Jesus. Those who remain connected to Jesus—who is the vine—will be sustained, nourished, and bound by selfless service and love.

Another important aspect of John's Last Supper Discourse is the way he addresses the role of the Holy Spirit. Sensing Jesus' impending departure, the disciples are afraid of what lies ahead. Jesus assures them they will not be left alone. They will receive the gift of the Holy Spirit, who is also called the **Paraclete.** The Holy Spirit, the Divine Third

Catholic Wisdom

Washing Feet

During the Last Supper, Jesus washed the feet of the Apostles. He did this so they would understand that they were called to be humble ministers to the world. On Holy Thursday foot washing is a part of the Mass. The priest washes the feet of parishioners. Participating in the Mass on Holy Thursday serves as a wonderful reminder of our call to serve others.

Person of the Trinity, will act as an advocate and counselor
for all who believe in Jesus Christ. ✝

Paraclete
A name for the Holy
Spirit, the Divine Third
Person of the Trinity,
whom Jesus promised
to the disciples as
an advocate and
counselor.

66 The Passion, Death, and Resurrection

The climax of the Gospel of John is Jesus' willingness to lay
down his life for the salvation of all. This moment embodies the most selfless act of love humans will ever witness.
The betrayer of Jesus, Judas, comes at night, representing
the power of darkness, but Jesus, as the power of light, is
fully aware and in charge of what is happening to him. The
Gospel of John does not focus on the tragedy of the Paschal Mystery. Rather, it portrays every moment, from Jesus'
betrayal to his Resurrection, God's glorious power at work in
Jesus. Jesus is glorifying his Father even when the forces of
evil seem to be winning.

Imminent Glory: From Passion to Death

The author of the Gospel of John recounts some events in
the Passion, death, and Resurrection of Christ differently
from the synoptic Gospels. For example, John's Passion narrative does not contain the account of the agony in the garden. Instead John focuses on when Jesus declares his identity
as "I AM" (John 18:5) to those who come to arrest him, and
they fall to the ground. The moment symbolically points to
Jesus as the one who is Lord of all. At being questioned by

Pray It!

Reflecting on the Passion of Jesus

A traditional Catholic prayer is called the "Prayer before Jesus Christ Crucified."
Take time to reflect on the sacrificial, loving action of Christ using this prayer:

My good and dear Jesus, I kneel before you, asking you most earnestly to engrave
upon my heart a deep and lively faith, hope, and charity, with true repentance for
my sins, and a firm resolve to make amends. As I reflect upon your five wounds, and
dwell upon them with deep compassion and grief, I recall, good Jesus, the words the
prophet David spoke long ago concerning yourself: "They have pierced my hands and
my feet; they have counted all my bones!"

(see Psalm 21:17–18)

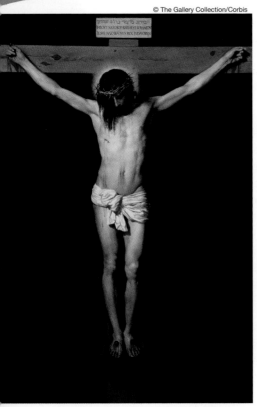

The chapters in John that tell of Jesus' Passion and death are sometimes called the Book of Glory. Why would we give this title to such sad and violent events?

Pilate, Jesus responds, "You would have no power over me if it had not been given to you from above" (19:11). After the inquisition by Pilate, Jesus is seated on the judge's bench. This symbolizes that Jesus is the judge of the world. He controls his own fate, as well as the fate of those who surround him. In John, Jesus does not cry out from the cross as he did in the synoptic Gospels. Instead, he simply states, "It is finished" (19:30).

The Gospel of John also includes an event in the Crucifixion of Jesus that does not appear in the other Gospels: a soldier pierces Jesus' side on the cross, "and immediately blood and water flowed out" (John 19:34). The blood and water that flow from the side of Jesus are signs of the salvation he won for us by his death and Resurrection. The blood and water symbolize the Sacraments of the Eucharist and Baptism. Through his death, Jesus offers his body for the salvation of the world and pours out his Spirit on his followers. His blood frees the human heart from the powers of sin and evil. Through his life-giving water, we are reborn as children of God. Jesus' death is not an ending but a beginning. John's Crucifixion account illustrates Jesus' triumph even at the moment of his death. Jesus' death is glorious, because through it the power of sin and death is shattered and God's love is revealed to all creation.

Triumphant Glory: Beyond Death to Resurrection

Five significant Resurrection appearance accounts appear in the Gospel of John. In two separate instances, Simon Peter and the Beloved Disciple find the tomb empty and believe Jesus has risen. Even though the tomb is empty, Mary Magdalene does not believe until she encounters the Risen Christ in the garden. The disciples recognize the Risen Christ by the wounds in his hands and feet. At touching his wounds, the Apostle Thomas exclaims, "My Lord and God!" (John 20:28). Each of these Resurrection appearances heralds the victorious and triumphant love of God. His powerful light burns away all darkness. No one can extinguish the light of his saving love.

One Message of Salvation

Though the Gospel of John differs from the synoptic Gospels in some significant ways, all four Gospels together announce the same Good News. Jesus Christ, the only Son of God, became man, and through his Passion, death, Resurrection, and Ascension, he makes it possible for us to share in the divine life of the Trinity. ✝

Review

1. What are two main reasons why the Gospel of John was written?

2. What is emphasized about Jesus Christ in the Gospel of John? Give some examples of how this is done.

3. Name four signs or miracles found in the Gospel of John but not in the synoptic Gospels.

4. What is the purpose of the seven signs or miracles in the Gospel of John?

5. What do we call the seven special statements that Jesus makes about himself in the Gospel of John? What do these statements indicate about Jesus?

6. How does John's account of the Last Supper differ from the accounts in the synoptic Gospels?

7. What is the emphasis in John's account of the Passion and death of Jesus? Describe one event that occurs in the Gospel of John that does not occur in the synoptic Gospels.

Part 4

Acts and Letters

Following the Gospels is a collection of books that give us insight into the spread of Christianity. These books also give an insight into the challenges the first Christians faced. In Acts of the Apostles, the Pentecost account tells about the Holy Spirit coming upon the Apostles and the Church. The Holy Spirit empowered the Apostles to proclaim the Good News. Later in Acts of the Apostles we see the spread of the Church through missionary journeys made with the goal of taking the Good News of Jesus Christ to the corners of the earth.

A key figure in the development of early Christianity was the missionary Saint Paul of Tarsus. Christian communities founded by Paul and other evangelizers needed wisdom and support to live out their faith. These communities faced internal strife and external persecution. The New Testament contains Paul's letters as well as the letters of other early Church leaders. These letters provided advice, pastoral encouragement, and support to the new Christian communities. The final book in the New Testament is the Book of Revelation. The Book of Revelation offers a message of hope to a people in crisis through highly symbolic language and vivid imagery.

The articles in this part address the following topics:

67 The Acts of the Apostles

Written around AD 80 by the Evangelist Luke, Acts of the Apostles is the second volume in the two-volume work known as Luke-Acts. Acts of the Apostles picks up where the Gospel of Luke ends. Beginning with the promise of the Spirit and the Ascension of Jesus, Acts of the Apostles recounts how the early Church grew under the guidance of the Holy Spirit. Acts of the Apostles begins with a small group of disciples in Jerusalem and ends with a Church spanning the Roman Empire, miraculously bridging the gap between the Jewish and Gentile worlds. Two significant events and movements form the backdrop of Acts: the coming of the Spirit at **Pentecost** and the evangelization and missionary efforts of early Christianity.

Pentecost
The fiftieth day following Easter, which commemorates the descent of the Holy Spirit on the early Apostles and disciples.

Gifts of the Holy Spirit

The Holy Spirit gives us special graces and tools that support spiritual growth, happiness, and wisdom to build a more just world in this life and to prepare us for full communion with God in Heaven. These graces and tools, called the Gifts of the Holy Spirit, help us to respond to God's call to holiness. The seven Gifts of the Holy Spirit are wisdom, understanding, counsel (right judgment), fortitude (courage), knowledge, piety (reverence), and fear of the Lord (wonder and awe).

"Tongues as of Fire"

On the Feast of Pentecost, an Israelite agricultural celebration, the house where the disciples gather is filled with the Holy Spirit in the form of a "strong driving wind" (Acts of the Apostles 2:2) that rests as "tongues as of fire" (verse 3) on each of them. This event marks the call of the disciples to go into the world, crossing borders and barriers, to spread the Good News of Christ. The Feast of Pentecost celebrates the fulfillment of Jesus' promise to send the Holy Spirit to guide the disciples and their followers as they proclaim the truth of salvation in Jerusalem and beyond. We commemorate Pentecost fifty days after Easter—some people call it the birthday of the Church. This is because even though the Church was founded by Christ, it was at Pentecost that the Holy Spirit revealed the Church to the world.

A Missionary Church

Three people stand out in Acts of the Apostles as models of Christian faith: Saint Peter, Saint Stephen, and Saint Paul. These three men embody the evangelization and missionary efforts of the early Church. Peter preaches a message of repentance and forgiveness. He calls disbelieving Israelites to a conversion of heart so the risen Messiah may wipe away their sins.

Pray It!

Saint Augustine's Prayer to the Holy Spirit

Just as the early Church did, we too must rely on the Holy Spirit for guidance in our lives. Saint Augustine of Hippo wrote this "Prayer to the Holy Spirit." Pray it often to ask the Holy Spirit for guidance in your life.

Breathe in me, O Holy Spirit,
    that my thoughts may all be holy,
Act in me, O Holy Spirit, that
    my work, too, may be holy.
Draw my heart, O Holy Spirit,
    that I love but what is holy.
Strengthen me, O Holy Spirit, to
    defend all that is holy.
Guard me then, O Holy Spirit,
    that I always may be holy.
Amen.

Filled with the power to do "great wonders and signs" (Acts of the Apostles 6:8), Stephen prophesies about how Jesus' life, especially his death and Resurrection, fulfills the Torah. His message is met with great resistance, eventually leading to his **martyrdom.**

After his dramatic conversion, Paul (known also as Saul) embarks on three missionary journeys to bring the Light of Christ to all. Some receive his message, but many reject it. He is persecuted, encircled by riots, and imprisoned. Peter's, Stephen's, and Paul's experiences of teaching, persecution, and suffering parallel those in the life of Christ. True discipleship is missionary in nature and risks all for the greater glory of God.

The Holy Spirit empowers and guides the Church from her humble beginning until she is perfected in the glory of Heaven. The Church is the means of God's plan. Through her the Good News is preached to all people and all people are invited into the Body of Christ. But the Church is also the goal of God's plan. Through her we participate, however imperfectly, in the joy of communion with God, which we will experience in complete glory in Heaven. ✝

martyrdom
Witness to the saving message of Christ through the sacrifice of one's life.

The Fruits of the Holy Spirit

The Gifts of the Holy Spirit produce positive virtues, known as the fruits of the Holy Spirit, in a person's life. We are told in Paul's Letter to the Galatians that people who open their minds and lives to God the Holy Spirit are blessed with the following fruits of the Holy Spirit: "love, joy, peace, patience, kindness, generosity, faithfulness, gentleness, self-control" (Galatians 5:22–23).

68 The Pauline Letters

After his conversion, during which he encounters the risen Christ on the road to Damascus, in Syria, Paul embarks on three missionary journeys to found new Christian communities and spread the Good News of Christ. Once he establishes a community, he moves on. Sometimes he is forced to leave. He travels to other cities to further his mission. To remain in

Pauline letters

Thirteen New Testament letters attributed to Paul or to disciples who wrote in his name. They offer advice, pastoral encouragement, teaching, and community news to early Christian communities.

contact with the communities he helps form, Paul writes letters, offering advice, pastoral encouragement, and teaching.

Some of Paul's letters are collected and shared with other Christian communities and become part of the collection of sacred writings that later become the New Testament. The thirteen letters in the New Testament attributed to Paul or to disciples who wrote in his name are called the **Pauline letters.** These letters are Romans, 1 and 2 Corinthians, Galatians, Ephesians, Philippians, Colossians, 1 and 2 Thessalonians, 1 and 2 Timothy, Titus, and Philemon. Nine of the letters are addressed to communities and four to individuals. The letters Paul wrote are the oldest Christian documents we have, even older than the four Gospels.

Some of the Pauline letters are grouped into two subcategories: the captivity letters and the pastoral letters. The captivity letters (Ephesians, Philippians, Colossians, and Philemon) are attributed to Paul's writing from jail. The pastoral letters (First Timothy, Second Timothy, and Titus) are attributed to Paul and his companions while on mission. Most of Paul's letters address some common themes. Two recurring themes are (1) Jesus the Christ is the path to salvation and (2) the Church is the Body of Christ.

The Common Pattern of New Testament Letters

All the Pauline letters are different from one another in content. Yet all share a common pattern:

1. Each begins with a greeting from the sender to the receiver or receivers.
2. Following the greeting, a prayer is offered.
3. Then the body of the letter addresses a particular issue and offers advice.
4. Each letter closes with greetings and instructions to specific people and then a final blessing.

Jesus Is the Path to Salvation

In regard to the first theme, Paul presents Jesus as the New Adam. Referring to the Fall of Adam and Eve, Paul asserts, "For just as through the disobedience of one person the many were made sinners, so through the obedience of one the many will be made righteous" (Romans 5:19). According to Paul, by accepting death on a cross, Jesus models perfect obedience, unlike Adam and Eve. Jesus' obedience makes salvation possible for all people.

Paul uses three Christological titles to highlight the role of Christ in God's plan of salvation. He uses *the Son* to point to Jesus as God's Divine Son, who is with God from the beginning of time. He employs the title of *the Christ* to show that Jesus fulfills the hope of Israel. The third title, *Lord*, is the way Paul refers to the risen Christ's dominion over creation won through obedience and death. The title *Lord* expresses Jesus' divinity. God exalted and raised up Jesus as the Lord of all creation, because Jesus emptied himself, "taking the form of a slave / . . . becoming obedient to death, even death on a cross" (Philippians 2:7–8).

The Church Is the Body of Christ

Paul's teaching that the Church is the Body of Christ, rings loudly throughout most of his letters. Paul's communities were dealing with the pangs of everyday living, sometimes resulting in disunity and discord. Paul uses an analogy of the human body to teach an important lesson. He says that all parts—the head, the hands, the heart, and the feet—are necessary for the body to fully function. If one part of the body is cut off, the rest of the body suffers. In the same way, all people, with their varied gifts and talents, are essential to the Body of Christ. The entire Body of Christ suffers

Live It!

Unity and Variety

High school can be a rough social scene. It is a tough place to be weak or different. People can be shunned because of the clothes they wear, the thoughts they reveal, their inadequacies, their race, or just because they hang around the "wrong" crowd. Being different is usually not cool.

Apparently some of the early Christians were going through similar problems. In his First Letter to the Corinthians, Saint Paul tells them that they are one body with different gifts and talents. He counsels them not to say to one another, "I do not need you" (First Corinthians 12:21). He even says that "the parts of the body that seem to be weaker are all the more necessary" (verse 22). Everyone thinking, looking, and acting the same is not beneficial for a community. Cutting out the weak is also not good. In what ways do you need to respect the differences among your classmates? How might weaknesses help unify a group?

when one of its parts, its people, is broken or cut off from the whole. Paul proclaims that Christians are one Body, the Church, of which Jesus is the head. The Church is a visible sign of God's presence in the world. Therefore she must be joined and knitted together in Christ, building "itself up in love" (Ephesians 4:16).

From his prolific writings to his lasting influence on early Christianity and beyond, Paul is one of the most important figures in the formation of the early Church. It is obvious from his writings and missionary journeys that Paul was profoundly affected by Jesus' message and mission, and by all he did for our salvation. The thirteen Pauline letters continue to plant the seeds of faith today, just as they planted faith beyond the limits of Judaism. ✝

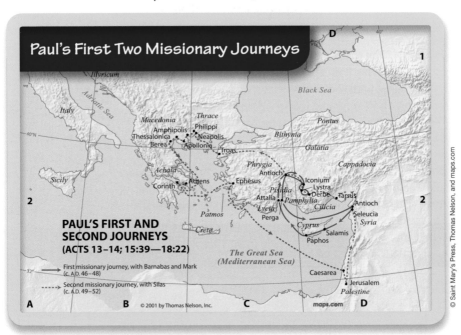

Paul's First Two Missionary Journeys

PAUL'S FIRST AND SECOND JOURNEYS
(ACTS 13–14; 15:39—18:22)

First missionary journey, with Barnabas and Mark (c. A.D. 46–48)

Second missionary journey, with Silas (c. A.D. 49–52)

© 2001 by Thomas Nelson, Inc.

maps.com

© Saint Mary's Press, Thomas Nelson, and maps.com

69 The Catholic Letters

In addition to the thirteen Pauline letters, there are seven other letters, or **epistles,** in the New Testament. These seven non Pauline letters, with the exception of the Letter to the Hebrews, are named for an Apostle or disciple of Jesus. However, biblical scholars believe anonymous authors wrote the letters, using the pseudonym of one of Jesus' Apostles or disciples. The seven letters attributed to the Apostles and disciples (James; First and Second Peter; First, Second, and Third John; and Jude) are known as the catholic letters. The word *catholic* here means "universal" or "general." Unlike Paul's letters, which originally were addressed to particular faith communities (although now they are addressed to the universal Church), the catholic letters were originally intended for a general audience or unnamed individual. Similar to Paul's letters, they offer advice, encouragement, and teaching about community life and faith in Jesus Christ. As we read the catholic letters, we must remember they were originally written for new believers living in a world that did not necessarily accept the truth of Jesus Christ.

The importance of the catholic letters is often not recognized. In fact, some scholars have noted that sometimes the catholic letters are overlooked altogether. The catholic letters, like the Pauline letters, are invaluable to our faith. Although short, the catholic letters complement Paul's letters by providing a unique perspective on how to be authentic witnesses to Christ in a divided and disbelieving world.

epistle
Another name for a New Testament letter.

Important Teachings

Numerous important teachings appear in the catholic letters. The Letter of James stresses the importance of both faith and good works for salvation. James says, "A person is justified by works and not by faith alone" (2:24). According to James true faith leads to good works. In other words, good works are the fruit of faith in Christ. In James 5:13–15, we find the biblical basis for the Sacrament of Anointing of the Sick: "Is anyone among you suffering? He should pray. Is anyone in good spirits? He should sing praise. Is anyone among you sick? He should summon the presbyters of the church, and they should pray over him and anoint with oil in the name of the Lord, and the prayer of faith will save the

The Letter of James gives directions for anointing the sick, providing the biblical basis for the Sacrament of Anointing of the Sick.

© Bill Wittman

sick person, and the Lord will raise him up. If he has committed any sins, he will be forgiven."

First Peter encourages suffering Christians not to lose faith and to keep their hearts rooted in Christ. The author affirms that followers of Christ are "a chosen race, a royal priesthood, a holy nation" (2:9), called from darkness into the amazing light of God. Second Peter preaches against false teachers who claim that Christ will not come again. He reminds his readers to remain true to the teachings of Jesus, including the proclamation of his second coming.

Writing to a divided Christian community being influenced by **Gnosticism,** First and Second John tell the community to beware of community members who have fallen

What about Hebrews?

There has been great debate over the origins of the Letter to the Hebrews (written about AD 80–90). In the past Hebrews has been identified as a catholic letter. For two reasons many biblical scholars do not include it in the catholic letters. First, it was originally circulated as a Pauline letter. Second, Hebrews does not follow the literary form of a traditional letter. As a matter of fact, it is written in the form of a homily and is much longer than the other catholic letters. What is most important, though, is its message. The author of Hebrews uses typical Jewish argumentation to show that Jesus is the new and perfect High Priest and the perfect sacrifice, thus embodying the New Law. Hebrews emphasizes the divinity of Christ, as well as the redeeming power of his death on the cross. Hebrews heralds the saving plan of God revealed in his Son.

Catholic Wisdom

Anointing of the Sick

The Sacrament of Anointing of the Sick brings special grace to those who suffer from serious illness or who are in danger of death due to sickness or old age. The celebration consists essentially in the anointing by the priest with oil blessed by the bishop, called the Oil of the Sick, and the priest's special prayer asking for the grace of the Sacrament. The Sacrament strengthens the sick and prepares the dying for death.

prey to the deceitful ways of the world. John warns against allowing deceivers to disrupt and destroy the community of Christ. Both First and Second John speak of the **antichrist,** which can be defined as any human being who puts himself or herself in the place of God or declares himself or herself to be a new messiah. Further reinforcing the message of First and Second John, Third John warns against evil by saying, "Whoever does what is good is of God; whoever does what is evil has never seen God" (verse 11). Last, but not least, Jude challenges Christians to remain firm in their beliefs and to emulate the mercy of Jesus Christ to their opponents. ☩

70 The Book of Revelation

Confusion often surrounds the interpretation of the Revelation to John, also called the Book of Revelation. Due to its highly symbolic language and placement at the end of the New Testament, Revelation is often interpreted as prophetic predictions and visions about the end of the world. However, it is necessary to place the Book of Revelation within its historical context for a proper understanding. When we do this, it is clear that the original author, rather than predicting the future, spoke to the experience of the Christian Churches in **Asia Minor** (modern Turkey). These churches were being persecuted during the time of the Roman Emperor Domitian (AD 81–96). Revelation was composed somewhere around AD 92–96. It was written by a Jewish-Christian prophet identified as John, not to be confused with the author of the Gospel of John.

Visions and Voices

The Book of Revelation, parts of the Book of Daniel, and parts of Matthew's Gospel are a literary form called **apocalyptic literature.** Apocalyptic literature was written during a time of crisis. This literary form predicts cosmic battles between good and evil, with good always winning in the end. As is the case in Revelation, apocalyptic literature contains visions, voices, and angelic messengers. It has symbolic numbers and colors. It also contains other extraordinary phenomena.

Gnosticism
A group of heretical religious movements that claimed salvation comes from secret knowledge available only to the elite initiated in that religion.

antichrist
A pseudo-Messianism whereby a human being puts himself or herself in the place of God or declares himself or herself to be a new messiah.

Asia Minor
An area corresponding roughly to modern Turkey.

apocalyptic literature
A literary form that uses dramatic events and highly symbolic language to offer hope to a people in crisis.

The language of apocalyptic literature tends to have a futuristic tone, especially in regard to the end of one time and the beginning of another. This can sometimes cloud our understanding of the purpose and intent of Revelation. Just because Revelation is written in this literary form does not mean its purpose is to predict the end of the world. Rather the veiled language of apocalyptic literature provides an outlet of communication. It presents information in a form that early Christians at the time could understand. It allowed the author to criticize the Roman authorities without putting his readers at risk of further persecution. It also allowed the author to communicate messages about the situation of his readers. Consistent with the style of apocalyptic literature, Revelation cannot be read as a continuous story with a beginning, middle, and end. It is instead a series of visions the author receives. The author may introduce an idea or image in an early vision and build on it later. The temptation to read Revelation as a chronological story often leads to a distortion of its meaning.

© Bildarchiv Preussischer Kulturbesitz / Art Resource, NY

This painting portrays a symbolic battle between good and evil described in the Book of Revelation. Whom might the various figures in the image represent?

Hope for All Time

The Book of Revelation provides hope for a people in crisis. A renewed commitment to faith, a message of consolation, and a call to maintain hope are the three main themes of the prophecy in the Book of Revelation. This message of hope is revealed in both the present and future. Through the symbolic language of his visions, John assures the persecuted Christians of Asia Minor that God has not abandoned them in their suffering. God is always present to those who trust and are faithful. The readers are also encouraged to renew their commitment to the life and teachings of Jesus Christ even in the face of the harsh reality of persecution. Focusing on the future, Revelation proclaims the justice and sovereignty of God. The plight of those being persecuted is short because God will triumph over evil at the end of time. Christ will come again in glory. Notice that the message of Revelation does not predict when or how the final coming will happen. Rather it speaks of a time when God will "make all things new" (Revelation 21:5). At the end of time, the King-dom of God will be fully realized. The faithful will live with Christ forever, glorified in body and soul, and all creation will be renewed. This is a time when all tears will be wiped away and death will no longer have the last word. The Book of Revelation also tells of the torment of those who follow Satan and reject the love of God. Revelation warns us of the sad reality of Hell, which is eternal separation from God and the Communion of Saints.

The message of the Book of Revelation is timeless. It was written in a particular time and place but declares a mes-sage of hope to all people of faith. God is with us in the trials

Numbers and Colors

Numbers and colors appear frequently in the visions and writings of Revela-tion. People mistakenly interpret the numbers and colors literally rather than symbolically. The author uses them symbolically to communicate a message to his hearers. Here are some symbolic numbers and colors with brief descrip-tions of their meanings:

Numbers

- **3:** a limited amount of time
- **4:** fullness, universality
- **7:** perfection
- **10:** sometimes denoting a limited number; at others meaning oppressors
- **12:** fullness, completeness
- **1,000:** countless, innumerable

Colors

- **white:** victory, triumph, conquest
- **red:** violence, conflict, bloodshed
- **scarlet:** royalty, bloodshed
- **purple:** sovereignty, royalty
- **black:** famine, plague
- **pale green:** death, the end

(Adapted from *The Book of Revelation*, pages 12–13)

and tribulations of life. All faithful members of the Body of Christ—the persecuted, the suffering, and the martyrs—will be among God's elect in the end. In the end God rewards the righteous and punishes the unjust. ♱

Review

1.   What two significant events and movements form the backdrop of Acts of the Apostles? Why are these events important?

2.   In what ways do the graces and tools given by the Holy Spirit help us?

3.   What is the purpose of Paul's letters?

4.   Name and briefly describe two recurring themes in Paul's letters.

5.   What important teaching is found in the Letter of James? in First Peter?

6.   What literary form is the Book of Revelation? What are some of the characteristics of this literary form?

7.   What are the three main themes of the Book of Revelation?

The Scriptures and the Life of Faith

Part 1

The Scriptures and the Life of the Church

The Scriptures are important in the life of the Church. As followers of Christ, we are called to study them so we discover "the supreme good of knowing Christ Jesus" (Philippians 3:8). The Good News of the Gospel nourishes our sacramental and liturgical celebrations. Our mornings, afternoons, evenings, and nights are made holy by praying Psalms and reading the Scriptures in the Liturgy of the Hours. The basis for our understanding of perfect prayer is found in Matthew's and Luke's depictions of Jesus' teaching the disciples the Lord's Prayer. Saints incorporate the teachings of the Bible into their spiritual writings. The Scriptures are also included in the formulations of religious rules for communities' living the evangelical counsels. Any time the Church gathers, the living Word of God is present.

The articles in this part address the following topics:

71 The Study of the Sacred Scriptures

We live in what is often called "the information age." More people have access to more information than any other time in the world's history. But when looking for answers to life's big questions, whom do you trust? Many people spend their lives pursuing the latest fads and "experts" in happiness. And they overlook the true and inerrant compass God has provided to guide us, the Sacred Scriptures.

The Scriptures support and strengthen the Church as she seeks to carry on her mission to announce the Good News of salvation. The divinely inspired words of the Sacred Scriptures provide "food of the soul, the pure and everlasting source of spiritual life" (*Divine Revelation*, 21). At the heart of the Scriptures is the Revelation of God as Father, Son, and Holy Spirit, a communion of Divine Persons.

Saint Jerome emphasized the importance of studying the Sacred Scriptures. He believed that "ignorance of the Scriptures is ignorance of Christ"[1] (*CCC*, 133). Knowledge of the Scriptures is essential if someone wants to understand the saving action of God. Vatican Council II, in the document *Divine Revelation,* asserts that the Christian faithful should have access to the life-giving words written in the pages of the Bible. Frequent reading and study of the Old and New Testaments help us to know Christ. We encounter the truth of Jesus' identity. We also see his mission in a profound and very real way. To study the Scriptures is to embark on a journey of continual discovery of God's presence. It also enables us to see his action in human history. Each time we read the Bible, the human heart and soul are further enlightened and directed toward their Maker.

Regarding the sacredness of Scripture, *Divine Revelation* states, "the Church has always venerated the divine Scriptures just as she venerates the body of the Lord" (21). The Sacred Scriptures inform every aspect of the Church. The Magisterium is charged with the important responsibility of interpreting, teaching, and proclaiming the Word. The Magisterium is the minister and servant of the Word. Those entrusted with preaching are called to break open the Word of God in new and enlightening ways. As minister and interpreter of the Word, the Church "forcefully and specifically exhorts all the Christian faithful"[2] (*CCC*, 133) to heed God's saving message manifested in his Son, the Incarnate Word. ✝

Saint Jerome

Saint Jerome was an early Christian apologist and Doctor of the Church. He was known for his intelligence and knowledge of the Sacred Scriptures. His love of learning far surpassed many of his contemporaries. In fact Saint Augustine is attributed with saying, "If Jerome doesn't know, nobody does, or ever did" (*The Catholic Source Book*, page 137). An exceptional scholar, Jerome is well known for preparing a translation of the entire Bible. His translation came to be known as the Vulgate. Jerome translated the Old Testament from its original Hebrew into Latin. He also translated the New Testament from Greek into Latin. The Vulgate is extremely important for two reasons. First, the Council of Trent promulgated the Vulgate as the official text of the Church. Second, Jerome's translation was more faithful to the original Old Testament and New Testament languages than earlier translations.

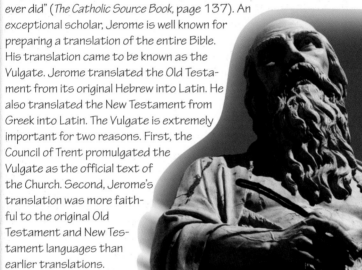

© Remi Benali/Corbis

72 The Centrality of the Scriptures in the Mass and Other Liturgies

A common misconception about Catholics is that we do not regularly use or read the Sacred Scriptures. Nothing could be more untrue! As a matter of fact, the Bible is an integral part of the life of the Church. Even though the Bible contains accounts and teachings from particular moments in time, its message is timeless and universal. God continues to speak to us through the Scriptures. Therefore the liturgies of the Church are founded on and sustained primarily by the Word of God. In fact, the heart of the Mass and all other sacramental celebrations is the living Word of God.

One Table

When we gather for the Mass, we are nourished by "the bread of life, taken from the one table of God's Word and Christ's Body"[3] (*CCC*, 103). In other words, both the sacred words of the Scriptures and the Eucharist feed us. The two parts comprise one celebration. The Word of God prepares and readies the heart for participation in **Holy Communion.** During the Mass we are truly blessed to encounter Jesus Christ in both the Word and the Eucharist. The two main parts of the Mass are the **Liturgy** of the Word and the Liturgy of the Eucharist. These two parts draw "their inspiration and their force" (*Constitution on the Sacred Liturgy* [*Sacrosanctum Concilium,* 1963], 24) from the Scriptures. Integral to the celebration of the Eucharist is the Liturgy of the Word. The words and actions present in the Liturgy of the Word nourish our faith. Through the Word of God, the deep meaning of the Eucharistic celebration is expressed in both proclamation and the response of the faithful.

On most Sundays and Solemnities, the Liturgy of the Word contains an Old Testament reading, a responsorial Psalm, a New Testament reading, and a passage on the life of Jesus taken from the Gospels. During the Easter Season, the first reading is from Acts of the Apostles. Daily Mass readings have one reading, a Psalm, and a reading from one of the Gospels. The Liturgy of the Word also includes a **homily,** or brief sermon, given by a priest to explain the Scripture readings. It also gives the priest an opportunity to encourage people to put the teachings of the Scriptures into practice. Finally, the Liturgy of the Word includes the profession of faith and the prayers of the faithful.

Holy Communion
Another name for the Sacrament of the Eucharist.

liturgy
The Church's official, public, communal prayer. It is God's work, in which the People of God participate. The Church's most important liturgy is the Eucharist, or the Mass.

homily
A brief liturgical sermon that explains the Scripture readings, helps the people of God accept the Scriptures as the Word of God, and encourages them to put the teachings of the Scriptures into practice in their daily lives.

Catholic Wisdom

A, B, or C?

The *Lectionary* is a book that contains the Scripture readings for the Mass. The *Lectionary* for Sundays has a three-year cycle of readings, denoted by the letter A, B, or C. The Gospel readings in the year A cycle are mostly from the Gospel of Matthew. The Gospel readings in the year B cycle are mostly from Mark. The Gospel readings in the year C cycle are mostly from Luke. Readings from John are inserted at appropriate times, especially during Lent and the Easter season.

Sacred Scripture is present in the Liturgy of the Eucharist. The **Eucharistic Prayer** during the Liturgy of the Eucharist recalls saving events from Scripture. In addition to the Liturgy of the Word and the Liturgy of the Eucharist, the introductory and concluding rites of the Mass also are formed in light of God's Word.

Along with the Mass, other sacramental and liturgical celebrations draw their inspiration and strength from the divine Scriptures. From the Sacrament of Baptism and the Sacrament of Matrimony, to the Sacrament of Penance and Reconciliation, the Scriptures are the focal point. When the Christian community gathers for liturgical celebrations in the name of Jesus, the Sacred Scriptures provide the foun-

More Than Just a Building

In the document *Built of Living Stones: Art, Architecture, and Worship* (2000), the United States Conference of Catholic Bishops (USCCB) states: "The church building is a sign and reminder of the immanence and transcendence of God" (50). We gather in our churches to be nourished by the Word of God and the Body and Blood of Christ. According to the bishops, when a church is

being designed and built, special attention must be given to the placement of the ambo (the lectern from which the Word of God is proclaimed) and the altar (the place where the sacrifice of the cross is made present and truly encountered). The altar is also the table of the Lord to which the People of God are called to celebrate the Mass within the sanctuary. The design and placement of the ambo and altar should emphasize the "harmonious and close relationship" (*Lectionary for Mass*, page 19) between the Word and the Eucharist.

© Bill Wittman

dation for the celebration. God—the Father, Son and Holy Spirit—is the center of our celebration. Thus we must speak and proclaim his Word.

With Joyful Song

The Sacred Scriptures also serve to enhance the music that is an integral part of our liturgical celebrations. Some liturgical celebrations tap into the rich tradition of sacred music, including **psalmody** and **Gregorian chant.** Liturgical music is steeped in the Sacred Scriptures. Sacred music should mirror salvation history. Numerous Church documents, especially *Sacred Liturgy*, address the intimate connection between the Word of God and the writing and singing of sacred music. In fact, the music that is part of the Mass "should be drawn chiefly from holy scripture and from liturgical sources" (*Sacred Liturgy*, 121). ✝

73 The Liturgy of the Hours: A Window into the Daily Rhythms of Life

Saint Paul exhorts the early Christian community of Thessalonica to "pray without ceasing" and "in all circumstances give thanks" (1 Thessalonians 5:17,18). This message was meant not only for the Thessalonians but also for Christians everywhere. Drawing on the ancient Jewish practice of sanctifying days and hours by reciting the Psalms, the Church developed the **Liturgy of the Hours**. This prayer is also known as the Divine Office. The Liturgy of the Hours is the official, public, daily prayer of the Catholic Church. It is composed of standard prayers, Scripture readings, and reflections at regular hours throughout the day. The Liturgy of the Hours makes holy the cycle of life with its many hours and days. Through the celebration of this official prayer of the Church, the mystery of Christ "permeates and transfigures the time of each day" (*CCC*, 1174). By stopping at various times during the day to pray, we remember Christ's continual work of redemption in the ordinariness of life.

Eucharistic Prayer
The part of the Mass that includes the Consecration of the bread and wine, beginning with the Preface and concluding with the Great Amen.

psalmody
From the Greek word *psalmos,* meaning "a song sung to a harp," and *aeidein,* meaning "to sing." The word has multiple meanings: the art of singing psalms, the arranging or composing of psalms for singing, or a collection of psalms for singing or reciting.

Gregorian chant
A monophonic, unaccompanied style of liturgical singing that takes its name from Pope Gregory the Great (540–604).

Liturgy of the Hours
Also known as the Divine Office, the official public, daily prayer of the Catholic Church. The Divine Office provides standard prayers, Scripture readings, and reflections at regular hours throughout the day.

breviary
A prayer book that contains the prayers for the Liturgy of the Hours.

opus dei
A Latin phrase meaning the "work of God."

The Word of God at Each Hour

"Seven times a day I praise you" (Psalm 119:164). Following this wise counsel, the Liturgy of the Hours can be prayed seven times a day. However, the primary hours, or "hinges" of each day, are morning and evening prayer. The Liturgy of the Hours follows a four-week cycle. The four-week cycle has adjustments for the feasts and seasons of the liturgical year. Central to the Divine Office is the Word of God, especially the recitation or singing of Psalms and the reading of the Scriptures. Although the Liturgy of the Hours has gone through many transformations in Church history, the Psalms have remained the heart of the prayer. The reading of the Psalms brings into harmony all that was revealed to our ancestors under the Old Covenant with all that was disclosed in Jesus Christ, the New Covenant. To meditate on the Psalms is to meditate on God's unified, saving action in human history. The Liturgy of the Hours integrates "the prayer of the psalms into the age of the Church" (*CCC*, 1177).

Scripture readings, from both the Old and New Testaments, are a central aspect of the celebration of the Liturgy of the Hours. The reading of the Sacred Scriptures at the principal hours of the day invites us to enter more deeply into relationship with our Triune God: Father, Son, and Holy Spirit. Praying the Liturgy of the Hours moves us to a deeper

The Liturgy of the Hours reminds us that prayer should be a daily practice. How do you make prayer a part of your daily routine?

© Bill Wittman

understanding of the Liturgy and the Sacred Scriptures. Seconds, minutes, hours, and days possess eternal significance when molded by the living Word of God. Along with the Sacred Scriptures, the Divine Office is composed of other key elements. These include canticles (biblical hymns and songs), antiphons (sung responses), a meditation (reflection on the Scriptures), and the Lord's Prayer. The prayers of the Liturgy of the Hours are found in the **breviary**.

The *Opus Dei*

The Benedictines are religious communities that follow the Rule of Saint Benedict. They refer to the Liturgy of the Hours as the ***opus dei*** (from the Latin for "work of God"). Benedict believed that the primary work of his community was to pray the Divine Office. Vatican Council II acknowledged the special call of priests and religious to pray the Liturgy of the Hours but proclaimed it must "become the prayer of the whole People of God" (*CCC*, 1175). It con-

Pray It!

The Canticle of Mary

The Canticle of Mary, or *Magnificat*, is prayed during evening prayer and can be found in Luke 1:46–55. This beautiful prayer can be recited or sung.

My soul proclaims the greatness of the Lord,
　　my spirit rejoices in God my savior.
For he has looked upon his handmaid's lowliness;
　　behold, from now on will all ages call me blessed:
The Mighty One has done great things for me,
　　and holy is his Name.
His mercy is from age to age
　　to those who fear him.
He has shown might with his arm,
　　dispersed the arrogant of mind and heart..
He has thrown down the rulers from their thrones,
　　but lifted up the lowly.
The hungry he has filled with good things;
　　the rich he has sent away empty.
He has helped Israel his servant,
　　remembering his mercy,
according to his promise to our fathers,
　　to Abraham and to his descendants forever.

tinues Christ's "priestly work through his Church"[4] (*CCC*, 1175). We must all participate in this wonderful work of God so his name may resound in every moment of every day. We mark our time with prayer, not with a clock. ✞

The Liturgy of the Hours		
Term	**Latin Name**	**Themes**
Morning Prayer	*Lauds*	Christ's Resurrection, praise for creation, dedication, light, dawn
Midmorning Prayer	*Terce*	New life, beginnings
Midday Prayer	*Sext*	Renewed commitment to the mission of Christ
Midafternoon Prayer	*None*	Awareness of the end of life and time
Evening	*Vespers*	Gratitude for Christ, reflection of Christ's Passion and burial, thanksgiving for the day, repentance for sin
Night Prayer	*Compline*	Divine protection and peace, restful sleep and happy death
Office of Readings	*Matins*	Wisdom revealed in the words of the Scriptures, writings of the Church Fathers, and lives of the Saints

prayer

Lifting up of one's mind and heart to God in praise, petition, thanksgiving, and intercession; communication with God in a relationship of love.

74 The Lord's Prayer: Rooted in the Scriptures

God created us to be in communion with him. Even though Original Sin separates us from the full communion God intended, God continues to call us into relationship and human beings continue to seek him. All salvation history reveals the importance of **prayer** as God calls to us and we search for him. Prayer, as communication and conversation with God, nourishes the seeds of faith.

Throughout the Gospels Jesus modeled deep and meaningful prayer. Before almost every significant event in Jesus' life, the Gospel of Luke mentions that Jesus prayed to his Father in Heaven. Realizing Jesus' true identity and affinity for prayer, one of the disciples said to him, "Lord, teach us to pray just as John taught his disciples" (Luke 11:1). In response to this request, Jesus taught the disciples the Lord's Prayer, also called the Our Father. It is called the

The Lord's Prayer

Our Father who art in heaven,
hallowed be thy name.
Thy kingdom come.
Thy will be done on earth, as it is in
    heaven.
Give us this day our daily bread,
and forgive us our trespasses,
    as we forgive those who
    trespass against us,
and lead us not into temptation,
but deliver us from evil.

(CCC, page 661)

© Pascal Deloche /Godong/Corbis

Lord's Prayer because the Lord Jesus gave it to us. Jesus also revealed to us who God is so we can call on God as Father. When we pray to the Father, we are in communion with him and with his Son, Jesus Christ. When we pray to our Father, we should develop the will to become like him.

The Lord's Prayer is "truly the summary of the whole gospel"[5] (CCC, 2774) and the "most perfect of prayers"[6] (2774). Christians highly esteem the Lord's Prayer because it came to us directly from Jesus and lays the foundation for all our desires in the Christian life. Along with the Psalms, the Lord's Prayer is a biblical prayer all Christians share. As Catholics we recognize the Lord's Prayer to be the "quintessential prayer of the Church" (2776). We recognize it as an integral part of the Liturgy of the Hours and of the Sacraments of Christian Initiation (Baptism, Confirmation, and the Eucharist).

hallowed
Regarded as holy; revered and respected.

temptation
An invitation or enticement to commit an unwise or immoral act that often includes a promise of reward to make the immoral act seem more appealing.

Satan
The fallen angel or spirit of evil who is the enemy of God and a continuing instigator of temptation and sin in the world.

Seven Petitions, Seven Requests

The Lord's Prayer unfolds for us a model of prayer and devotion to God. The Lord's Prayer as written in the Gospel of Matthew is the one used with the Church's liturgical tradition. The Lord's Prayer is made up of seven petitions. A petition is a prayer that requests a grace or blessing from God. In her spiritual memoirs, Saint Teresa of Ávila wrote that asking great things of God is a compliment to him. The seven petitions in the Lord's Prayer are no ordinary requests but rather models of Christian prayer. The first petition, "**Hallowed** be thy name," asks that our words and deeds radiate respect and reverence for the name of God. When we speak the second petition, "Thy kingdom come," we pray for the fulfillment of the Reign of God through the second coming of Christ, or the Parousia. As a Church we also pray for the strength to be a visible sign and presence of the Reign of God in the world. The third petition, "Thy will be done on earth, as it is in heaven," asks for obedient and trusting hearts so our desires may never stand in the way of God's plan of salvation. Together the first three petitions focus on the glory of God the Father.

"Give us this day our daily bread." In this fourth request, we pray for an even greater awareness of our absolute and total dependence on God. In this petition we acknowledge God as the source of all we need. We pray not only for our needs but for those of everyone in the world. The fifth petition, "Forgive us our trespasses, as we forgive those who trespass against us," centers on the intimate connection between God's forgiveness and our willingness to forgive others. To be forgiven we must forgive those who "trespass against us." In the sixth petition, we pray that God will not allow us to be led "into temptation." A **temptation** is an invitation or enticement to commit an unwise or immoral act. Our prayer asks for a wise and vigilant heart that is able to identify and resist temptation. Continuing the theme of the sixth petition, the final petition requests that God "deliver us from evil." As individuals and a collective whole, we petition God to deliver us from **Satan,** the evil one, the fallen angel who is the enemy of God and a continuing instigator of temptation and sin in the world. We pray with confidence that good will triumph over evil. ☩

75 The Scriptures and the Rules of the Saints

Saint Augustine, Saint Benedict, and Saint Francis are three well-known saints who founded religious communities. The members of these communities publicly profess the evangelical counsels of poverty, chastity, and obedience. They also lead lives in common as a public witness to Christ. Each religious community has its own particular history, charism, and rules. Founders of religious communities write a Rule of Life. The Rule of Life provides practical guidelines and rules for day-to-day life in community. The heart of any Rule of Life is the Sacred Scriptures.

The Rule of Saint Augustine: Community

Saint Augustine of Hippo wrote one of the earliest and best-known religious Rules. Throughout the ages numerous religious communities have adopted his Rule. It has influenced the extraordinary writings of the saints. A strong theme in Augustine's Rule is the importance of community. Drawing on Acts of the Apostles, Augustine maintains that the community of brothers be "of one heart and mind" (Acts of the Apostles 4:32) in God. The community must "live harmoniously in this house" ("The Rule of Our Holy Father Augustine," 3). The members of the community must have compassion and love for one another. This compassion and love will be visible signs of Christ's love for humanity. Harmony rings through the house when all things are shared in common and the only thing one possesses is love.

The Rule of Saint Benedict: Hospitality

Saint Benedict of Nursia (480–547) is considered the founder of Western Monasticism. His Rule was instrumental in the foundation of many religious communities during the Middle Ages—roughly the fifth century to the beginning of the sixteenth century. The Rule of Saint Benedict lifts up the value of hospitality. Chapter 53 of the Rule states, "Let all guests who arrive be received like Christ" ("The Order of Saint Benedict: The Rule of Saint Benedict," chapter 53). The Benedictine vision of hospitality is based on Matthew 25:35:

© Philippe Lissac/Godong/Corbis

Monks are not the only people who practice community, hospitality, and simplicity. How are these values part of your family life? your parish life?

"For I was hungry and you gave me food, I was thirsty and you gave me drink, a stranger and you welcomed me." Benedict wanted his monks to be men of hospitality so all would know and heed the saving message of Christ.

The Rule of Saint Francis: Simplicity

After hearing a sermon on Matthew 10:9–10, where Jesus tells the Twelve Apostles to leave everything behind to proclaim the Reign of God, Saint Francis of Assisi (ca. 1182–1226) responded by founding a religious community dedicated to poverty and simplicity. In his Rule, Francis asserts that if someone wants to join the community, the person's life must be modeled on the poor and crucified Christ. People called to live the simple life "should go and sell all that is their own and strive to give it to the poor" ("The Rule of St. Francis—1223" chapter II). Francis wanted his fellow brothers to rid themselves of material wealth. By simplifying and removing the distractions from their lives, they could more easily know and proclaim the wealth of God's mercy. ✝

Review

1. Why did Saint Jerome say the Scriptures were so important in the life of the Christian faithful?

2. What is a common misconception about Catholics and their relationship to the Scriptures? Why is it a misconception?

3. What are the two main parts of the Mass? How do we encounter Jesus Christ in each part?

4. In what ways do the Scriptures influence Catholic worship besides being actually read in the Liturgy?

5. What is the Liturgy of the Hours? What is its purpose?

6. Why is the Lord's Prayer so important?

7. What role do the Sacred Scriptures play in the Rules of Saint Augustine, Saint Benedict, and Saint Francis?

Live It!

Oblates and Third Orders

Some Catholics are formally associated with religious communities even though they are not sisters, brothers, or priests. They are sometimes called oblates or third orders. They make promises to follow a community's rule in ways their lives allow.

For example, those who are married with children cannot live in a Benedictine community, but as lay oblates they can still follow the Rule of Saint Benedict by feeding those who are hungry. Those with families to support might not be able to take on the poverty required of the Franciscans, but they can still promise to live simply and care for those who are poor. Each community's Rule of Life is an attempt to guide its members to live as Christ did. That is something all of us are called to do.

Part 2

The Scriptures and the Life of the Individual

People have pondered the Word of God made known to us through the Scriptures ever since they were written. The Word of God can support us in difficult times, guide us in making good decisions, and unite us as children of God. Spending time with the Scriptures also brings us closer to God. The Church "forcefully and specially exhorts"[7] *(CCC, 2653)* Christians to reflect on the Scriptures. Not only should we reflect on them, we also should pray with them. Through ancient traditions of prayer, specifically *lectio divina,* we awaken to God's Holy Word on a more personal level. In facing difficult moral situations, the Word of God enlightens us to know and choose the way of righteousness. Participation in Bible study groups and prayer groups at our parishes and schools invites us into deeper relationship with the Lord and one another. Religious expression in the form of devotions stems from and points to the Word of God. As Catholics we view the Word of God as integral to our everyday lives. Reading, studying, and praying the Sacred Scriptures makes the most ordinary moments of life extraordinary.

The articles in this part address the following topics:

76 Lectio Divina

Responding to the Sacred Scripture's command to "be still" (Psalm 46:11) to hear the "whispering sound" (1 Kings 19:12) of God's voice, the monastic monks developed the prayer form known as *lectio divina*. **Lectio divina** (from the Latin for "divine reading") is a slow, contemplative praying of the Scriptures so the Word of God may penetrate our hearts, leading us to a deeper relationship with the Lord. Within monastic communities the practice of divine, or holy, reading, along with manual labor and participation in liturgical life, is the foundation of the monastery and the monk. Regarding the larger Church, Pope Benedict XVI said of *lectio divina*, "If it is effectively promoted, this practice will bring to the Church—I am convinced of it—a new spiritual springtime" ("Address of His Holiness Benedict XVI to the Participants in the International Congress Organized to Commemorate the 40th Anniversary of the *Dogmatic Constitution on Divine Revelation 'Dei Verbum'*"). *Lectio divina* is not only a spiritual practice of monasticism but also a practice of the entire Church. In fact, *lectio divina*, "where the Word of God is so read and mediated that it becomes prayer, is thus rooted in the liturgical celebration" (*CCC*, 1177).

lectio divina
A Latin term meaning "divine reading." *Lectio divina* is a form of meditative prayer focused on a Scripture passage. It involves repetitive readings and periods of reflection and can serve as either private or communal prayer.

Practicing *lectio divina* can better prepare us to hear the Sunday Gospel. Find the Gospel reading for the coming Sunday and pray with it, using the steps described in the sidebar on the next page.

© iStockphoto.com / Dawna Stafford

lectio
Slow and attentive reading of a passage from the Sacred Scriptures.

meditatio
Ruminating on the passage to understand what God is trying to communicate.

oratio
Speaking to God in prayer.

contemplatio
Simply and silently resting in the presence of God.

actio
Action and life changes that result from *lectio divina.*

The Four Rungs

During the twelfth century, a Carthusian monk named Guigo II wrote the book *The Ladder of Monks,* in which he describes the following four stages, or rungs, of *lectio divina:*

- *lectio* (reading)
- *meditatio* (meditation)
- *oratio* (prayer)
- *contemplatio* (contemplation)

The first stage, **lectio,** involves the slow and attentive reading of a particular passage from the Sacred Scriptures. The deliberate and reverential reading of the Scriptures cultivates an ability, as the Prologue to the "Rule of Saint Benedict: Prologue" says, to "listen carefully . . . with the ear of your heart."

Moving to the second stage, **meditatio,** we are invited to meditate on the chosen Scriptures to understand what God is trying to communicate to us. Through meditation on the mysteries of Christ, we gain knowledge of his love and grow in union with him. Meditation engages the intellect by allowing the Word of God to interact with our thoughts, memories, desires, and hopes. When we ponder the words of the Sacred Scriptures, we will discover God's intended message.

Following meditation we enter the third stage, **oratio,** where we simply let our hearts speak to God in prayer.

Lectio Divina Made Easy

Following are some simple steps for engaging in the ancient practice of *lectio divina:*

1. **Choose** a passage of the Scriptures from the Eucharistic liturgy of the day or from the upcoming Sunday.
2. **Find** a comfortable and quiet place to pray.
3. **Take** a few moments of silence to settle your inner chaos.
4. **Read** the Scripture passage slowly and attentively.
5. **Focus** on a word or phrase from the Scripture reading. Memorize or repeat it several times.
6. **Communicate** with God in prayer.
7. **Experience** God's calming and loving presence.

Through prayer we respond to what we have received in meditation. We allow the Word of God to touch and change our real selves.

The fourth and final stage, **contemplatio,** is simply and silently resting in the presence of God, the Father, Son, and Holy Spirit, who loves us. Contemplation puts all words and thoughts aside to experience the transforming embrace of God. The journey through the four stages of *lectio divina* results in **actio,** Latin for "action." What happens during *lectio divina* changes us. It affects how we live our lives and may call us to further action regarding ourselves, the Church, or the world.

God and Self

Lectio divina can be compared to a classroom where God— the Father, Son, and Holy Spirit— is the teacher and we the students. The ancient practice of divine reading teaches us about God and self. Lying at the heart of *lectio divina* is God, our Teacher, who truly loves us and longs to reveal himself to us in the sacred pages of the Bible. As his beloved students, we are called to offer ourselves to him, allowing his Word to inform even the darkest corners of our lives. We are called to consecrate our entire lives—our wills, memories, hopes, and dreams—to him.

Pray It!

Practice, Practice, Practice!

Engaging in *lectio divina* can seem difficult. The best way to get comfortable with this form of praying with the Scriptures is to practice continually. Follow the steps in the "*Lectio Divina* Made Easy" sidebar. Use those steps as you read the following Scriptures:

- Genesis 45:4–8 (Joseph reunites with his brothers.)
- Jeremiah 1:4–10 (Jeremiah is called by God.)
- Mark 2:1–12 (Jesus heals a paralyzed man.)
- Mark 4:35–41 (Jesus calms a storm at sea.)

It is also good to keep a journal handy should you feel like writing down something that touched your heart. If at first you find yourself easily distracted, do not worry about it. Simply continue following the steps. The more you return to this style of prayer the more comfortable you will feel with it.

morality
Referring to the goodness or evil of human acts. The morality of an act is determined by the nature of the action, the intention, and the circumstances. Human freedom enables us to judge the morality of acts we choose.

77 The Scriptures and Morality

Every day we face tough decisions between what is right and wrong. When we talk about right and wrong, we are talking about **morality.** Morality can be defined as dealing with the goodness or evil of human acts, attitudes, and values. By our capacity to reason, we are "capable of understanding the order of things established by the Creator" (*CCC*, 1704). Through our free will, God has given us the capacity to choose what is truly good for ourselves and for others. One way we direct ourselves to God's true good is through reflection and prayer with the Sacred Scriptures.

"The Light for Our Path"

The *Catechism* is clear that learning to do what is right is a "lifelong task" (1784). It is a difficult task because the world is filled with conflicting voices about right and wrong. One voice we can turn to, is the Word of God. The Church points to God's Word as "the light for our path"[8] (*CCC*, 1785). God's Word assists us in learning to live moral lives. Therefore the Word must be read, studied, and prayed. By reading about salvation history, particularly of the life of Christ, the wisdom of our Creator is revealed. We encounter the Law of God revealed in the Ten Commandments (see Exodus 20:1–17) and the Beatitudes (see Matthew 5:3–12). The Ten Commandments and the Beatitudes direct us toward the true path of happiness. Jesus Christ, the Incarnate Word, walked this earth preaching and teaching about the holy will of the Father. The Paschal Mystery reminds us that the path of righteousness is not always easy and often meets great resistance. The Sacred Scriptures can help us to make virtuous choices.

"How I love your teaching, LORD! / I study it all day long. . . . Your word is a lamp for my feet, / a light for my path" (Psalm 119:97,105).

© Remi Benali/Corbis

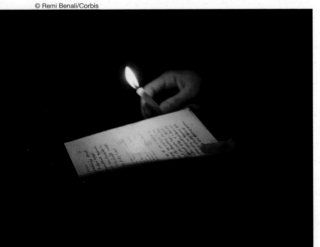

Praying with the Scriptures directs us to the goodness of God. By participating in the Eucharist, Sacraments, Liturgy of the Hours, *lectio divina,* and other prayers with the Scriptures, we come face to face with God's saving Word. Grounded in the Sacred Scriptures, liturgy and prayer challenge us to delve deeper into the absolute and definitive truth of Christ. Praying with the Word of God, both individually and communally, strengthens us in our ability to recognize the morality of a particular act and to choose what is good. When we pray with the Scriptures, we unite ourselves more closely to God—the Father, Son, and Holy Spirit. ✝

© Lincoln Rogers / shutterstock.com

"The Holy Spirit is the living water 'welling up to eternal life'[9] in the heart that prays."

(CCC, 2652)

78 Individual and Communal Prayer with the Scriptures

We are blessed to have the Holy Spirit to guide us and teach us how to pray. We can pray both individually and in groups at school, with family, and with our church youth groups. We

Saint Alphonsus Liguori

Saint Alphonsus Liguori (1696–1787) was a Roman Catholic bishop. He was also a prolific spiritual writer and founder of the Religious Congregation of the Most Holy Redeemer (Redemptorists). He was raised in a devout Catholic family and began his studies in law when he was sixteen years old. He eventually became a well-known lawyer. Feeling discontent with his life as a lawyer, Liguori decided to study for the priesthood and was ordained at the age of thirty. His life was remarkable from start to end, especially during his years of priesthood.

After Liguori was ordained, he chose to live with the homeless and marginalized youth of Naples, Italy. He founded evening chapels. These chapels provided young people a place to pray, participate in social activities, and receive education. As a great moral theologian, Liguori counseled priests and bishops on how to approach moral matters in a spirit of compassion rather than from the rigid and legalistic perspective that was characteristic of the time. He felt that neither a rigorous nor a lax approach to moral theology allowed the Gospel message to permeate the lives of the faithful. Because of his lasting influence on spirituality and moral theology, Liguori was declared a Doctor of the Church in 1871 and Patron of Confessors and Moralists in 1950.

> *"For where two or three are gathered together in my name, there am I in the midst of them."*
>
> (Matthew 18:20)

> *"Prayer should accompany the reading of Sacred Scripture, so that God and man may talk together; for 'we speak to Him when we pray; we hear Him when we read the divine saying.'"*
>
> (*Divine Revelation*, 25)

can also pray with friends, with our sports teams, and in countless other ways. When we gather as small Christian communities and in other groups, such as at school or in our parishes, we are called to have the Scriptures as the basis for our prayer. Every opportunity to gather as a faith community finds its strength in the "'surpassing knowledge of Jesus Christ' (Philippians 3:8)"[10] (*CCC*, 2653). This surpassing knowledge is made known to us through reading the Scriptures. ✝

© James L. Amos/CORBIS

Live It!

Harsh Words

"Anyone who curses his father or mother shall be put to death" (Leviticus 20:9). After reading this you might be thinking: "Wow! That is harsh. I better watch what I say to my parents from now on!" The Scriptures are an excellent source to reference for moral advice. We must be careful, though, to avoid taking certain passages out of context.

In biblical cultures to curse someone was more than just a moment of anger. It expressed a desire to see serious harm come to the person and such curses were taken very seriously. In addition, parents were to be treated with the utmost respect. So cursing your parents was almost the moral equivalent of physically attacking or killing them. Cursing your parents today is not good, but it certainly is not the same thing as cursing parents in biblical times! Reading and quoting from the Bible requires a careful understanding of the biblical cultures, as well as the overall message of the Bible.

79 Two Devotional Prayers and Their Scriptural Connections

Devotional prayers are personalized prayers that have developed outside of, but should lead to, the Liturgy of the Church. The Stations of the Cross and the Rosary are two popular devotional prayers that are based on the Scriptures.

The Stations of the Cross

The life and Passion of Jesus are the focus of many traditional devotions of the Church. One of the most notable devotions, the Stations of the Cross, centers on the Passion of Christ. The Stations of the Cross are rooted in the scriptural accounts of the persecution and Crucifixion of Jesus. The stations commemorate fourteen stops, or stations, along the *Via Dolorosa,* Latin for "way of sorrow." By meditating on the chief scenes of Christ's Passion and death, beginning with his condemnation and ending with the placement of

devotional prayers
Also known as devotions, these are personalized prayers that have developed outside, but should lead to, the liturgy of the Church.

Via Dolorosa
Latin for "way of sorrow," referring to the path Jesus journeyed in the last few moments of his life, which is commemorated in the devotion of the Stations of the Cross.

Stations of the Cross

1. Jesus is condemned to death.
2. Jesus bears his cross.
3. Jesus falls the first time.
4. Jesus meets his mother.
5. Simon of Cyrene helps Jesus carry his cross.
6. Veronica wipes the face of Jesus.
7. Jesus falls a second time.
8. Jesus meets the women of Jerusalem.
9. Jesus falls a third time.
10. Jesus is stripped of his garments.
11. Jesus is nailed to the cross.
12. Jesus dies on the cross.
13. Jesus is taken down from the cross.
14. Jesus is placed in the tomb.

© Bill Wittman

Rosary
A devotional prayer that honors the Virgin Mary and helps us meditate on Christ's life and mission. We pray the Rosary using rosary beads, which are grouped into "decades." Each decade consists of praying the Lord's Prayer followed by ten Hail Marys and the Glory Be while meditating on an event from Christ's life and mission.

his body in the tomb, we commemorate the sacrifice of Jesus and can better experience God's redemptive love. In the Stations of the Cross, stations 3, 4, 6, 7, and 9 do not have clear scriptural foundations but are supported by Tradition. Taken from the Scriptures and Tradition, the Stations of the Cross enrich the spiritual lives of the faithful by inviting them to delve into and experience the Word of God in a unique way.

In 1991 Pope John Paul II introduced a new devotion as an alternative to the traditional stations. He called it the Scriptural Way of the Cross. This way more accurately reflects Christ's Passion as recounted in the Scriptures.

The Rosary

Within the Church Tradition are several devotions focusing on Mary, the Mother of God. The most popular devotion to Mary is praying the **Rosary** (from the Latin *rosarium*, meaning "garland of roses"). The Scriptures are the basis of the Rosary. The prayers and mysteries of Jesus that are reflected on are rooted in the Scriptures. In fact, before Pope John Paul II announced the Luminous Mysteries in 2002, the Rosary consisted of 150 prayers to mirror the 150 Psalms. This structure of 150 prayers came about because of the laity's desire to have a prayer that matched Psalms chanted by monks. The Rosary also begins with the praying of the Apostle's Creed, which is based on the Scriptures.

Praying the Rosary involves reciting five sets of ten Hail Marys (each set is called a decade). Each new decade is begun by saying the Lord's Prayer once and concludes with a Glory Be. Those praying trace their prayers along a small chain of beads with a crucifix, called a rosary. While

Catholic Wisdom

Stations of the Cross

Have you noticed the Stations of the Cross in your church? Most Catholic churches have paintings or statues representing the stations on their walls. The Stations originated centuries ago with Christian pilgrims who traveled to the Holy Land to retrace the steps of Jesus on his way to Calvary. The next time you are at your church, take time to pause before each station, study the art depicting the station, and silently say a short prayer.

praying the Rosary, we are invited to meditate on the mysteries of the life of Jesus. These mysteries are also collected into several series of five—called the five Joyful, five Sorrowful, five Glorious, and five Luminous Mysteries. One recitation of the Rosary is dedicated to each set of mysteries. The mysteries of the Rosary are based on events recounted in the Sacred Scriptures and transmitted through Tradition. The Joyful Mysteries center on Jesus' birth, the Sorrowful Mysteries on his death, the Glorious Mysteries on his Resurrection, and the Luminous Mysteries on his public ministry. ✝

© iStockphoto.com / Peter Zelei

Praying the Rosary is another way we can integrate the Scriptures into our prayer life. If you are not familiar with praying the Rosary, ask someone who knows how to pray it to show you how.

The Scriptural Way of the Cross

1. Jesus is in the garden at Gethsemane.
2. Jesus is betrayed by Judas and is arrested.
3. Jesus is condemned by the Sanhedrin.
4. Jesus is denied by Peter.
5. Jesus is judged by Pilate.
6. Jesus is scourged and crowned with thorns.
7. Jesus bears the cross.
8. Jesus is helped by Simon the Cyrenian to carry the cross.
9. Jesus meets the women of Jerusalem.
10. Jesus is crucified.
11. Jesus promises his Kingdom to the good thief.
12. Jesus speaks to his mother and the disciple.
13. Jesus dies on the cross.
14. Jesus is placed in the tomb.

The Mysteries of the Rosary

The Joyful Mysteries
- The Annunciation
- The Visitation
- The Birth of Our Lord
- The Presentation of Jesus in the Temple
- The Finding of Jesus in the Temple

The Sorrowful Mysteries
- The Agony in the Garden
- The Scourging at the Pillar
- The Crowning with Thorns
- The Carrying of the Cross
- The Crucifixion

The Glorious Mysteries
- The Resurrection of Jesus
- The Ascension of Jesus into Heaven
- The Descent of the Holy Spirit on the Apostles (Pentecost)
- The Assumption of Mary into Heaven
- The Crowning of Mary as Queen of Heaven

The Luminous Mysteries
- The Baptism of Jesus
- Jesus Reveals Himself in the Miracle at Cana
- Jesus Proclaims the Good News of the Kingdom of God
- The Transfiguration of Jesus
- The Institution of the Eucharist

Review

1. What is *lectio divina*?

2. Name and describe the four stages of *lectio divina*.

3. Why does the Church exhort Christians to read the Sacred Scriptures?

4. How can the reading of Scripture influence our moral life?

5. What is a devotional prayer?

6. How are the Scriptures used in the devotional prayers of the Stations of the Cross and the Rosary?

Glossary

A

actio: Action and life changes that result from *lectio divina*. *(page 227)*

allegory: A literary form in which something is said to be like something else, in an attempt to communicate a hidden or symbolic meaning. *(page 188)*

analogy of faith: The coherence of individual doctrines with the whole of Revelation. In other words, as each doctrine is connected with Revelation, each doctrine is also connected with all other doctrines. *(page 66)*

anawim: A Hebrew word for the poor and marginalized. *(page 171)*

Annunciation: The event in which the Archangel Gabriel came to Mary to announce that she had found favor with God and would become the mother of the Messiah. *(page 173)*

antichrist: A pseudo-Messianism whereby a human being puts himself or herself in the place of God or declares himself or herself to be a new messiah. *(page 205)*

apocalyptic literature: A literary form that uses dramatic events and highly symbolic language to offer hope to a people in crisis. *(page 205)*

Apostolic Succession: The uninterrupted passing on of apostolic preaching and authority from the Apostles directly to all bishops. It is accomplished through the laying on of hands when a bishop is ordained in the Sacrament of Holy Orders as instituted by Christ. The office of bishop is permanent, because at ordination a bishop is marked with an indelible, sacred character. *(page 42)*

Ark of the Covenant: A sacred chest that housed the tablets of the Ten Commandments. It was placed within the sanctuary where God would come and dwell. *(page 125)*

Asia Minor: An area corresponding roughly to modern Turkey. *(page 205)*

B

Baal . . . Asherah: Two Canaanite gods of earth and fertility that the Israelites worshiped when they fell away from the one true God. *(page 116)*

Babylonian Exile: In 587 BC the Babylonians pillaged Judah, destroyed the Temple and the city of Jerusalem, and banished the people in chains to serve as slaves in Babylon. The Exile lasted until 539 BC. *(page 129)*

Beatitudes: The teachings of Jesus that begin with the Sermon on the Mount and that summarize the New Law of Christ. The Beatitudes describe the actions and attitudes by which one can discover genuine happiness and they teach us the final end to which God calls us: full communion with him in the Kingdom of Heaven. *(page 175)*

Beloved Disciple: A faithful disciple in the Gospel of John who is present at critical times in Jesus' ministry. The Beloved Disciple may have been the founder of the Johannine community. *(page 185)*

biblical exegesis: The critical interpretation and explanation of a biblical text. *(page 64)*

biblical inerrancy: The doctrine that the books of the Scriptures are free from error regarding the truth God wishes to reveal through the Scriptures for the sake of our salvation. *(page 50)*

breviary: A prayer book that contains the prayers for the Liturgy of the Hours. *(page 217)*

C

canon: The collection of books the Church recognizes as the inspired Word of God. *(page 56)*

canticle: From the Latin *canticum,* meaning "song." It usually refers to biblical hymns (other than the Psalms), such as those found in the Song of Solomon in the Old Testament and the hymns of Mary (see Luke 1:46–55) and Zechariah (see 1:68–79) in the New Testament. By extension, *canticle* is sometimes used to describe other hymns in the liturgy. *(page 171)*

Christological: Having to do with the branch of theology called Christology. Christology is the study of the divinity of Jesus Christ the Son of God and the Second Divine Person of the Trinity, and his earthly ministry and eternal mission. *(page 69)*

conscience: The "interior voice," guided by human reason and divine law, that leads us to understand ourselves as responsible for our actions, and prompts us to do good and avoid evil. To make good judgments, one needs to have a well-formed conscience. *(page 30)*

contemplatio: Simply and silently resting in the presence of God. *(page 227)*

contextualist approach: The interpretation of the Bible that takes into account the various contexts for understanding. These contexts include the senses of Scripture, literacy forms, historical situations, cultural backgrounds, the unity of the whole of the Scriptures, Tradition, and the analogy of faith. *(page 70)*

covenant: A solemn agreement between human beings or between God and a human being in which mutual commitments are made. *(page 37)*

creed: A short summary statement or profession of faith. The Nicene and Apostles' Creeds are the Church's most familiar and important creeds. *(page 91)*

D

Deposit of Faith: The heritage of faith contained in Sacred Scripture and Sacred Tradition. It has been passed on from the time of the Apostles. The Magisterium takes from it all that it teaches as revealed truth. *(page 43)*

desire: From the Latin *desidero,* "to long for what is absent or lost." *(page 11)*

devotional prayers: Also known as devotions, these are personalized prayers that have developed outside, but should lead to, the liturgy of the Church. *(page 231)*

Divine Inspiration: The divine assistance the Holy Spirit gave the authors of the books of the Bible so the authors could write in human words the salvation message God wanted to communicate. *(page 50)*

Divine Revelation: God's self-communication through which he makes known the mystery of his divine plan. Divine Revelation is a gift accomplished by the Father, Son, and Holy Spirit through the words and deeds of salvation history. It is most fully realized in the Passion, death, Resurrection, and Ascension of Jesus Christ. *(page 34)*

Doctor of the Church: A title officially bestowed by the Church on those saints who are highly esteemed for their theological writings, as well as their personal holiness. *(page 94)*

dogma: Teachings recognized as central to Church teaching, defined by the Magisterium and accorded the fullest weight and authority. *(page 43)*

E

Ecumenical Council: A gathering of the Church's bishops from around the world to address pressing issues in the Church. Ecumenical councils are usually convened by the Pope or are at least confirmed or recognized by him. *(page 30)*

epistle: Another name for a New Testament letter. *(page 202)*

Essenes: A group of pious, ultraconservative Jews who left the Temple of Jerusalem and began a community by the Dead Sea, known as Qumran. *(page 74)*

Eucharist, the: The celebration of the entire Mass. The term sometimes refers specifically to the consecrated bread and wine that have become the Body and Blood of Christ. *(page 57)*

Eucharistic Prayer: The part of the Mass that includes the Consecration of the bread and wine, beginning with the Preface and concluding with the Great Amen. *(page 214)*

Evangelists: Based on a word for "good news," in general, anyone who actively works to spread the Gospel of Jesus; more commonly and specifically, the persons traditionally recognized as authors of the four Gospels, Matthew, Mark, Luke, and John. *(page 161)*

exegete: A biblical scholar attempting to interpret the meaning of biblical texts. *(page 68)*

F

Fathers of the Church (Church Fathers): During the early centuries of the Church, those teachers whose writings extended the Tradition of the Apostles and who continue to be important for the Church's teachings. *(page 24)*

fidelity: Faithfulness to obligation, duty, or commitment. *(page 136)*

fundamentalist approach: The interpretation of the Bible and Christian doctrine based on the literalist meaning of the Bible's words. The interpretation is made without regard to the historical setting in which the writings or teachings were first developed. *(page 70)*

G

garden at Gethsemane: An olive grove near the Mount of Olives, where Jesus gathered with the Apostles to pray and prepare for his Crucifixion on Calvary. *(page 180)*

Gentiles: Non-Jewish people. *(page 166)*

Gnostic: Referring to the belief that salvation comes from secret knowledge available to only a select few. *(page 57)*

Gnosticism: A group of heretical religious movements that claimed salvation comes from secret knowledge available only to the elite initiated in that religion. *(page 204)*

Golgotha: A Hebrew word meaning "place of the skull," referring to the place where Jesus was crucified. *(page 170)*

Gospels: Translated from a Greek word meaning "good news," referring to the four books attributed to Matthew, Mark, Luke, and John, "the principal source for the life and teaching of the Incarnate Word"[3] (CCC, 125) Jesus Christ. *(page 157)*

Gregorian chant: A monophonic, unaccompanied style of liturgical singing that takes its name from Pope Gregory the Great (540–604). *(page 215)*

H

hallowed: Regarded as holy; revered and respected. *(page 220)*

Hebrew people: The descendants of Abraham and Sarah who become known as the Israelites after the Exodus and who later were called Judeans or Jews. *(page 78)*

Hellenism: The acceptance of Greek culture, language, and traditions. *(page 85)*

herald: To proclaim or announce a saving message. *(page 134)*

Holy Communion: Another name for the Sacrament of the Eucharist. *(page 213)*

homily: A brief liturgical sermon that explains the Scripture readings, helps the people of God accept the Scriptures as the Word of God, and encourages them to put the teachings of the Scriptures into practice in their daily lives. *(page 213)*

hymns: Poetic song lyrics written to honor God. *(page 145)*

I

idolatrous: Worshipping false gods. *(page 120)*

Immanuel: A Hebrew word meaning "God is with us." *(page 138)*

Incarnation: From the Latin, meaning "to become flesh," referring to the mystery of Jesus Christ, the divine Son of God, becoming man. In the Incarnation, Jesus Christ became truly man while remaining truly God. *(page 14)*

Infancy Narratives: The accounts of Jesus' birth and early childhood. *(page 173)*

J

Johannine: Related to the author of the fourth Gospel. *(page 185)*

judges: The eleven men and one woman who served the Hebrew people as tribal leaders, military commanders, arbiters of disputes, and enliveners of faith. *(page 119)*

K

kerygma: A Greek word meaning "proclamation" or "preaching," referring to the announcement of the Gospel or the Good News of divine salvation offered to all through Jesus Christ. *Kerygma* has two senses. It is both an event of proclamation and a message proclaimed. *(page 161)*

L

lament: A Psalm that conveys mourning and petitioning of God in times of need (see, for example, Psalm 38). *(page 145)*

Law of Moses: The first five books of the Old Testament, which are also called the books of the Law or the Torah. God gave Moses the tablets containing the Law (see Exodus 31:18), which is why it is also called the Law of Moses, or the Mosaic Law. *(page 85)*

lectio: Slow and attentive reading of a passage from the Sacred Scriptures. *(page 226)*

lectio divina: A Latin term meaning "divine reading." *Lectio divina* is a form of meditative prayer focused on a Scripture passage. It involves repetitive readings and periods of reflection and can serve as either private or communal prayer. *(page 225)*

liturgy: The Church's official, public, communal prayer. It is God's work, in which the People of God participate. The Church's most important liturgy is the Eucharist, or the Mass. *(page 213)*

Liturgy of the Hours: Also known as the Divine Office, the official public, daily prayer of the Catholic Church. The Divine Office provides standard prayers, Scripture readings, and reflections at regular hours throughout the day. *(page 215)*

Logos: A Greek word meaning "Word." Logos is a title of Jesus Christ found in the Gospel of John that illuminates the relationship between the three Persons of the Holy Trinity. (See John 1:1,14.) *(page 185)*

M

Magi: Wise men of the East who followed a new star that directed them to the birth of Jesus. *(page 174)*

Magisterium: The Church's living teaching office, which consists of all bishops, in communion with the Pope. *(page 43)*

Magnificat: This is the first Latin word (from *magnus*, meaning "great," and *facere*, meaning "to make") of the prayer of Mary in response to the Annunciation of the birth of Jesus in the Gospel of Luke (see Luke 1:46–55). *(page 172)*

manna: Little flakes the Israelites collected and boiled or baked into a breadlike substance, symbolizing God as the sole sustainer of life. *(page 110)*

martyrdom: Witness to the saving message of Christ through the sacrifice of one's life. *(page 199)*

Matthean: Related to the author of the first Gospel. *(page 166)*

meditatio: Ruminating on the passage to understand what God is trying to communicate. *(page 226)*

messianic hope: The Jewish belief and expectation that a messiah would come to protect, unite, and lead Israel to freedom. *(page 138)*

messianic secret: A theme in the Gospel of Mark that portrays the disciples and others as recognizing Jesus' identity as the Messiah. However, Jesus directed them not to tell anyone else. *(page 169)*

Middle Ages: Also known as the medieval period, the time between the collapse of the Roman Empire in the fifth century AD and the beginning of the Renaissance in the fourteenth century. *(page 27)*

millennium: A period of one thousand years, also referring in modern usage to the transition from the year 1999 to 2000. *(page 77)*

miracles: Marvelous and unexpected events that manifest the presence and power of God. *(page 177)*

monarchy: A government or a state headed by a single person, like a king or queen. As a biblical term, it refers to the period of time when the Israelites existed as an independent nation. *(page 122)*

morality: Referring to the goodness or evil of human acts. The morality of an act is determined by the nature of the action, the intention, and the circumstances. Human freedom enables us to judge the morality of acts we choose. *(page 228)*

N

Nag Hammadi manuscripts: Fourth-century writings discovered in 1945 near the village of Nag Hammadi in Upper Egypt, that are invaluable sources of information regarding Gnostic beliefs, practices, and lifestyle. Gnosticism was an early Church heresy claiming that Christ's humanity was an illusion and the human body is evil. *(page 73)*

natural revelation: The process by which God makes himself known to human reason through the created world. Historical conditions and the consequences of Original Sin, however, often hinder our ability to fully know God's truth through natural revelation alone. *(page 22)*

Near East: In biblical times the region commonly known today as the Middle East, including the modern countries of Iraq, Iran, Syria, Lebanon, Israel, and Jordan. *(page 97)*

New Testament: The twenty-seven books of the Bible written in apostolic times, which have the life, teachings, Passion, death, Resurrection, and Ascension of Jesus Christ and the beginnings of the Church as their central theme. *(page 82)*

O

opus dei: A Latin phrase meaning the "work of God." *(page 217)*

oral tradition: The handing on of the message of God's saving plan through words and deeds. *(page 53)*

oratio: Speaking to God in prayer. *(page 226)*

Original Sin: From the Latin *origo,* meaning "beginning" or "birth." The term has two meanings: (1) the sin of the first human beings, who disobeyed God's command by choosing to follow their own will and thus lost their original holiness and became subject to death, (2) the fallen state of human nature that affects every person born into the world. *(page 37)*

P

parables: Short stories that use everyday images to communicate religious messages. *(page 177)*

Paraclete: A name for the Holy Spirit, the Divine Third Person of the Trinity, whom Jesus promised to the disciples as an advocate and counselor. *(page 192)*

Parousia: The second coming of Christ at the end of time, fully realizing God's plan and the glorification of humanity. *(page 87)*

Paschal Lamb: In the Old Testament, the sacrificial lamb shared at the seder meal of the Passover on the night the Israelites escaped from Egypt;

in the New Testament, the Paschal Lamb is Jesus, the Incarnate Son of God who dies on a cross to take away "the sin of the world" (John 1:29). *(page 163)*

Paschal Mystery: The work of salvation accomplished by Jesus Christ mainly through his Passion, death, Resurrection, and Ascension. *(page 83)*

Passion: The sufferings of Jesus during his final days in this life: his agony in the garden at Gethsemane, his trial, and his Crucifixion. *(page 179)*

Passover: The night the Lord passed over the houses of the Israelites marked by the blood of the lamb, and spared the firstborn sons from death. It also is the feast that celebrates the deliverance of the Chosen People from bondage in Egypt and the Exodus from Egypt to the Promised Land. *(page 108)*

patriarch: The father or leader of a tribe, clan, or tradition. Abraham, Isaac, and Jacob were the patriarchs of the Israelite people. *(page 38)*

Pauline letters: Thirteen New Testament letters attributed to Paul or to disciples who wrote in his name. They offer advice, pastoral encouragement, teaching, and community news to early Christian communities. *(page 200)*

Pentateuch: A Greek word meaning "five books," referring to the first five books of the Old Testament. *(page 79)*

Pentecost: The fiftieth day following Easter, which commemorates the descent of the Holy Spirit on the early Apostles and disciples. *(page 197)*

personification: A literary technique that uses human characteristics to describe nonhuman realities. *(page 152)*

pharaoh: A ruler of ancient Egypt. *(page 105)*

polytheistic beliefs: Beliefs in many gods and goddesses. *(page 116)*

praise: A prayer of acknowledgment that God is God, giving God glory not for what he does, but simply because he is (see, for example, Psalms 113 and 114). *(page 145)*

prayer: Lifting up of one's mind and heart to God in praise, petition, thanksgiving, and intercession; communication with God in a relationship of love. *(page 218)*

primeval history: The time before the invention of writing and recording of historical data. *(page 91)*

Promised Land: The land (Canaan) God promised to the children of Abraham. *(page 101)*

prophecy: A message communicated by prophets on behalf of God, usually a message of divine direction or consolation for the prophet's own time. Because some prophetic messages include divine direction, their fulfillment may be in the future. *(page 129)*

prophet: A person God chooses to speak his message of salvation. In the Bible, primarily a communicator of a divine message of repentance to the Chosen People, not necessarily a person who predicted the future. *(page 39)*

psalmody: From the Greek word *psalmos,* meaning "a song sung to a harp," and *aeidein,* meaning "to sing." The word has multiple meanings: the art of singing psalms, the arranging or composing of psalms for singing, or a collection of psalms for singing or reciting. *(page 215)*

Psalms: Hymns or songs of prayer to God that express praise, thanksgiving, or lament. *(page 145)*

Psalter: The Book of Psalms of the Old Testament, which contains 150 Psalms. *(page 145)*

Q

Qoheleth: A Hebrew word for *Ecclesiastes,* meaning "preacher" or "one who convokes an assembly." *(page 147)*

Quelle: Also called the Q Source, a theoretical collection of ancient documents of the teachings of Jesus shared among the early followers of Christianity. *(page 162)*

R

rabbi: An honored teacher in the Jewish tradition. *(page 167)*

redact: To select and adapt written material to serve an author's purpose. *(page 74)*

redemption: From the Latin *redemptio,* meaning "a buying back," referring, in the Old Testament, to Yahweh's deliverance of Israel and, in the New Testament, to Christ's deliverance of all Christians from the forces of sin. *(page 45)*

remnant: A prophetic term for the small portion of people who will be saved because of their faithfulness to God. *(page 136)*

Rosary: A devotional prayer that honors the Virgin Mary and helps us meditate on Christ's life and mission. We pray the Rosary using rosary beads, which are grouped into "decades." Each decade consists of praying the Lord's Prayer followed by ten Hail Marys and the Glory Be while meditating on an event from Christ's life and mission. *(page 232)*

S

Sacred Tradition: From the Latin *tradere,* meaning "to hand on." Refers to the process of passing on the Gospel message. It began with the oral communication of the Gospel by the Apostles, was written down in the Scriptures, and is interpreted by the Magisterium under the guidance of the Holy Spirit. *(page 41)*

salvation: From the Latin *salvare,* meaning "to save," referring to the forgiveness of sins and assurance of permanent union with God, attained for us through the Paschal Mystery—Christ's work of redemption accomplished through his Passion, death, Resurrection, and Ascension. Only at the time of judgment can a person be certain of salvation, which is a gift of God. *(page 14)*

salvation history: The pattern of specific events in human history in which God clearly reveals his presence and saving actions. Salvation was accomplished once and for all through Jesus Christ, a truth foreshadowed and revealed throughout the Old Testament. *(page 34)*

Samaritan: An inhabitant of Samaria. The Samaritans rejected the Jerusalem Temple and worshipped instead at Mount Gerizim. The New Testament mentions the Jewish rejection of Samaritans in both the parable of the Good Samaritan (see Luke 10:29–37) and the account of Jesus' speaking with the Samaritan woman at the well (see John 4:1–42). *(page 171)*

Satan: The fallen angel or spirit of evil who is the enemy of God and a continuing instigator of temptation and sin in the world. *(page 220)*

scholastic theology: The use of philosophical methods to better understand revealed truth. The goal of scholastic theology is to present the understanding of revealed truth in a logical and systematic form. *(page 27)*

scribes: People associated with the Pharisees or Sadducees who were skilled copyists, professional letter writers, and interpreters and teachers of the Law. *(page 167)*

Semitic: A term referring to Semites, a number of peoples of the ancient Near East, from whom the Israelites descended. *(page 97)*

servant leadership: A type of leadership based on humble service to all God's people. *(page 126)*

sign: The Johannine name for a miracle of Jesus. *(page 187)*

Sinai Covenant: The Covenant established with the Israelites at Mount Sinai that renewed God's Covenant with Abraham's descendants. It establishes the Israelites as God's Chosen People. *(page 112)*

stump of Jesse: A phrase taken from Isaiah 11:1 that traces Jesus' lineage to Jesse's son, King David. *(page 139)*

synoptic Gospels: From the Greek for "seeing the whole together," the name given to the Gospels of Matthew, Mark, and Luke, because they are similar in style and content. *(page 162)*

Syrophoenician: A person from the Phoenician cities of Tyre and Sidon. Jews considered Syrophoenicians "outsiders" because of their idolatrous practices. *(page 170)*

T

temptation: An invitation or enticement to commit an unwise or immoral act that often includes a promise of reward to make the immoral act seem more appealing. *(page 220)*

Ten Commandments: Sometimes called the Decalogue, the list of ten norms, or rules of moral behavior, that God gave Moses and that are the basis of ethical conduct. *(page 112)*

thanksgiving: A prayer of gratitude for the gift of life and the gifts of life (see, for example, Psalm 47). *(page 145)*

theocracy: A nation ruled by God. *(page 122)*

theophany: God's manifestation of himself in a visible form to enrich human understanding of him. An example is God's appearance to Moses in the form of a burning bush. *(page 35)*

Torah: A Hebrew word meaning "law," referring to the first five books of the Old Testament. *(page 79)*

Trinity: From the Latin *trinus,* meaning "threefold," referring to the central mystery of the Christian faith that God exists as a communion of three distinct and interrelated divine Persons: Father, Son, and Holy Spirit. The doctrine of the Trinity is a mystery that is inaccessible to human reason alone and is known through Divine Revelation only. *(page 40)*

V

Vatican Council II: The Ecumenical or general Council of the Roman Catholic Church that Pope John XXIII (1958–1963) convened in 1962 and that continued under Pope Paul VI (1963–1978) until 1965. *(page 30)*

venerated: Respected and given devotion. *(page 158)*

Via Dolorosa: Latin for "way of sorrow," referring to the path Jesus journeyed in the last few moments of his life, which is commemorated in the devotion of the Stations of the Cross. *(page 231)*

vocation: A call from God to all members of the Church to embrace a life of holiness. Specifically, it refers to a call to live the holy life as an ordained minister, as a vowed religious (sister or brother), in a Christian marriage, or in single life. *(page 11)*

W

wisdom literature: The Old Testament Books of Proverbs, Job, Ecclesiastes, Sirach, and the Wisdom of Solomon. *(page 39)*

written tradition: Under the inspiration of the Holy Spirit, the synthesis in written form of the message of salvation that has been passed down in the oral tradition. *(page 53)*

Y

Yahweh: The most sacred of the Old Testament names for God, which he revealed to Moses. It is frequently translated as "I AM" or "I am who am." *(page 107)*

Index

Page numbers in italics refer to illustrations.

Q

Qoheleth, 147
Quelle, 162
Qumran, 74

R

rabbis, 167
Rachel, 100
Rahab, 118
Rahner, Karl, 30–31
rainbows, 37, 95
ransoms, 165, 180, 181
reason, human, 21, 22, 24, 27, 29–31, 49, 61, 71. *see also* history; science
redaction, 74
redemption. *see also* salvation
  basics, 45
  Hebrews, Letter to, and, 204
  love and, 181
  Luke's Gospel and, 172
  Paschal Mystery and, 82, 182
  prophets and, 129–131
  Resurrection and, 181
Redemptorists (Religious Congregation of the Most Holy Redeemer), 229
Red Sea crossing, 69, 104, 108–109. *see also* water parting
Reformation, Protestant, 186
Reign of God. *see* Kingdom of God
Reign of Terror, 106
relationships, 69, 94, 114, 145, 185. *see also* God (Lord), relationship with
religious communities, 221–223, 225. *see also specific orders*
Religious Congregation of the Most Holy Redeemer (Redemptorists), 229
remnant, 136–137
repentance. *see also* Sacrament of Penance and Reconciliation
  David and, 123, 124, 125, 126
  Liturgy of the Hours and, 218
  Peter and, 198
  prayer and, 193, 218
  prophets and, 39, 80, 129, 136, 137
respect and dignity, 15, 18, 93, 134, 135
"resurrection and the life," 190
Resurrection of Christ. *see* Jesus Christ, Resurrection of
Revelation, Book of, 67, 86, 87, 196, 205–208
Revelation, Divine
  analogy of faith and, 65
  basics, 7, 10–20, 33–36, 49, 56
  Church and, 45–47, 63, 211
  history and science and, 71, 74
  interpretation of, 74
  Jesus as, 39–41, 157, 189
  New Testament and, 82, 83, 85, 157–208
  Old Testament and, 36–39, 77, 83
  private, 36
  translations and, 58
  transmission of, 41–45
revelation, natural, 21–33
Risen Christ, 194–195. *see also* Jesus Christ, Resurrection of
Roman centurion, 167
Romans, 55, 168, 170, 180, 206
Romero, Oscar, 131, 133
Roncalli, Angelo Giuseppe, 14
Rosary, 44, 231, 232–233
Rose of Lima, 181
Rules of Life, 221–222, 226

S

Sacrament of Anointing of the Sick, 203, 204
Sacrament of Baptism, 43–44, 69, 97, 175, 214, 219
Sacraments of Christian Initiation, 219
Sacrament of Confirmation, 219
Sacrament of the Eucharist, 57, 111, 175, 180, 213, 219, 228–229. *see also* Mass
Sacrament of Holy Orders, 42
Sacrament of Matrimony, 214
Sacrament of Penance and Reconciliation, 96, 137, 214
Sacraments, 228–229
Sacred Liturgy, 215
sacrifices
  Abraham's, 98, 99
  Cain and Abel and, 95
  friendship and, 125
  Passover and, 109
  prayer and, 98
  Saul and, 122
  Stations of the Cross and, 232
  Temple of Jerusalem and, 124
Sadducees, 85, 167, 168
saints, 12, 13, 121, 210, 218. *see also individual saints*
salvation. *see also* redemption
  Apostles and, 33
  Crucifixion and, 57, 179
  defined, 14
  Ezekiel and, 134
  Gnosticism and, 57
  John's Gospel and, 195
  Lord's Prayer and, 220
  love and, 19
  Mary and, 44

Acknowledgments

The first "Salt and Light" excerpt on page 59 is from the New Revised Standard Version of the Bible, Catholic Edition (NRSV). Copyright © 1993 and 1989 by the Division of Christian Education of the National Council of the Churches of Christ in the United States of America. All rights reserved.

The "Salt for the Earth and Light for the World" excerpt on page 59 is from the *New Jerusalem Bible (NJB)*. Copyright © 1985 by Darton, Longman and Todd, London; and Doubleday, a division of Bantam Doubleday Dell Publishing Group, New York. All rights reserved.

The second "Salt and Light" excerpt on page 59 is from the Good News Translation in Today's English Version, Second Edition (GNT). Copyright © 1992 by the American Bible Society. Used with permission.

All other scriptural quotations in this book are from the New American Bible with Revised New Testament and Revised Psalms. Copyright © 1991, 1986, and 1970 by the Confraternity of Christian Doctrine, Washington, D.C. Used by the permission of the copyright owner. All rights reserved. No part of the New American Bible may be reproduced in any form without permission in writing from the copyright owner.

The excerpts marked *Catechism* and *CCC* are from the English translation of the *Catechism of the Catholic Church* for use in the United States of America, second edition. Copyright © 1994 by the United States Catholic Conference, Inc.—Libreria Editrice Vaticana. English translation of the *Catechism of the Catholic Church: Modifications from the Editio Typica* copyright © 1997 by the United States Catholic Conference, Inc.—Libreria Editrice Vaticana. Used with permission of the United States Conference of Catholic Bishops.

The definitions in this book are taken from *The Catholic Faith Handbook for Youth*, second edition (Winona, MN: Saint Mary's Press), copyright © 2008 by Saint Mary's Press; *Saint Mary's Press® Essential Bible Dictionary*, by Sheila O'Connell-Roussell (Winona, MN: Saint Mary's Press), copyright © 2005 by Saint Mary's Press; and *Saint Mary's Press® Glossary of Theological Terms*, by John T. Ford (Winona, MN: Saint Mary's Press), copyright © 2006 by Saint Mary's Press. All rights reserved.

The poetic lines of Saint John of the Cross on page 13 are from *The Collected Works of Saint John of the Cross*, revised edition, translated by Kieran Kavanaugh and Otilio Rodriguez (Washington, DC: ICS Publications, 1991), pages 358–359. Copyright © 1964, 1979, 1991 by the Washington Province of Discalced Carmelites. Used with permission of ICS Publications, 2131 Lincoln Road NE, Washington, D.C. 20002-1199, USA, *www.icspublications.org*.

The excerpts on pages 14, 15, and 32 are from *Pastoral Constitution on the Church in the Modern World* (*Gaudium et Spes*, 1965), numbers 19, 4, and 11, respectively, at *www.vatican.va/archive/hist_councils/ii_vatican_council/documents/vat-ii_cons_19651207_gaudium-et-spes_en.html*.

The excerpts on pages 43, 45, 50, 61, 67, 68, 72, 82, 211, and 230 are from *Dogmatic Constitution on Divine Revelation* (*Dei Verbum*, 1965), numbers 9, 9, 10, 8, 11, 12, 12, 12, 12, 17, 21, and 25, respectively, at *www.vatican.va/archive/hist_councils/ii_vatican_council/documents/vat-ii_const_19651118_dei-verbum_en.html*.

The excerpts on pages 45 and 111 are from *Dogmatic Constitution on the Church* (*Lumen Gentium*, 1964), numbers 12 and 11, at *www.vatican.va/archive/hist_councils/ii_vatican_council/documents/vat-ii_const_19641121_lumen-gentium_en.html*.

The quotation by Pope John Paul II on page 77 is from "15th World Youth Day: The Holy Father's Address at the Welcoming Ceremony," number 4, at *www.vatican.va/holy_father/john_paul_ii/speeches/documents/hf_jp-ii_spe_20000815_gmg-accoglienza1_en.html*.

The quotation by Archbishop Romero on page 131 was found at *www.utcatholic.org/document_repository/8/161.pdf*.

The quotations on pages 159 and 183 are from *The Roman Missal* © 1973 International Commission on English in the Liturgy (ICEL). English translation prepared by the ICEL (New York: Catholic Book Publishing Company, 1985), pages 567 and 437. Illustrations and arrangement copyright © 1985–1974 by the Catholic Book Publishing Company, New York. Used with permission of the ICEL.

The first quotation on page 167 is from *The Collegeville Bible Commentary*, Dianne Bergant and Robert J. Karris, general editors (Collegeville, MN: The Liturgical Press, 1989), page 861. Copyright © 1989 by the Order of Saint Benedict, Collegeville, MN.

The second quotation on page 167 is from *Saint Mary's Press® College Study Bible* (Winona, MN: Saint Mary's Press, 2007), page 1419. Copyright © 2007 by Saint Mary's Press. All rights reserved.

The lists of numbers and colors on page 207 are adapted from *The Book of Revelation*, by Catherine Cory (Collegeville, MN: The Liturgical Press, 2006), pages 12–13. Copyright © 2006 by the Order of Saint Benedict, Collegeville, MN.

The quotation about Saint Jerome, attributed to Saint Augustine, on page 212 is found in *The Catholic Source Book*, third edition, by Peter Klein (Orlando, FL: Harcourt Religion Publishers, 2000), page 137. Copyright © 2000 by Harcourt Religion Publishers.

The excerpts on pages 213 and 215 are from *Constitution on the Sacred Liturgy* (*Sacrosanctum Concilium*, 1963), numbers 24 and 121, at *www.vatican.va/archive/hist_councils/ii_vatican_council/documents/vat-ii_const_19631204_sacrosanctum-concilium_en.html*.

The first excerpt on page 214 is from *Built of Living Stones: Art, Architecture, and Worship*, number 50, by the United States Conference of Catholic Bishops (USCCB), at *www.usccb.org/liturgy/livingstones.shtml*. Copyright © 2000 by the USCCB. All rights reserved.

The second excerpt on page 214 is from *Lectionary for Mass: For Use in the Dioceses of the United States of America*, second typical edition, volume one, by the USCCB (New Jersey: Catholic Book Publishing Company, 1998), page 19. Copyright © 1998, 1997, 1970 by the Confraternity of Christian Doctrine, Washington, D.C. All rights reserved.

The first excerpt on page 221 is from "The Rule of Our Holy Father Augustine," number 3, found at *www.norbertines.co.uk/Rule.htm*.

The second excerpt on page 221 is from "The Order of Saint Benedict: The Rule of Benedict," chapter 53, found at *www.osb.org/rb/text/rbeaad1.html*.

The excerpt on page 222 is from "The Rule of St. Francis — 1223," chapter II, found at *www.thenazareneway.com/rule_of_st_francis.html*.

The excerpt from Pope Benedict XVI on page 225 is from "Address of His Holiness Benedict XVI to the Participants in the International Congress Organized to Commemorate the 40th Anniversary of the *Dogmatic Constitution on Divine Revelation 'Dei Verbum*,'" at *www.vatican.va/holy_father/benedict_xvi/ speeches/2005/september/documents/hf_ben-xvi_spe_20050916_40-dei-verbum_ en.html.* Copyright © 2005—Libreria Editrice Vaticana.

The excerpt on page 226 is from the "Rule of Saint Benedict: Prologue," found at *www.bluecloud.org/rule.html.*

To view copyright terms and conditions for Internet materials cited here, log on to the home pages for the referenced Web sites.

During this book's preparation, all citations, facts, figures, names, addresses, telephone numbers, Internet URLs, and other pieces of information cited within were verified for accuracy. The authors and Saint Mary's Press staff have made every attempt to reference current and valid sources, but we cannot guarantee the content of any source, and we are not responsible for any changes that may have occurred since our verification. If you find an error in, or have a question or concern about, any of the information or sources listed within, please contact Saint Mary's Press.

Endnotes Cited in Quotations from the *Catechism of the Catholic Church, Second Edition*

Section 1
1. Cf. *1 Corinthians* 6:19–20; 15:44–45.
2. St. Thomas Aquinas, Summa Theologiae I, 2, 3.
3. Vatican Council I, *Dei Filius* 2: Denzinger-Schönmetzer, *Enchiridion Symbolorum, definitionum declarationum de rebus fidei et morum* (1965) 3004; cf. 3026; Vatican Council II, *Dei Verbum* 6.
4. *Dei Verbum* 2; cf. *Ephesians* 1:9; 2:18; *2 Peter* 1:4.
5. *Dei Verbum* 3; cf. *John* 1:3; *Romans* 1:19–20.
6. Cf. *Ezekiel* 36; *Isaiah* 49:5–6; 53:11.
7. *Dei Verbum* 8 § 1.
8. *Dei Verbum* 8 § 1.
9. *Dei Verbum* 8 § 3; cf. *Colossians* 3:16.
10. *Matthew* 28:20.

Section 2
1. *Dei Verbum* 12 § 3.
2. Cf. *Dei Verbum* 8 § 3.
3. *Dei Filius* 4: Denzinger-Schönmetzer, *Enchiridion Symbolorum, definitionum declarationum de rebus fidei et morum* (1965) 3017.
4. *Dei Verbum* 10 § 2.
5. *Dei Verbum* 10 § 2.
6. Cf. *Dei Verbum* 12 § 1.
7. *Dei Verbum* 12 § 3.
8. Cf. *Luke* 24:45.
9. *Dei Verbum* 12 § 3.

10. Littera gesta docet, quid credas allegoria, moralis quid agas, quo tendas anagogia. Augustine of Dacia, *Rotulus pugillaris*, I: ed. A. Walz: Angelicum 6 (1929) 256.
11. *Dei Filius* 4: Denzinger-Schönmetzer, *Enchiridion Symbolorum, definitionum declarationum de rebus fidei et morum* (1965) 3017.
12. Cf. *Dei Verbum* 12 § 1.
13. *Dei Verbum* 15.
14. Cf. *Dei Verbum* 14.
15. *Dei Verbum* 15.
16. *Dei Verbum* 15.
17. Cf. *Dei Verbum* 14.
18. Cf. *Mark* 12:29–31.
19. Cf. St. Augustine, *Quaest. in Hept.* 2, 73: J. P. Migne, ed., Patrologia Latina 34, 623; cf. *Dei Verbum* 16.
20. Cf. *Dei Verbum* 20.

Section 3
1. Cf. Council of Trent: Denzinger-Schönmetzer, *Enchiridion Symbolorum, definitionum et declarationum de rebus fidei et morum* (1965) 1511–1512.
2. Cf. *Ezekiel* 36; *Isaiah* 49:5–6; 53:11.
3. *Lumen gentium* 6; cf. *Galatians* 4:26; *Revelation* 12:17; 19:7; 21:2, 9; 22:17; *Ephesians* 5:25–26, 29.
4. *Lumen gentium* 6; cf. *Galatians* 4:26; *Revelation* 12:17; 19:7; 21:2, 9; 22:17; *Ephesians* 5:25–26, 29.

Section 4
1. *Dei Verbum* 18.
2. St. Caesaria the Younger to St. Richildis and St. Radegunde, Sources Chrétiennes (Paris: 1942–) 345, 480.
3. *Dei Verbum* 18.
4. *Dei Verbum* 18.
5. *Sacrosanctum concilium* 56.
6. Cf. *Dei Verbum* 21.
7. *Dei Verbum* 19.
8. *Dei Verbum* 19.
9. *Dei Verbum* 19.
10. *Dei Verbum* 15.
11. *Matthew* 3:15; cf. 26:39.
12. *Acts of the Apostles* 2:22; cf. *Luke* 7:18–23.
13. Cf. Council of Trent (1547); Denzinger-Schönmetzer, *Enchiridion Symbolorum, definitionum et declarationum de rebus fidei et morum* (1965) 1529.
14. St. Rose of Lima, cf. P. Hansen, *Vita mirabilis* (Louvain, 1668).
15. Cf. *John* 10:17–18; 15:13; *Hebrews* 9:14; *1 John* 4:10.

Section 5
1. *Dei Verbum* 25; cf. *Philippians* 3:8 and St. Jerome, *Commentariorum in Isaiam libri xviii* prol.: J. P. Migne, ed., Patrologia Latina (Paris: 1841–1855) 24, 17b.

2. *Dei Verbum* 25; cf. *Philippians* 3:8 and St. Jerome, *Commentariorum in Isaiam libri xviii* prol.: J. P. Migne, ed., Patrologia Latina (Paris: 1841–1855) 24, 17b.
3. Cf. *Dei Verbum* 21.
4. *Sacrosanctum concilium* 83.
5. Tertullian, *De orat.* 1: J. P. Migne, ed., Patrologia Latina (Paris: 1841–1855) 1, 1251–1255.
6. St. Thomas Aquinas, Summa Theologiae II–II, 83, 9.
7. *Dei Verbum* 25; cf. *Philippians* 3:8; St. Ambrose, *De officiis ministrorum* 1, 20, 88: J. P. Migne, ed., Patrologia Latina (Paris: 1841–1855) 16, 50.
8. Cf. *Psalm* 119:105.
9. *John* 4:14.
10. *Dei Verbum* 25; cf. *Philippians* 3:8; St. Ambrose, *De officiis ministrorum* 1, 20, 88: J. P. Migne, ed., Patrologia Latina (Paris: 1841–1855) 16, 50.

Glossary
1. *Dei Verbum* 18.